∞

Spiritual Secrets of
a Trappist Monk

Father M. Raymond, O.C.S.O.

Spiritual Secrets
of a
Trappist Monk

The Truth of Who You Are
and What God Calls You to Be

SOPHIA INSTITUTE PRESS®
Manchester, New Hampshire

Spiritual Secrets of a Trappist Monk: The Secret of Who You Are and What God Calls You to Be was originally published in 1957 by the Bruce Publishing Company, Milwaukee, Wisconsin, under the title *You*. This 2000 edition by Sophia Institute Press® contains editorial revisions to the original text.

Sophia Institute Press®
Box 5284, Manchester, NH 03108
1-800-888-9344
www.sophiainstitute.com

Nihil obstat: Fr. M. Gabriel O'Connell, O.C.S.O., *Censor*
Fr. M. Thomas Aquinas Porter, O.C.S.O., *Censor*
Imprimi potest: Fr. M. Gabriel Sortais, O.C.S.O., *Abbas Generalis*
Nihil obstat: Rev. John A. Schulien, S.T.D., *Censor Librorum*
Imprimatur: Albert G. Meyer, D.D. Archbishop of Milwaukee
October 8, 1957

Library of Congress Cataloging-in-Publication Data

M. Raymond, Father, O.C.S.O., 1903-
      Spiritual secrets of a Trappist monk : the truth of who you are and what God calls you to be / Father M. Raymond.
            p.   cm.
      Rev. ed. of: You. 1957.
      Includes bibliographical references.
      ISBN 1-928832-07-5 (pbk. : alk. paper)
      1. Man (Theology) 2. Catholic Church — Doctrines. I. M. Raymond, Father, O.C.S.O., 1903- You. II. Title.

BT701.2.M2   2000
233 — dc21   00-034448

To the honor of
Mary Immaculate,
Mother of Christ and of all His members,
and to the memory of
Michael Joseph Henry, M.D.,
stalwart member of Christ's Mystical Body
and sterling friend

"Know thyself!"

is a precept that
binds the whole world.

Every man, whether Christian or
non-Christian, should know himself.

He can and ought to know himself free — and that is his
greatness, to be free and to know that he is so — but he ought
also to understand that he is himself the author neither of his
being nor of his liberty, nor of his knowledge of the one or
the other. And thence arises for every man equally the strict
obligation to love God with his whole soul and his whole
heart, and above all things, whether he be Christian or not.

We have no need to know Christ to recognize this duty;
we have only to know ourselves.

Etienne Gilson
The Mystical Theology of St. Bernard

∞

Contents

∞

Spiritual Secrets of
a Trappist Monk

Publisher's Note

Father M. Raymond, the author of *Spiritual Secrets of a Trappist Monk*, is a soul aflame with love for God. This love often impels him to verbal heights that, to some, may seem to border on the unacceptable, e.g., his statements in these pages about the divinity and priesthood of every individual. He was, however, a loyal son of the Catholic Church; he wanted all who encounter these pages to understand his words in full accord with the mind of the Church.

Accordingly, please read these chapters completely and carefully before forming any judgments about what Father Raymond is saying. In all cases, as you will see, he explains his verbal enthusiasms according to the teaching of the Church's Magisterium.

Editor's Note

Except where otherwise noted, the biblical quotations in the following pages are based on the Kleist-Lilly translation of the New Testament and the Knox translation of the Old Testament. Where applicable, quotations have been cross-referenced with the differing names and enumeration in the Revised Standard Version, using the following symbol: (RSV=).

Who are you?

Do something that brings comfort, convenience, or practical use-fulness to your fellowmen, and, according to Antoine de Saint-Exupéry, in *The Wisdom of the Sands*,[1] you have done nothing. But raise them a pedestal, build them a stairway, make them a ship that will bring them to God, and you have produced.

This book is made to be a high pedestal, a steep stairway, a ship strong enough to plow life's roughest, deepest seas and never founder; and the pedestal, the stairway, and the ship are yours, for this book has been written exclusively for, and entirely about, you.

But, who are you?

That question sounds simple. But be not deceived by its sound. It is one of the most penetrating questions you will ever face, one of the most difficult you will ever attempt to answer. For it probes more than your mind and your memory. It searches — as God is said to search — the deepest secret of your being. And that is one secret too often kept, even from yourself.

Arthur Schopenhauer, who tried to teach philosophy at the University of Berlin in the middle of the nineteenth century, was

[1] New York: Harcourt, Brace, 1950.

3

one day walking down the street buried in thought. In his abstraction, he accidentally bumped into a pedestrian. Irritated by the jolt, and by the seeming indifference of the philosopher, the pedestrian angrily demanded, "Who are you, anyhow?" Schopenhauer, still deep in his meditation, replied, "Who am I? How I wish I knew!"

That answer gives insight into the root cause of many of Schopenhauer's dark and dismal philosophical aberrations. It is an admission of ignorance that accounts, in no slight degree, for Schopenhauer's whole system of pessimism. For any man's answer to the question "Who are you?" lays bare the very essence of his philosophy of life.

Nothing more personal could ever be asked, nor anything more important. Yet, few indeed are they who have a ready reply to the question, and fewer still are they who grasp its transcendent import. Many people today have wide and, occasionally, deep knowledge of countless things outside themselves; but pitiful, and even frightening, is the knowledge they have of themselves.

Recently several hundred average Americans were stopped on the street, visited in their homes, confronted in their offices or other places of employment, and asked to help out in a survey that was being conducted by some university psychologists. These people were handed a plain sheet of paper, then told that they would be rendering a real service if they would write on that paper three replies to a very simple question. It was: *Who are you?*

Most people gasped. Some started stuttering. Not a few exclaimed, "Who am I? Why, this is the queerest question I ever heard!" Undoubtedly, it was for hundreds. But from the replies submitted, it was evident to the psychologists in the University of California at Los Angeles that at last, after months of seeking, they had found what they desired: the single question which, in the shortest space of time, will reveal most about the individual interrogated. "Who am I?" wrote one man. "Why, I don't know. I see myself a little inferior to others. . . . I guess I am something put on this earth to make it a better place for those who come after me." That man was a builder. One wonders how much building of his own life, of his own character, he had done.

A bank cashier did somewhat better. "I am a soul gaining the experiences of mortality," was his first response. "I am a person progressing with an ultimate goal in mind, but not progressing as rapidly as I desire," was his second. His third answer read, "I am an individual getting an awful lot of fun out of life." How much, we wonder, was that person putting into life?

A tailor simply stared from the paper to the investigator, then back to the paper again. Finally, while scratching his head, he said, "Who am I? I never asked myself that question before. . . . It kinda stops me. . . . I guess I don't know who I am, except that I am kinda all mixed up. . . . I feel alone, all by myself, and that most people have it in for me. I feel like I gotta hold tight to everything I got, or somebody'll take it away from me." When he noted that the investigator was busy jotting all this down, he grew excited and cried, "You're writing all that down!" He ripped the top page from the investigator's book and fled.

From an office came these three replies: "I am an architect. I design office buildings. I am forty-five."

It was a simple housewife who gave the psychologists what they claim is the best revelation of a person fully aware of herself, consequently, quite intimately acquainted with herself, and, therefore, one who most likely would *be* herself, and thus know happiness. Her replies ran, "I'm Mary N. I'm me. I'm myself."

Now, inadequate as that sounds, it certainly was better than the ones already quoted and far better than what the man offered who gave his street address, his army serial number, and his social security number. That man seemed to consider himself only a number! But you may be wondering how the psychologists could ever come to such conclusions about Mary N. from the seemingly obvious and almost meaningless replies that she gave. The explanation is not difficult. They claim that, to be happy, you must be able to express yourself fully, must be able to externalize your personality with ease and adequacy. But they also claim that, before you will ever be able to do that, you will have to *know yourself* — and know yourself intimately.

Looking at the replies of the housewife, they see that uppermost in her consciousness is the fact that she *is* herself. This indicates that she is quite well acquainted with what it is that makes her Mary So-and-So and nobody else. Hence, she really knows something of her inner drives, impulses, urges, and desires. Consequently, she will be able to express herself outwardly with ease and adequacy.

Naturally, you will ask if there is anything in such a claim. The answer is: Much! For it cannot be questioned that you tend to act externally in close accord with the mental picture you habitually have of yourself. "We are what our thoughts are." A thought almost inevitably gives birth to an act; if you repeat that act often enough, you generate a habit; if you consciously cultivate that habit, you will fashion a character.

∞

Psychology cannot tell you of yourself

That is why psychologists like to get an insight into your habitual way of thinking. Give them what spontaneously rises to your consciousness, and they will surprise you by going down to dark depths within you that you have never fathomed, measuring in you distances you had always thought measureless, calling back to consciousness things that you had completely forgotten. These men can tell you a startling amount *about* you, but how much can they tell you *of* you?

Thales of Miletus, considered one of the seven wise men of Greece, who lived five centuries before Christ — and fully twenty-five centuries before your modern psychiatry and psychology — was once asked, "What is most difficult?" His reply was: "To know thyself."

When the Greeks built a temple to Apollo at Delphi, they immortalized the wisdom of that reply by cutting deep into the marble that crowned the entrance the bold imperative "Know thyself." With that penetration which was the genius of the Greeks, these ancient pagans clearly recognized the fundamental character of this very personal problem. But they never found its solution.

Some moderns think they have. Certain present-day scientists claim that they have gone deeper into the study of man than any of the moralists or philosophers before them. They say they now know how to probe not only what lies below the level of your conscious mind, but quite easily can go far below your subconscious, and fathom the deep, deep reaches of your unconscious. And they do it. And yet, as far as the question "Who are you?" is concerned, they no more than scratch the surface.

Dr. Karl Stern was most emphatic in stating that "clinical concepts lose their significance when we enter the life of the spirit." In one place, he unqualifiedly admitted that "psychiatry and psychoanalysis are unable to penetrate the mystery of the *person*."[2] Yet, ultimately, the question "Who are you?" asks about nothing else. Hence, you can see that it can be answered adequately only by those who have learned what Dr. Karl Stern so repeatedly stressed:

[2] *The Third Revolution* (New York: Harcourt, Brace, 1954), 246.

namely, that there is something — there is definitely very much — "beyond the psychological."

A few decades back, the witty popularizer of science told you that your body was composed of lime enough to make six bars of soap, iron enough to fashion a half-dozen tenpenny nails, phosphorous enough for twenty boxes of matches, sugar enough to sweeten ten cups of coffee, just enough potassium to explode a toy cannon, and sufficient sulphur to deflea one fair-size dog. The price of those chemicals would be very little.

Today, while neither the physical nor the chemical constituents of man are neglected, ever heavier and heavier stress is being placed on the psychological. Too many modern scientists, however, stop short of the last logical step which would lead them to that broad, indestructible base on which rests the whole truth about the human individual. No one will deny that, today, more is known about your body and your mind, more about your emotions, instincts, sensations, desires, and drives, than, perhaps, was ever known before. Clearer insight into the unity of the human composite has been gained. This, in its turn, has generated a sharper awareness of the composite that makes the human individual. That is why it is something in the nature of an education to be examined in a modern clinic, for you learn an amazing amount not only about your physical constitution and your psychological makeup, but are told some astonishing truths about their constant interaction. You may come out a bit bewildered, but it will not have been the fault of the specialists who examined you if you do not come out pondering many definite truths about yourself as a psychological personality. But that is all these specialists do tell you about: your psychological personality. And that is something distinctly different from telling you anything about yourself as an ontological person. Yet, until this last depth is probed, you will never be able to answer that question which, by this time, has become a disturbing question: "Who are you?"

Specialists in the material sciences cannot help you. Psychologists who are not also real philosophers will be greater hindrances than helpers. And the psychologist-philosopher, if he is to be of any real assistance, will have to be something of a theologian; for this question about you as a human being cannot be answered without touching the Divine. Therefore, the only "ology" that can ever give proper reply to the question "Who are you?" is theology — a theology that teaches that each of us is a child of God who, under God's loving guidance and with God's generous help, is working out a God-given destiny.

∞

You must discover yourself with childlike faith

It sounds simple — almost too simple. It strikes you as something that would come only from the mouth of a child. But never forget: "Unless you become as little children, you shall not enter the kingdom of God."[3]

Note also just where the stress lies in the solution given — not on the word *child*, but on the phrase *of God*. For whenever you look at yourself and do not see the Love, Liberty, Power, Goodness, Greatness, and fierce Possessiveness who is God, you do not see yourself. Failing to see yourself aright, you will never come to the stimulating knowledge of just how important you are — and important to Almighty God — at this very moment of time, on this very crowded globe, whirling as a tiny speck in His almost limitless universe. What would it matter even if it did come from the lips of a child, so long as it is truth?

[3] Cf. Matt. 18:3.

Father Vincent McNabb, O.P., certainly one of the most zealous and keen-minded, priests of recent times, once tore the top page from a book written for children. That page held eight short questions and answers. Each question and answer had much to do with you and the query you are facing. Yet these questions and answers were not prepared for adults at all, but only for those who had just reached the age of the use of reason. "In sheer philosophic gratitude," Father McNabb wrote, "let me set down the first eight questions of this appeal made by dear Mother Church to the philosophical intelligence of her children of seven."

The man is not fooling. He knew philosophy as only those know it who have devoted a lifetime to its study. Here are the questions and answers:

Who made you?
God made me.

Why did God make you?
God made me to know Him, love Him,
and serve Him in this world, and to be
happy with Him forever in the next.

To whose image and likeness did God make you?
God made me to His own image and likeness.

Is this likeness to God in your body or in your soul?
This likeness is chiefly in my soul.

How is your soul like to God?
My soul is like to God because it is a spirit and is immortal.

What do you mean when you
say your soul is immortal?
When I say my soul is immortal,
I mean that it can never die.

Of which must you take most care,
of your body or of your soul?
I must take most care of my soul, for Christ has said,
"What doth it profit a man if he gain the whole world
and suffer the loss of his own soul?"[4]

What must you do to save your soul?
To save my soul, I must worship God by faith.

Looking at these questions from a book for children, would you consider them a "priceless gem of literature and philosophy"? Father McNabb did and justified his estimate by asking, "In the realm of letters, is there any masterpiece in any language that opens so dramatically as this, with its almost fierce accost, 'Who made you?' If since the time of Genesis and Plato, dialogue has been looked upon as a supreme form of literature, is there any more dramatic dialogue than this traffic of question and answer between the wisest institution in the world and a child of seven?"

He concludes, "Notice that the great truths underlying these questions are all within the discovery of human reason, yet human reason is not merely patient but expectant of faith."[5]

Human reason — *your* human reason — is not merely patient but expectant of faith.

∽

Reason and faith reveal your true self
The best brief reply ever given to the question "Who are you?" came from human reason illumined by faith: *I am a son of God.*

---

[4] Matt. 16:26.
[5] *Father McNabb Reader* (New York: P. J. Kenedy and Sons, 1954), 15, 16, 17.

Know thyself, and you will arrive at the thrilling knowledge that Y-O-U spells God! That is true not only in the alphabet of the theologian, who sits enraptured as God quietly tells how He composed that lyric we men call creation, but also in the alphabet of the philosopher, whose hands must ever go groping for ultimates. Four distinct times, the fingers of the philosopher must feel their way down those far reaches that wise men have named causes as he seeks for what is formal, what is final, what is efficient, and what is material about man.[6] Each time, those fingers will go on and on until they finally touch *God!*

Y-O-U must spell God in your alphabet if your days and nights are to be anything more than the passing of time. Know thyself, and you will become a garnerer who every day goes forth to a fresh field for God and is found at nightfall still busy binding sheaves that will stay tight for all eternity. Know thyself, and there will be no footstep in your life that will be without specific godly meaning. Know thyself, and you will come to some knowledge of the Infinite.

All your thinkers are forced by the stern, unyielding evidence of fact to admit that you are a creature and, therefore, were created; but too often many of them stress the wrong element in creation and, hence, tell but half the truth about you. Nothing could be more dangerous, for, while all half-truths are dangerous, there is none more dangerous than the one that says, "Creation is the production of something from nothing." That is no indication of whence you came. That is a shattered mirror that can hold only a distortion of what you are. Creation is not the production of

---

[6] Philosophers traditionally explained things in terms of what they called the four causes: formal cause, final cause, efficient cause, and material cause.

something from nothing; it is the production of something from nothing by the almighty *fiat* of Him who is your eternal and ever-loving Father.

Too often and too clearly, spiritual writers tell you truths about yourself that you need never be told. You know you have been fashioned from clay. Daily experience tells you how prone you are to evil, how weak is your will, and how dark your intellect. But just as it is impossible to handle pitch and come away with clean hands, so it is impossible to ward off disgust, discouragement, and even despair if you focus forever on the fact that you are "slime of the earth."[7]

That is not even half the truth of your origin. Revelation tells you that God made man on the sixth day. It was not on the first day, when He shattered the impenetrable darkness with His "Let there be light";[8] nor on the second, when He canopied earth with the heavens; nor on the third, when He separated land from the sea; nor was it on that fourth day, when He placed the sun and the moon in His sky; nor was it yet on the fifth, when He put life into the waters of the sea and filled the air with the flashing wings and the songs of birds. Only after He had filled His world with wonders did He set about fashioning that masterpiece that was to be the crown of His visible creation.

On that sixth day, the unchangeable God changed His manner of making. He did not say, "Let man be made," as He had said about light and the firmament and all the other creatures. He said, "Let us make man."[9] The difference is highly significant and tells you precisely why and how Y-O-U spells God. This text set St.

[7] Gen. 2:7.
[8] Gen. 1:3.
[9] Gen. 1:26.

John Chrysostom[10] exclaiming, "What wonder is this? Who is he for whose production God takes counsel and Sovereign Wisdom enters into deliberation?" This same text set King David singing, "It was your hands, O God, that formed and fashioned me."[11] This was the text that caused St. Ambrose[12] to remark that what was sufficient to give being to the great universe was not enough to give being to man; for while, with one of His hands, God made the heavens and rendered them incorruptible, it took two of His hands to fashion man.

The story of your beginning as told by God the Holy Spirit in the first book of the Bible is essential for any intelligent and true reply to the question "Who are you?" For, while reason might lead you on, as it led Plato, and have you calling yourself "the horizon of the universe" as this wise old pagan did, because in you the two spheres of the angelic and the animal meet, reason alone would never lead you on to the vision of the divine sculpting that took place on the sixth day. Nor would it tell you how the Sculptor Divine bent over that clay and breathed His own breath into it so that man might be.

Reason might tell you that you are from God, but revelation alone explains how Y-O-U spells God. And you must know how to spell before you can reply to "Who are you?"

Y-O-U spells God now just as it has, and will, at every moment of your existence. For you are a breath of God that He is still breathing. Your continuance in being is as dependent on God's continual breathing as the liquid beauty in a thrush's note is dependent on that thrush and its singing.

---

[10] St. John Chrysostom (c. 347-407), Bishop of Constantinople.

[11] Ps. 118:73 (RSV = Ps. 119:73).

[12] St. Ambrose (c. 339-397), Bishop of Milan.

Y-O-U will go on spelling God so long as God is God, for "Heaven and earth shall pass away," but His Word will never pass away[13] — and you are a syllable in His Word!

That is the ultimate answer this book shall give to the question "Who are you?" It is a reply different from any you may obtain from men who know your body inside out and your psyche to its last and least movement. It is a reply that comes from those who are wise with the wisdom that teaches that life is not something, but Someone. It is the only reply that can be given in a book that is to be a pedestal, a stairway, and a ship.

But while it is different from the replies so many modern men will give you, there is nothing really new about this reply. It is almost as ancient as the sun. Yet, like all living truth, it is as fresh as this morning's dawn. Like God's own beauty, it is something "ever ancient, ever new,"[14] for its most sublime phrasing fell from the lips Wisdom Incarnate used to articulate His message of love. It came from them just before those lips were blistered by the kiss of the traitor, broken and bloodied by the blows of the soldiers, and finally blackened by death. Thus, it is a reply that forms part of the last testament given to man by God — a final bequest, as it were, from Him who "emptied Himself"[15] so that you might be filled. Hence, it is something transcendently sacred. It is Christ with almost His last breath saying, "You are a branch of that Vine which is I."[16]

Think of it: you, with all your lusts, angers, envies, jealousies, and sloth; you with all your meanness, pettiness, and towering

---

[13] Matt. 24:35; Mark 13:31; Luke 21:33.

[14] St. Augustine (354-430; Bishop of Hippo), *Confessions*, Bk. 10, ch. 27.

[15] Phil. 2:7.

[16] Cf. John 15:5.

pride; you with all your covetousness; you who can be such a glutton; you with all your secret ambitions for earthly glory, your sly schemings for passing honors, your craving for worldly wealth; you who so reek of the earthy earth — you are *His* member!

The answer to the question "Who are you?" should be given on your knees; for it is sacred with the very sanctity of God. You are a syllable in that Word God spoke in the unbeginning of eternity.

You are a branch in that Vine God planted in time, setting it out on a Judean hillside so that it might one day climb the trellis of the Cross.

You are a living stone in that temple whose cornerstone is the never-dying Christ.

You are a member of that Body whose Head is "God from God, true God from true God."

To know yourself intimately, learn first that you are *one sent by God.*

Chapter One

∞

You are one sent by God

You are one sent by God: such words startle when you find them applied unqualifiedly to yourself. For they are rich with the sound of Sacred Scripture and conjure up scenes of both time and eternity. They show the bronzed Baptist standing by the Jordan, telling men fearlessly of the One in their midst whom they knew not. They open the very heavens for you, let you hear God the Father speaking of His Son and let you see God the Holy Spirit descending as a dove. Thus, they take you back through two thousand years of time and bring you to the beginning of Christ's public life.

But they do more than that. They take you back through all time and bring you face-to-face with that beginning which was "the unbeginning of endlessness and eternity" as they show you the blissful Trinity. Yet these words are spoken unequivocally about you. You are one sent by God.

That should neither frighten you nor fill you with awe, because if you but knew yourself, you would ever be conscious not only of your origin but of your mission as well; and beating in your blood would be the realization that you have a dignity and a destiny that are divine. You are one sent by God.

∞

You didn't come to be by chance ˎ

The truth is old as old as creation. But because man has been, and still is, such a heresiarch, this old and utterly unassailable truth about yourself strikes your ears now with some of the stridency of blasphemy. Yet, this was the answer given by Pius XII[17] to the question "Who are you?" He was addressing university professors, telling them just exactly what the university's task was, when suddenly he broke off and used as a climax to a very earnest argument about their God-given assignment these words: "You are one sent by God."

Other explanations of your origin have been given, it is true; but they have never explained it. It may amuse you to read today what Cicero had to say about atoms a full half-century before Christ and more than twenty centuries before Einstein or Hiroshima. He was talking to the materialists of his day. Very quietly, but with deep earnestness, he asked them, "If the clash of atoms could create a world, why can it not produce a colonnade, a temple, a house, a city — things less indeed than the world, and much less difficult to make?" The materialists of your day, who can split atoms and shatter a universe, will stand mute before that question as stood the materialists of Cicero's time; for no mature mind will attribute to dead, unthinking matter, even if filled with energy, light, and whirling electrons, an omnipotence that any adolescent mind will refuse to Almighty God — namely, the power to produce something infinitely greater than itself.

Sound philosophy, which always squares with sanity and common sense, teaches apodictically that no effect can ever be greater than its cause. The clay does not shape the potter. Matter never

---

[17] Pius XII (1876-1958), Pope from 1939.

makes a mind. The light in your eyes was kindled and could only be kindled by Him who dwells in light inaccessible.[18]

Some moderns may still apotheosize chance by giving it a capital letter. But few will adore such a deity; and fewer still accept it as explanation of your existence. Centuries ago, the able and eloquent François Fénelon[19] argued that it would be as logical to propose chance as the explanation of the universe (or of any individual in the universe) as it would be to suppose the *Iliad* came into being by taking the letters of the alphabet, tossing them into the air, letting the winds sport with them for a while, then having them come down arranged in the perfection of that fascinating Greek epic.

You would never credit chance with the ability to shape so much as the last joint in the little finger of a tiny child. How could it ever organize, then, anything like your complex nervous system or arrange so much as the cortex of your brain with its two billion cells?

It was an American psychiatrist who remarked that, at every moment of your existence, there are going on in one single nerve cell of yours processes of such great complexity that an assembly of all the Nobel Prize winners in chemistry could not re-create them. A French biophysicist calculated the time necessary for one protein molecule to occur as a chance combination of atoms and found that the theoretical age of the earth — something like 4.5 billion years — would not be long enough. A German neurologist once pointed out that the mere fact that you are reading this page and understanding it is proof of the existence of a First Cause and an unchallengeable proof that you have been created by a Spirit: you think; therefore, He is! Indeed, you are one sent by God.

---

[18] Cf. 1 Tim. 6:16.

[19] François Fénelon (1651-1715), Archbishop of Cambrai.

Those words are scriptural. They come to you from God the Holy Spirit, the Author of Scripture. Yet they come to you also with somewhat similar majesty and imperious truth from that God-given gift of common sense and ordinary sanity. Look at yourself in the light of reason, and if you do not see that you are a casement opening wide on Divinity, blind indeed is your vision. If you study yourself and do not see the ever-living, immense, all-wise, all-powerful, all-beautiful God within you, without you, above you, and below you, you have not studied yourself at all. For to what revelation so majestically testifies, reason joyfully concurs.

☙

You as an individual are important

You are one sent by God. The truth cannot be repeated often enough. For there is a strong, almost universal modern heresy that somehow seeps into the mental atmosphere even of the most orthodox. It is that heresy which teaches that the human individual is of no importance.

That *is* heresy — monstrous heresy. For it makes the infinitely wise God witless. It shows Him crowning His wondrous visible creation with that which is negligible. It has Him stamping His own image and likeness on wax that is worthless. The longer you look at this heresy, the larger its horrors loom. Actually, it attributes to God what basest man would not attribute to an imbecile, namely, the deliberate bestowal of what is most intimate and which He alone can grant — eternal life — on one who is unworthy of any regard.

Yet that heresy is practically universal. In present-day economics, what are you, as an individual, accounted? At best, exploitable and dispensable. In statecraft, be the issue war or peace, you are looked upon as readily expandable. In international and national society, you are rated as practically negligible. There are the facts: as an individual, you simply do not count with "the lords of this earth."[20] Yet the truth remains: *you are one sent by God.*

For the sake of argument — or for the sake of avoiding truth-giving argument — some of the followers of this heresy may admit that you are one sent by God, but they will quickly add, "God has not yet created the indispensable man or woman." That, too, is heresy. The exact opposite is the truth: never yet has God created a man or a woman who *is* dispensable! There is not a single person on the face of the earth this moment who is not, in the strictest sense of the word, necessary to Omnipotence. You would not now be breathing, your heart would not be beating if the all-sufficient and only self-sufficient God did not have vital need for you at this very moment. You are not only one sent by God, but one sent *for a purpose.*

Sound philosophy, ever striving to articulate truth with conciseness and crystal clarity, says that no intelligent person acts without a purpose. God is infinite Intelligence. He acted to create you. He still acts to keep you in creation. Now, if this philosophic axiom falls with full force upon the inventor of so simple a thing as a common pin, with what weight must it fall on the Creator of the universe and the Maker of all men? If you, despite your limited intelligence, do not so much as blink an eye or move a finger without definite purpose, what of Him who moves the heavens and the earth and continually "stirs the ever-beating sea"? God had a purpose — an all-wise purpose — for saying *fiat* on that first day of creation, when "the earth was void and empty, and darkness was upon the face of the deep";[21] He had the same purpose — and be it

[20] Cf. 1 Cor. 8:5.
[21] Gen. 1:2.

said again: it was an all-wise purpose — for saying *fiat* on creation's final day, when He "created man to His own image."[22]

∞

God created to communicate His goodness

Philosophers have long wondered just why God ever said *fiat* at all. They know He had a reason, for sanity demands it. But they are nonplused to say precisely what that reason could have been. Certainly it was nothing outside Him, for there *was* nothing outside Him. They are equally certain that there was nothing inside Him that could have *necessitated* the utterance of that creating word, for God is liberty itself.

Some have said — among them Bishop Fulton J. Sheen — that "God was in love, and could not keep the secret. The telling of it was creation." That is a fetching solution, and very happily phrased. It has much truth in it. But the trouble with that solution is that God did not have to tell His secret to anyone or anything outside Himself. God is a Triunity. The Father tells all He knows to the Son, and the love story He had to tell was expressed eternally in the Holy Spirit. So, while God is love, and love is ever diffusive of self, God's infinite love was infinitely and eternally diffused within Himself. It needed no expression in sun, moon, stars, or sea; it felt no need to tell its secret in majestic mountains or in even more majestic man.

There is the philosophical and theological fact: God did not have to create you, the world, or anything! He created freely, for there is no other way God could act and still remain God. But because He created freely, it does not follow that He created arbitrarily or without set purpose; for that, too, would be contrary to His

---

[22] Gen. 1:27.

very being, which is supreme intelligence and absolute holiness of will.

Why, then, did God call to the depths of nothingness and summon you into everlasting being? What was the reason for that specific *fiat* which created your soul? It has to be a reason that will square with God's infinite intelligence and spotless sanctity. Reason can assign only one — and that is the one that revelation joyfully confirms. It explains the all-but-invisible pulse beat at your temple this moment, just as it explains that mysterious movement of the Spirit over the waters back in that dark before light was made. That one purpose was, and is, and can only be *Himself*.

God made you for Himself. God made everything else — day, night, the firmament, the waters above and under the firmament, the atom and the sun, the star-choked Milky Way, oxygen and hydrogen, everything — all for *Himself*.

But when it is said that God made you and everything else for Himself, it is not said that He was or is selfish. Just the opposite. When you act for yourself, you always act to *acquire*. You have to, for such is the nature of an imperfect being. You always reach out to get something that will increase your perfection. But when God, the perfect Being, acts, even though He does and must act for Himself, He does not act to acquire, but to *communicate*. He reaches out to give something away. For such is the nature of the perfect act and of the action of the perfect Being. He communicates goodness.

That is what philosophers and theologians mean when they say God's purpose in creating was Himself. Love acted. Love acted for Himself. Love acted out of goodness, which is Himself. Love acted to manifest His love. That means only one thing: God acted to communicate His goodness. That is why, when you look closely enough, you find a strong family resemblance in everything that is. You and they are not only from God, but from Him for the same purpose. The Vatican Council[23] says that that purpose is to "manifest His perfection." To stress that truth, the same council pronounced an anathema on all who would dare deny that you, and everything else in creation, is to "show forth God's glory" each in its own particular way.

∞

God continuously keeps you in existence

Now, here is life's most exciting truth: You are one sent by God to manifest Him in a manner no human before you, no human on earth with you, and no human who may come after you, could, or ever can, manifest Him! You have something of God in you that no one else in creation can display. You have something to manifest that, if you fail to show it, will be lost to man, to the world, and, in one sense, even to God Himself for all eternity. That is how important you are as an individual — and important to Omnipotence Himself. You are one sent by God — *for a very specific purpose*.

Strange as it may sound, that is the only explanation of your present existence that can do justice to God's intelligence or to your own. If Omnipotence did not have a personal and very special purpose for you this very moment, you simply would not be. If Omniscience did not have some personal and specific demand for you on earth as an intellectual being at this particular moment of time, you would not now be enjoying your intellectuality. All that has been said about the necessity for God's having some reason for your coming into being holds true for every split second of your *continuance* in being.

[23] The author refers to the First Vatican Council. — ED.

That is a truth you seldom bring to mind. Yet it is a truth that can do wonders to your heart. In a world where you as an individual are made to feel utterly unimportant, how stimulating it is to realize that you are:

A breath of God, which God
must keep on breathing;

A syllable in that Word of God,
which God must go on pronouncing;

An image and likeness to God,
which God must go on producing;

A very specific manifestation of God's glory,
which God must keep on showing;

A creature of God, whom God
must keep on creating.

That final fact is the one that brings all the other facts into sharpest focus. You are a created being. Therefore, you are a product that only God could bring forth. But since you are such a product, you can continue to exist only so long as God continues to create you.

That idea is, at first, positively baffling. For you are so very conscious of your own individual existence, and so completely unconscious, in any physical sense, of anyone sustaining you in existence, that you simply refuse to believe that the ever-living God must keep on working if you are to keep on living. Your heart keeps beating, your lungs go on breathing, all your bodily processes go on working, and since you help these life-sustaining systems by taking air and food and sleep, you subconsciously think that you are the one who keeps yourself in being. But no. You are as dependent on God for continuance in life as the sunbeam is on the sun for its continuance in shining.

This fact, irrefutable though it be, can, and often does, stir resentment — especially in those who live in a land that was brought into political being by a very forthright Declaration of Independence. But that is only because these same people have failed to note that the Preamble to that declaration contains, as a solid foundation stone, a very positive declaration of dependence. "We hold these truths to be self-evident," said our Founding Fathers, "that all men are *created*" and "that they are endowed by their *Creator* . . ." Actually, it is this continued dependence that gives you your continual independence. Far from being an affront to your individuality, it is that individuality's glory: for you are yoked to no one less than God. You who were called into being in time, and who live in time, are one who is ever linked to the Eternal. In very truth, your eternity has already begun.

You may have seen a fog upon a mountain, but you have never seen a mountain upon a fog. You may meet a singer who is momentarily without his song, but you will never, at any moment, meet a song without a singer. For while there can be light without a shadow, there never was, and there never will be, a shadow unless there is a light.

Now, you are "one sent by God to give testimony to the Light!"[24] What greater thrill could you desire than to realize that you will never again cast the slightest shadow upon the earth unless the Light of the World keeps shining and illuminating you? Grasp this fact firmly: God could, and did, exist without man, but no man ever could, no man now can, and no man ever will, for so much as a measureless flash of time, exist without God.

[24] Cf. John 1:8.

26

This truth needs repeating. By your very nature, you are a dependent being. Your every breath calls out to Omniscience for attention if there is to be another. For just as your lungs must have a supply of air from moment to moment if they are not to collapse, so you must have a supply of existence from split second to split second if you are not to vanish completely, slipping back to that abysmal void which was your original nothingness. God alone can furnish you with that supply of existence, just as it was He alone who could give you existence in the first place.

To realize that you are so vitally linked to the Almighty that your next breath and your next heartbeat depend entirely upon Him should enable you to see that when Pius XII called you a "precious person," he was actually making an understatement. But what word can describe you who, in God's infallible scale of values, far outweigh the entire universe? What phrase will fittingly describe you who live only because God is somehow breathing in your body and pulsing in your blood? It is no easy matter to express your worth, but the fact that it is God who keeps you alive ought to furnish you with some idea of your own personal value and the pricelessness of each moment of time. Every passing second has for its backdrop eternity; for it is from the infinite wisdom and the ever-purposeful will of the Eternal One that each comes.

∞

God created you for a specific purpose

Creation tells you that you are one sent by God. With perhaps greater force, conservation insists that you are one sent *for a purpose*. Without these two truths as foundation, you cannot build your life even on shifting sand.

But it is not enough for you to be vibrantly conscious of the fact that you are one sent by God, and sent for a purpose; you must also know precisely what that purpose is. For only thus will you learn your exact stature and be able to give the lie to that modern and almost universal heresy that would take you — who have come from the infinite mind and omnipotent will of the eternal God — and make you infinitesimal.

Astronomers demonstrate that you and your tiny earth are all but lost in a corner of this ever-expanding universe. Mathematically, their proofs are unassailable. The picture they present of you and your earth is true to figures and to the facts generated by those figures. But the conclusion they draw from such figures and facts is utterly false. They would have you deem yourself and your earth next to worthless. That conclusion, false though it be, can have a soul-destroying effect on you if you do not keep on reminding yourself that it was in this all-but-lost corner of the universe that God became man — and became man for you; that it was here that God became a corpse — and became a corpse for you; that here everlasting life with God the all-holy was made possible by God for you. Then you can go on reminding yourself that it is here in this tiny corner that God keeps on creating you so that you may, in your own specific manner, fulfill the special function that the omnipotent Maker of this ever-expanding universe had in mind when He said *fiat* for you.

To know that on this whirling bit of burned-out stardust, you have a mission from Almighty God and for Almighty God, which no one else in the universe can discharge, is a challenge to the best that is in you. You who, but a few short years ago, were absolutely nothing are now throbbing with life so that you may radiate the Eternal; you who are considered by the powerful of earth as completely negligible, are now on earth by God's command and thanks to God's continued action so that you might show forth some shadow of Omnipotence and make manifest in your own particular way that goodness which is the very essence of God. What a mission is yours!

But how can you fulfill it? How can you, who know something of your ever-wavering will and your other weaknesses, ever measure up to the demand made by the omniscient and omnipresent God?

That question brings you face-to-face with the only problem of your life: How are you ever to be true to yourself?

To be true to yourself is a challenge of staggering proportions. It is a demand that you be godlike — that you, a mortal of but a few years, give the ever-immortal God glory. Well might you wonder how to do it, had not God given you detailed direction on just how you are to fulfill the sublime mission He has entrusted to you.

A shackled man once became an amanuensis for God the Holy Spirit. He had been imprisoned by the Romans, but the message he sent from his prison cell is one that will enable you to keep your soul, and the soul of every other believer, in the most complete freedom, no matter what fetters may be placed on your flesh. It is a message that has not only outlasted the mighty world empire that had imprisoned the man, but is destined to outlive every empire this world will ever see, for it is a message from God and of God.

Paul, the prisoner, addressed it long ago to his Ephesian converts, but God the Holy Spirit, the real Author of the message, was addressing it very directly and very purposefully to you who call yourself modern. Both God the Holy Spirit and the prisoner Paul had but one end in view: to kindle in you a confidence that nothing on earth will ever be able to quench. It is for you to let the reality they portray sink into your soul so that you may really live.

"Peace be yours from God, our Father, and from the Lord Jesus Christ."[25] Thus begins Paul at the dictation of the Holy Spirit.

---

[25] Eph. 1:2.

Now, greetings from God are never mere conventional phrases. They burn with a sincerity that gave being to the seraphim. God wants you to have peace — that "tranquillity of order" which can be enjoyed only when God is in His place and you are in yours. Those places are specified by Paul and the Holy Spirit when they mention your "Father" and your "Lord Jesus Christ." With an insistence that is almost alarming, the Holy Spirit repeats these words, which show forth so intimate a relation between you and Divinity that the human intellect staggers back in what is close to unbelief. "Blessed be that God, that Father of our Lord Jesus Christ, who has blessed you, in Christ, with every spiritual blessing, higher than Heaven itself. He has chosen you out, in Christ, before the foundation of the world, to be a saint, to be blameless in His sight, for love of Him; marking you out beforehand (so His will decreed) to be His adopted child through Jesus Christ."[26]

Before that passage, Pope St. Leo the Great[27] once sat in profoundest awe. He was hearing God's protest of everlasting love in that choice He made of you "in Christ, before the foundations of the world." But he also heard God's plea for a return of love in that "marking you out beforehand to be His adopted child through Jesus Christ." Truly it is bewildering: the length of it, the love of it, the infinite intimacy of it! St. Leo finally sat back and exclaimed, "Surely, the right to call God 'Father' is the greatest of gifts!"

Now, why did God bestow this "greatest of gifts" on you? What was His purpose in selecting you before the foundations of the world to be His child? Paul told his Ephesians. The Holy Spirit tells you. "Thus He would manifest the splendor of that grace by

---

[26] Cf. Eph. 1:3-5 (Knox translation). The second-person form of the pronoun has been substituted for *us* in the original.

[27] St. Leo I (d. 461), Pope from 440.

which He has taken you into His favor in the person of His be-loved Son."[28] The Holy Spirit then goes on to reveal the reason for the constant repetition of the words *Jesus Christ* and *beloved Son* as He spreads wide for you the overall plan of God, saying, "It was His loving design, centered in Christ, to give history its fulfillment by resuming everything in Him, all that is in Heaven, all that is on earth, summed up in Him."[29]

All things in Christ — that is the loving design of God. And that design, drawn up in eternity, includes you who live in these days of airplanes. That eternal design, which sums up A-bombs, H-bombs, and supersonic speeds in Christ Jesus, is the plan of God for you. That is why the Holy Spirit inspired Paul to write, "In Him it was your lot to be called, singled out beforehand to suit His purpose," which is "to manifest His glory."[30]

There is God's eternal purpose underlined: You are to manifest His glory by *living in Christ Jesus*.

But those directives from Paul to his Ephesians, and from God the Holy Spirit to you, seem only to pile mystery on mystery. For secular history tells you that Jesus Christ lived and died two thou-sand years ago. Sacred history tells you that He rose from the dead, ascended into Heaven, and sits now at the right hand of the Fa-ther. Yet you are told that you are to live in this same Jesus Christ, for, in Him, you were "chosen out before the foundations of the world."

All this astounded Paul as much as it bewilders you. That is why he prayed, "So may He who is the God of our Lord Jesus

---

[28] Eph. 1:6 (Knox translation).

[29] Eph. 1:9-10 (Knox translation).

[30] Cf. Eph. 1:11 (Knox translation). The second-person form of the pronoun has been substituted for *our* in the original.

Christ, the Father to whom glory belongs, grant you a spirit of wisdom and insight, to give you fuller knowledge of Himself. May your inward eye be enlightened, so that you may understand to what hopes He has called you, how rich in glory is that inheritance of His found among the saints, what surpassing virtue there is in His dealings with us who believe."[31]

It *is* a matter of belief. But let no one ever speak to you of "blind" belief. Faith opens your eyes; it does not close them. Faith gives vision; and without vision men die, for they become nothing more than cattle. Faith is that gift of God which allows you to see through appearances and to focus on substance; it is that special God-given grant which gives you evidence of things that cannot be seen. That is exactly how God the Holy Spirit once described faith through this same St. Paul. "It is the substance of things to be hoped for," He said, "the evidence of things that are not seen."[32] Faith is a gift and a grant that defies evaluation, for it enables you to see beyond that last horizon where burning sand and flaming sky blur into one and to rest your eyes on the only Oasis where exiled man will find the water that will let him live. It is no mirage. It will never induce desert madness: for it is God.

∞

You are called to help complete Christ's work

Do you wish to know the height and the depth and the breadth of your God-given vocation? "Measure it," say Paul and the Holy Spirit, "by that mighty exercise of power which He [God] showed when he raised Christ from the dead, and bade Him sit on His right hand above the heavens, high above all Princedoms and

---

[31] Eph. 1:17-19 (Knox translation).

[32] Heb. 11:1 (Confraternity translation).

Powers and Virtues and Dominations, and every name that is known, not in this world only, but in the world to come."[33]

Then comes the truth that is to be the foundation of your life and all your living: "He has put everything under His dominion, and made Him the head to which the whole Church is joined, *so that the Church is His Body,* the completion of Him who everywhere and in all things is complete."[34]

Christ is the Head to which you are joined. You are a member of that Church which is His Body. You are "the completion of Him who everywhere and in all things is complete."

That last puzzling phrase contains the heart of the solution to this whole problem of you, your life, and that life's work. The Greek verb found in the original may mean exactly what Monsignor Knox has set down — namely, "is complete." Knowing that Christ is God, you will have no difficulty in seeing that He is complete. But you may well wonder how He who "is complete" could ever need completion. Yet that is precisely what Paul and the Holy Spirit say: The Church is the completion of Christ. So you must realize that the same Greek verb can also mean "who completes." Then you will relish the footnote appended to the Kleist-Lilly translation of this passage, which reads: "Just as the head is completed by the rest of the body, so Christ is completed in His mission as Savior by the Church, which continues and prolongs His work through time and space. He, in turn, *supplies the members* with all needed grace." Thus you see that He completes and is completed. But the translation that will aid you most in knowing just who you are and what you are to do in life is the one added at the end of this same footnote. God, the Father has appointed the

---

[33] Eph. 1:19-21 (Knox translation).

[34] Eph. 1:22-23 (Knox translation; emphasis added).

Christ as universal head of the Church, which is "the complement of Him, who in all things *is made complete by means of us all.*"[35]

You are to complete Christ. You are to fill out the very Son of God. That is why you were born. That is why you were brought into this world. You are one sent by God to give testimony to the Light. That is why God, by that marvelous process which is called *conservation*, but which in reality is continued creation, keeps you in being. God is to shine out through you. You are a lamp for the Light of the World. You are a flame in that fire that Christ came to throw upon the earth, and which He was in agony to see ablaze.[36] "You were once darkness, but now you are light in the Lord. Walk, then, as children of light."[37]

To know yourself and understand your mission, go back now and read that magnificent prologue to St. John's Gospel, a passage that rings with the solemn tones of eternity. It begins:

> In the beginning was the Word,
> and the Word was with God,
> and the Word was God.
> He was in the beginning with God;
> all things were made through Him,
> and without Him was not anything
>   made that was made.
> In Him was life,
> and the life was the light of men.
> The light shines in the darkness,
> and the darkness has not overcome it.[38]

---

[35] Emphasis added.

[36] Cf. Luke 12:49.

[37] Eph. 5:8 (Knox translation).

[38] John 1:1-5 (Revised Standard Version).

But "Jesus Christ, the same yesterday, today, and forever"[39] would go on shining in the darkness. Did He not promise that He would be with us all days?[40] But how can He be, unless you let Him? He will not shine unless you "give testimony to the Light." He will not live on earth unless He lives in you.

There, then, is the all-but-unbelievable truth: You are one sent by God *to continue Christ's Incarnation and help Him complete His work of Redemption.* Believe that with all your being, and you will readily see that life has meaning — that you are *one whom Almighty God actually needs!*

[39] Heb. 13:8.
[40] Cf. Matt. 28:20.

Chapter Two

∞

You are one whom Almighty God needs

You are on a stairway that leads to God. You have mounted a pedestal that yearns toward God. You are on a ship that will plow steadily on and bring you to God. These truths are told so that God may become more real to you than the bread you eat — so that He may become more essential to you than the food and the air by which your body lives. For you must come to know what life is — and *have* it in abundance; you must never again be deceived by appearances or lured on by mere imitations. Hence, you are now taken to wells as deep as your eternal, invisible God and given what can become in you "a fountain of water welling up into eternal life."[41]

But what *is* life?

After reading these first two chapters, you know the only valid answer: Life is not something; it is *Someone*. It is He who said, "I am the bread of life. . . . I am the living bread that has come down from Heaven. If anyone eats of this bread, he will live forever."[42] It is He who said, "I am come that they may have life, and have it in

[41] John 4:14.
[42] John 6:51.

37

abundance."[43] It is He who, on the night before He died, said, "I will not leave you orphans; I am coming back to you . . . because I live, and you, too, will live."[44] It is He who, on that same sad yet wondrous night, said, "I am the vine; you are the branches."[45] It is He who flatly stated, "I am the Life."[46]

∞

God truly needs you

Yes, He is the Life; He is your life; yet it is He who actually *needs* you — so that He may *live!*

Do not let that paradox frighten you. You cannot confront the Divine without being faced with what is palpably paradoxical. The long history of God and man is nothing but a tissue of seeming contradictions. Did God not take the slime of the earth and make it the crown of His visible creation by shaping it into man? Then, did not this finite man, with his puny will, openly defy the only will that is infinite and omnipotent? Thereupon, did not God promise to empty Himself and become man so that man might be filled and become like unto God? Have you not been invited to the marriage of the Lamb in that city which has no lamp, yet is always brilliantly lighted?[47] Thus, from beginning to end, there is paradox. But, after all, that is but vivid proof that God is God and man is man, and the two are in intimate contact.

Once you grasp the paradox that says that the never-dying God needs you so that He may live, you will learn not only how near

---

[43] John 10:10.

[44] John 14:18-19.

[45] John 15:5.

[46] John 14:6.

[47] Cf. Rev. 19:9, 21:23.

God is to you but also how dear you are to God, and life will take on both meaning and beauty.

God needs you. The Creator actually needs the creature. The only independent Being in existence needs you whose very essence and existence spell dependence; and He needs you so that He may exist on earth. Omnipotence, then, is calling to impotence so that He may exercise His power. The Infinite leans on you who are finite so that the Eternal may have expression in time. Pile up the paradoxes; each is absolutely true. The uncaused First Cause needs you who are but a contingent effect of His creative action; and He needs you so that He may go on exercising His causality. The sole Redeemer of mankind needs you whom He has redeemed; and He needs you so that He may save — both you and others. The God-Man stands in actual need of you so that you and other men may become like God. Omniscience, Omnipotence, Immensity need you so that They may have space in that universe which They called into being from nothingness!

The longer the reflection, the more the paradoxes multiply. But religion without mystery would not be religion; conscious, intimate contact with the Divine without palpable paradox would not be contact with the Divine; life that raised no questions about the unknown factors in living would not be life. So face this fact squarely: the God who made you, the God who keeps you in being is the God who actually needs you this moment, so that He Himself may now go on living on this earth. Far from contradicting all you have known about God, this truth is but a complement to all you have just been learning about God and yourself. If He made you for a purpose, and keeps you in being to fulfill that purpose, that purpose can only be His actual need of you.

That fact, faced fully for perhaps the first time, most likely frightens you. But that fright is perfectly normal. To know that the breath of God is not only on your neck or on your face, but actually in your very breathing, to become conscious of the truth that your heart is beating only because you are pulsing somehow with the Divinity, can cause in you the same elemental fear you feel when face-to-face with a fire completely out of control, or when lost in a stormy sea.

This kind of fear seized those who saw Jesus walk up to the coffin in which the widow of Naim's only son lay, and after hearing Him say, "Young man, I command you, awake!" saw the boy sit up.[48] It is the same kind of fear that fell on those outside the tomb of Lazarus the day Jesus cried, "Come forth!" and a bound man, who had been four days dead, stumbled out to the light.[49] But, just as with those who saw Jesus' miracles, so, too, with you, this elemental fear will soon be followed by wonder, then admiration, and finally by grateful adoration. For, to learn that you mean much to God, to have your every moment of earthly existence pulse with purpose predetermined and prized by the infinite Mind and Will, to learn that Christ actually needs you is to learn why Mary sang, "*Magnificat*,"[50] why Zachary sang, "*Benedictus*,"[51] and why you can sing, "*Sanctus, sanctus, sanctus*."[52]

Yet, if this fear persists and does not quickly become wonder, gratitude, and adoration, it is proof positive that you never really learned what lay implicit in those questions and answers on that page Father McNabb tore from the child's catechism. It proves more. It proves that you have been taken in by the world — that

---

[48] Luke 7:14-15.

[49] John 11:43-44.

[50] "My soul magnifies the Lord . . ."; cf. Luke 1:46-55.

[51] "Blessed be the Lord . . ."; cf. Luke 1:68-79.

[52] "Holy, holy, holy"; cf. Isa 6:3; Apoc. 4:8 (RSV = Rev. 4:8).

you have been using a set of values that is false and scales that are anything but up to standard. It proves that you have not been living fully, no matter how alive you may have thought yourself to be.

For God is one, and God is life. Therefore, life is a unity. But what have you been making of it? Have you not divorced time and eternity? Have you not separated the natural from the supernatural? Have you not partitioned off your religion from your work, your play, your social contacts, your business world, and your weekday existence? What place has God held in your life from morning to night, from Sunday to Saturday, from year to year? Have you given so much as first place to Him who wants the only place?

∞

God must have the only place in your life

Prepare yourself at once to give a real assent to the truth that first place in your life is not enough for the God who made you! He has not loved you with an everlasting love just to have the first place in your life, ahead of many other loves and countless other interests. He does not now exert His omnipotence, nor every day, from dawn to dusk then on through the night, ply His Providence just to have first place in your life. He would never shatter nothingness with His creative cry of *fiat* just for first place. He merits and He wants the *only* place!

That does not mean that you are not to have other loves and other interests — far from it. Once you have given God the only place in your life, your loves are multiplied and your interests become innumerable; for you live fully, and the almost limitless capacity of your heart for loves and of your mind for interests, in God and under God and for God, will be receiving its fill.

But before that tide begins to swell, you will have to make your life the unity God planned it. You will have to integrate your whole day and your entire existence. You will have to blend into "perfect harmony," as Pope Pius XII put it, the many elements that make up your living. Since you are what your thoughts are, your first task is to realize, with a dynamic realization, that while you can legitimately talk of "this world" and "the other world," your Heaven actually begins on earth — or it does not begin at all. The same drive and dynamism must be present in your conviction that, while there is a real distinction between time and eternity, your eternity has already begun in time — all of which means that you are not only living face-to-face with God, but that you are actually living in God and God is actually living in you.

Blindness to this thrilling reality accounts for all the emptiness in life, all the restlessness of the human individual, and the gnawing dissatisfaction that eats at the human soul like some cancer. Forgetting that the God of nature and the God of supernature is the one, same, living, and only true God; forgetting that it is only on the natural that the supernatural can rest and from it arise; forgetting that the practical task of paramount importance in the world of today is the supernaturalizing of the natural, too many humans never know life, for they go seeking God where they never can find Him. They have divorced Him, the Source of all reality, from all the realities around them. They have separated the body of life from the Soul of life, and wonder why they have nothing in their hands but a corpse.

If you would live life as it is meant to be lived, you must never dare to put asunder what Almighty God has joined. Religion, or conscious, intimate contact with God, must not only dominate, but must penetrate and permeate all your living. That means you are not only to worship while at work, but your work itself must be worship; you are not to go from play to prayer or from prayer to play, but your play itself must be a form of prayer; you are to sleep, and sleep soundly, but all the while your heart is to be watching;[53] and when you are awake, you are to be wide awake to the God you are adoring with your entire being.

If that strikes you in any way as exaggerated, you have never known yourself or your God. Religion is no mere philosophy of life, no mere way of life, and not simply an accessory to living. Religion is life, or it is not religion; and life is religious, or it is a mere sham. Paul told you as much when he said, "Whether, then, you eat or drink, or do anything else, do everything for God's glory."[54]

∞

Christ expressed need in His life on earth

Once you follow that directive, your invisible God becomes the all-pervading Obvious One, and His Christ, who "was born of the Virgin Mary, suffered under Pontius Pilate, was crucified, died, and was buried,"[55] becomes your contemporary. Then your every footstep has meaning not only for yourself and your fellowman, but for the God who actually needs you. Then your every moment is pregnant with purpose and merits eternity; for it is being bartered, and bartered with energy and glad good will, on the actual need the great God has of you. Then, although the heavens fall, the stars burn out, the seven seas dry up, you will not be moved; for already you will have shared in the eternal immutability of Him who is your life, and whose need you serve with all your living.

[53] Cf. Song of Sol. 5:2.
[54] 1 Cor. 10:31.
[55] Apostles' Creed.

God actually needs your every moment, your every movement. That is something you must believe if you believe in God at all, for it was He Himself who said, "Behold, I am with you all days."[56]

Those words came from the lips of Him who spoke the Sermon on the Mount,[57] articulating the Beatitudes, which left His hearers "lost in admiration of His teaching," for He taught them "as one having authority, and not like their scribes and Pharisees."[58] Far better than they who heard, you know with what authority He spoke, for you know that Incarnate Truth was speaking. God was talking face-to-face with man. But the Jesus who delivered that sermon passed from Galilee and Judea, passed from this earth and the sight of men, on the day He ascended from a mount. Yet it was He who said, "I am with you all days."

He, "very God of very God," left footprints on the sands by the Sea of Tiberias again and again — not only when He called Simon and Andrew, James and John; not only when He spoke to the multitudes from Simon Peter's boat; not only after He had walked on the waters and stilled the storm by a gesture and a word; but even after He had risen from the dead. Yet, those footprints, made even by the glorified Christ, faded; and He was seen no more by friend or foe by those blue waters. Yet He said, "I am with you all days."

He had gone about doing good. Dust and human spittle, when touched by Him, took on divine power and were able to open eyes and unstop ears. The touch of His garment sent out virtue and cured the incurable. But the hands that had blessed little children, lifted the daughter of Jairus from her bed of death, and multiplied loaves and fishes, lest anyone faint on the way — those hands,

[56] Matt. 28:20.
[57] Matt. 5-7.
[58] Matt. 7:28-29.

stigmatized eternally with the signs of sin and salvation, were one day folded across a breast that was stilled in death. The eyes that had looked with love on the tears of Magdalene and had become wet with tears because of the blindness and lovelessness of Jerusalem, were sightless one Friday afternoon, for the Heart that had so often melted with pity for men had been pierced by men. Yet this God who died said, "I am with you all days."

Now, how are those feet to leave footprints on other sands than those by the sea of Tiberias? How are those hands to lift dust from other country lanes and even from city streets so that today's blind may see and today's deaf hear? How are modern Magdalenes to win pardon before the eyes of today's cynical scribes and sneering Pharisees, or modern women taken in adultery be spared their lives? How are the poor in city slums to know that theirs is the kingdom of Heaven, or the persecuted, those now being tortured, to know that they should be "glad and lighthearted" since "a rich reward awaits them"?[59] How are the hungry and thirsty of today to be filled, or the dying millions of your current civilization to have life and have it in abundance, unless He who said "I am with you all days" keeps His promise? And how can He keep that promise except through you?

To understand this truth, ponder now that happening which is commemorated every Palm Sunday. Jesus made a triumphal entry into Jerusalem that day. Do you know why? Read the account as Matthew gives it,[60] and you will see that this enthusiastic, noisy, tumultuous thing was anything but an accidental happening. Jesus knew beforehand exactly what was going to take place. He all but set the stage for it by sending two disciples from Bethphage to the

[59] Matt. 5:12.
[60] Matt. 21:1-11.

village opposite to find "an ass and a foal with her." These they were to untie and bring to Jesus. "And in case anyone says anything to you," ran the explicit instruction of the God-Man, "just say that the Lord has need of them."[61] There is your Gospel text: "The Lord has need."

The next several verses seethe with action. Cloaks are torn from shoulders and backs to be strewn on the ground under the donkey's feet. Palm branches are broken from the boughs of trees by the side of the road to be waved on high. Song breaks forth and enthusiastic shouts set the city walls and the Temple porches ringing.

Why this thunderous triumph? This does not seem at all in character with the Jesus who, from the time of the Jordan and John's baptism to this present hour, has been consistently shunning the plaudits and praises of men. This does not look at all like the Jesus who fled the multitudes when they wanted to take Him and make Him king. Yet, "when the high priests and scribes saw the astonishing activity He displayed, and heard the children cry out on the temple grounds, 'Hosanna to the Son of David,' they indignantly said to Him, 'Do you hear what they are saying?' " Jesus has only a crushingly short and sharp rejoinder for them. "Certainly," He replies; then, with some severity, immediately adds, "Did you never read this text: 'From the lips of infants and of babes you have drawn a fitting hymn of praise'?"[62]

Why did Jesus stage this triumph? Most assuredly not for Himself. Christ, who knew all things, who looked across time and space, who knew "what was in man,"[63] was not going to seek on Sunday loud hosannas from a people He knew would be crying,

[61] Matt. 21:2-3.
[62] Matt. 21:15, 16.
[63] John 2:25.

"Crucify Him! Crucify Him!"[64] on Friday. No, the triumphal entry was not for Himself.

Nor was it for His friends. That would have been deception, and Christ cannot deceive. Only a week previous to this day, He had taken the Twelve aside and said, "Listen! We are going up to Jerusalem, where the Son of Man will be betrayed to the high priests and scribes, and they will condemn Him to death, and hand Him over to the Gentiles to mock, and scourge, and crucify."[65] No, the waving palms and enthusiastic acclamations were not for His friends to whom He had always insisted, "My kingdom is not of this world."[66]

That leaves you with but one possibility. Since it was not for Himself nor His friends, this veritable uproar must have been staged by Christ *for the sake of His enemies*. Yes, He deliberately planned it for hateful high priest, scheming scribe, and haughty Pharisee. It was purposely produced for those who were plotting His capture and who had decreed His death. In short, Christ actually arranged this triumphal entry so as to fulfill an outstanding prophecy about the promised Messiah.

For almost three years now, the leaders of the people had been asking for a sign, and, for almost three years, Jesus had answered them with words from the prophets. This Sunday of the Palms, however, He gave neither promises nor predictions, but fulfillment. These leaders of the people knew the prophets. They knew that Isaiah had spoken in his Song of Victory about the entry of the Savior into Jerusalem.[67] But if there was some lack of clarity in

---

[64] Cf. Mark 15:13.

[65] Matt. 20:18-19.

[66] John 18:36.

[67] Cf. Isa. 40:9 ff.

Isaiah, there was none whatever in Zechariah, who explicitly stated, "Say to the daughter of Zion: Behold your King coming to you — gentle and seated upon an ass and a foal of the beast of burden."[68]

Christ was ever consistent. Christ was ever kind. Christ wanted Jerusalem. He wanted the hating Annas and hypocritical Caiphas. He wanted the sharply critical Pharisees along with the sneering scribes and Sadducees. He wanted everyone in the Holy City to recognize Him for what He was — not the prophet from Nazareth, not the wonder-worker from Galilee, but the Christ, the Son of the living God, their long-promised Messiah, their Savior. That is why He expressed His *need* for an ass and the foal of an ass. That is why He staged the triumphal entry — so that His foes might *see!*

∞

You can make Christ present today

But Jesus Christ is "the same yesterday, today, and forever."[69] He again has need. He would fulfill it for the same purpose He fulfilled the one just mentioned. He wants modern Annases and present-day Caiphases to *see*. He wants modern Jerusalems to recognize Him for what He is. He wants men and women of the present century to know that He lives and that He loves — them!

But the body He took from the womb of Mary is in Heaven. It can be seen only by the blessed who have left this earth. Hence, if He is to fulfill a prophecy today as He fulfilled one that Palm Sunday, He must have His need satisfied as fully now as it was when the two disciples brought back to Him the ass and her foal. How can that be done? How can Jesus Christ be seen by persons of

[68] Zech. 9:9; Matt. 21:5.
[69] Heb. 13:8.

the present day and thus keep the promise He made by saying, "Behold, I am with you all days"? Simply! Just as the invisible God became visible nine months after a Nazareth maid had said *fiat*, so the departed Christ can be made present today. He has only to do now what He did then: *assume a body!*

It will not be humility to liken yourself to "the ass and the foal of the beast of burden" that He needed two thousand years ago in order to fulfill a prophecy. Genuine humility, which is almost always a thrilling exaltation, will have you seeing that your role in the drama of salvation, which is now going on, is very similar to the role filled in the drama of the Redemption by that humblest of all human beings, the maid who sang, "*Magnificat*." For God needed Mary of Nazareth's yes in order to become incarnate and to redeem. He now needs your yes in order to continue that Incarnation and thus save. By her yes, Mary became Christ's Mother; by yours, you become Christ's member.

God's need now is just as real as when He "sent the Angel Gabriel to a city of Galilee called Nazareth, where a virgin dwelt."[70] He needed her yes so that He could live in a physical body, which He would assume from her virginal womb; He needs your yes so that He may live in that Mystical Body[71] which He assumes from the womb of mankind. Just as He could live a physical life only if Mary gave her consent, so now He can live a mystical life only if you acquiesce.

Humans should say yes to all the failures, frustrations, disappointments, trials, and contradictions that clutter their way of life, accepting them as from the hand of God, and as being for them the will of God. That is as true as the Gospel of Jesus Christ. But

[70] Luke 1:26.
[71] That is, the Church; cf. 1 Cor. 12:27.

life is ever so much more than a series of mistakes and a succession of failures. Still, if it is to be real life, if it is to be the full life such as is being here outlined for you, it must be nothing else but an acquiescence. It must be saying yes to God from moment to moment, for His need of you is real from moment to moment!

Mary's *fiat*, then, made it possible for the physical Christ to say that same word years later one night as olive trees were casting shadows on a face that was wet with blood; and this *fiat* of the God-Man was as potent as that first *fiat* of God, which brought your universe into being. For while that one was creative, Christ's was re-creative.

If you now make your life one long acquiescence to God, the mystical Jesus will be able to go on saying *fiat* and thus bring about the salvation of mankind. He longs for the ability to do this, for, as the drama of the Redemption closed, the drama of salvation began, and unless this latter is allowed to move along the lines drawn by the Father, the former, although infinite in worth, will somehow be incomplete. So, you see, God needs you to fill out His Christ.

The night before He died, Jesus Christ disclosed the deepest secret of life when He said, "I am the real vine, and my Father is the vinedresser. He prunes away any branch of mine that bears no fruit. . . . A branch can bear no fruit of itself, that is, when it is not united to the vine; no more can you, if you do not remain united with me. I am the vine; you are the branches. One bears abundant fruit only when he and I are mutually united; severed from me, you can do nothing, if one does not remain united with me, he is simply thrown away like a branch, and dries up. Such branches are gathered and thrown into the fire to be burned. As long as you remain united with me, and my teachings remain your rule of life, you may ask for anything you wish, and you shall have it. This is what glorifies my Father — your bearing abundant fruit and thus proving yourselves my disciples."[72]

That is one of the most important passages you will ever read. It means *life* for you. No branch can live unless united with the vine. So, you see your need for the Christ, who is God — you cannot live without Him.

But in this passage, which so conclusively proves your utter dependence on God, there lies implicit an undeniable proof of God's dependence on you. Christ says that a branch cannot live apart from the vine. That is true — unchallengeably true. The coming into being of the branch, its life, and all its living are due to the vine. But have you ever seen a vine that held fruit and yet had no branches? Have you ever seen a vine that could manifest the life within it except through its branches? Have you ever seen any vine that could live for any length of time unless it had branches?

Can't you hear, then, all that God is saying to you in what Christ has left unsaid? Christ must have Christians if the trellis of the Cross is to hold the Passion's purple harvest. Christ must have Christians if the omnipotent *fiat* of creation and the almighty *fiat* of re-creation are not to be rendered impotent. He is the Vine; you are the branches. You depend on Him for life. He depends on you for fruitful living.

Indeed, you are one whom Almighty God actually needs! As the Father needed Christ for Redemption, so Christ needs you for salvation. The task God gave to His only Son, that only Son has handed on to you; for the Incarnation must be made manifest far beyond tiny Judea and continued in times far distant from the short span of thirty-three years that Jesus lived.

[72] John 15:1-2, 4-8.

∞

God needs you to reveal Christ to others

There is your life's work. There is the need God has of you. You are to make God known to the world. You are to give a dying world not only life, but life that is eternal. For God Himself said, "This is the sum of eternal life — their knowing you, the only true God, and your ambassador Jesus Christ."[73] You are to open the eyes of the world to Jesus Christ.

But how can the world ever see Jesus Christ unless He walks your city streets, rides your subways, enters your slums, and speaks His parables in your stockyards and in your stock exchange? How will the world acknowledge the Christ to be what He is unless it sees Him "going about doing good,"[74] hears Him teaching "as one having authority,"[75] and watches Him doing works no mere man can do? But how can Christ do any of these things except through that Mystical Body of which He is the Head and you are a member?

The world must come to believe in Jesus Christ. The world must come to acknowledge Jesus Christ as God. It will do so only if you, in your way, answer the need that God has of you at this moment. It will do so only if you do your part by being your real self! Then modern man will have no reason to envy those who lived when Jesus made known the Father's name through the members of His physical body, for they will come to know the Father through Christ their contemporary.

Do your part. Then, if modern man misses God, it will not be because He has been too distant but because He is altogether too

[73] John 17:3.
[74] Acts 10:38.
[75] Matt. 7:29.

near! If you despair of ever having anyone recognize Jesus by looking at you, take heart by recalling that a dying thief once looked through a haze of blood and, in the tortured, unsightly, horribly bruised physical members of Christ, recognized God![76] Take heart, for it is God's work more than yours. But you must do your part. You must answer the very real need that Almighty God has of you. You must be His member!

Some psychiatrists may try to tell you that these truths are nothing but so much "bolstering of the ego," sheer "escapism," a pure "flight into religion" to compensate for frustration or to palliate some fear. But let them learn the imperative need God has of them, and they will know a fear so salutary that it will oust all other fears, for they will find within their souls something stronger than anything in their psyche; they will find a fear of God that will have them fearless of all men. For they will have recognized the triumphant truth that just as Christ was God's ambassador to men to make known the Father's name, they have been made Christ's ambassador for the same purpose. Once they accept and live that fact, they will become men and cease to be mere imitations of manhood.

In the midst of World War II, when civilization looked like a shambles, and the whole world seemed to be in its death agony, Pius XII, one of the most astute minds of this day and age, sent to the warring world his encyclical *Mystici Corporis Christi*.[77] He knew what embroiled mankind needed. He knew what alone can give lasting peace. So he gave that world the one thing that can really unify the very disorganized members of the human family — namely, the truth about Christ's Mystical Body, which teaches so clearly God's need of you.

[76] Cf. Luke 23:42.
[77] On the Mystical Body of Christ, June 29, 1943.

"Because Christ the Head holds such an eminent position," wrote the Pontiff, "one must not think that He does not require the Body's help. What Paul said of the human organism is to be applied likewise to the Mystical Body. 'The head cannot say to the feet: I have no need of you.' It is manifestly clear that the Faithful need the help of the Divine Redeemer, for He has said, 'Without me, you can do nothing. . . .' Yet, this, too, must be held, marvelous though it appear, *Christ requires His members.* . . .

"Deep mystery this," says His Holiness, "subject of inexhaustible meditation: that the *salvation of many* depends on the prayers and penance which the *members* of the Mystical Body offer for this intention."[78]

After reading that, can you ever again doubt your dignity or question your worth? The salvation of many depends on your fulfilling the need that Almighty God has of you.

You are one sent by God to help the Son of God save your fellowmen. But you can fulfill that destiny only if you have proper life in you; and that you can have only if you have been "raised from the dead."

[78] Emphasis added.

Chapter Three

∾

You are one whom Christ
raised from the dead

Your name is Lazarus — and you *live!* For you are one Christ raised from the dead.[79] You cost Almighty God His life. But He gave it without counting the cost; for He wanted you, who were dead, to know a resurrection — and never again die!

Those statements of historical and theological truth strike modern ears like so much vulgar sensationalism. Yet it was Jesus Christ, Incarnate Truth, "true God of true God," who said, "I am come that they may have life, and have it in abundance."[80] If you were not dead, what need would there have been for Him to come with life?

You were dead! How often did God the Holy Spirit, that Spirit of Truth, tell you so! "How rich God is in mercy, with what an excess of love He loved us!" He says to the Ephesians, "Our sins had made dead men of us, and He, in giving life to Christ, gave life to us, too."[81] The identical truth He told the Colossians, saying, "In giving life to [Jesus], He gave life to you, too, when you lay dead in

---

[79] Cf. John 11:14-44.
[80] John 10:10.
[81] Eph. 2:4-5.

your sins."[82] From the letter to the Romans you learn that, because you were a child of Adam, you were dead when you were born. "It was through one man that guilt came into the world, and since death came, owing to guilt, death was handed on to all mankind by one man."[83] The converted Saul could never forget the lesson he had learned on the road to Damascus, the lesson about the solidarity of mankind in both sin and salvation. That is why you read in his second letter to the Corinthians, "Just as in Adam all men die, so too in Christ, all men are made alive."[84]

After such testimony, can you question the fact that you are one Christ raised from the dead?

Since we are what our thoughts are, who can escape the conclusion that shallow thoughts can produce only shallow Christians? But in your world, shallow Christians cannot survive. The tide of anti-Christianity is too deep and too strong. Reality that is both naked and raw, ultimates that are ugly, absolutes both stark and bitter, are the life concern — and seemingly the only concern — of the members of the mystical body of anti-Christ; and with what looks like clearer vision and stronger faith, they are living up to the demands their "religion" makes on them as individual members. That fact is a fierce challenge to you.

You are one sent by God. You are an individual with a distinctly personal mission. You are one whom Almighty God actually needs — and needs in a specific manner. But you will never fulfill your mission, nor satisfy God's need, unless you are fully convinced that you are one whom Christ raised from the dead, that your name is Lazarus and you live.

---

[82] Col. 2:13.
[83] Rom. 5:12.
[84] 1 Cor. 15:22.

That last expression is borrowed from Gilbert K. Chesterton, the man who once said, "To become a Catholic is not to leave off thinking, but to learn how to think aright." He told, after his Baptism, how, once he had bowed his head for those life-giving waters, he looked up and found that his entire world had "turned over and come up right." He confessed that he went out and walked his old road, which had often enough been dark, and saw it now shining in clean white light. He listened to men talk and learned that now he could hear what they were actually saying. With crystal clarity he saw that while they were using reason, they were straining it out through a sieve that was holding all the sand as it let the gold fall through. The last line in that triumphant account of his Baptism is the grateful exclamation "My name is Lazarus, and I live!"

༺

Baptism gives you new life

The world in which you live is more upside-down than was the world of Chesterton before his Baptism. The men among whom you move are still using that same useless sieve, and it is holding more and more sand. Hence, you have even a greater obligation than Chesterton to think aright. Therefore, learn that while you can say with him truthfully that your name is Lazarus and you live, it will not be telling the full truth. For what happened to you — and to Chesterton — at Baptism was something far greater than what happened to Lazarus the day Christ cried to him, "Come forth!"[85] You have been raised from the dead, but from a deeper death than Lazarus knew the four days he was in the tomb. To bring you to life, Jesus had to cry to more than a bound corpse that had been hidden behind a stone; He had to cry to an abyss far

---

[85] John 11:43.

57

deeper than that fathomless abyss of nothingness to which He had cried for your creation. For, in a certain sense, you were farther from God after coming into being than you had been when you were nothingness, for now you were His enemy, estranged from Him whose love had given you existence.

The truth is that you had to be re-created, and that taxed Omnipotence almost infinitely more than the saying of *fiat* to nothingness and bringing a universe into being. For, before this second *fiat* of re-creation could be pronounced over you effectively, God had to be born of a woman. God had to live thirty and more years of frustration among men whom He had not only made, but had chosen as His people. God had to climb a Cross, and over a darkness more void, in its way, than the one over which He said, "Let there be light!"[86] He had to cry, "It is finished."[87] God had to die so that you might live. Actually, God had to go into the grave so that you might be raised from the dead.

"Know thyself!" The tighter you grip reality and the more vigorously you wrestle with truth, the larger that command looms until, finally, it fills your every horizon. Obeying it, you not only come to know yourself, but also your God; and once you know Him with any intimacy, you learn the fascinating truth that life is love which was and is proved by a death and a resurrection — His and yours!

You were born twice. And your second birth was a veritable resurrection. It had to be, for your first birth was a stillbirth. You were born dead despite the fact that, as you came from your mother's womb, you were pronounced alive. That pronouncement was true only of your body. That body had a soul that was its vital

---

[86] Gen. 1:3.
[87] John 19:30 (Revised Standard Version).

principle. But that soul was as much a corpse as is the body of a stillborn baby. And a corpse it stayed until Christ came and called you back from the dead by His Baptism.

That concept of actuality, which is not very common among modern men and women, all-Catholic though it be, should open your eyes to the two realities that fill your world: death and life — really synonyms for *sin* and *salvation;* and these, in their turn, are but abstractions of the two concrete realities: yourself and your Savior.

∞

You have been "born of God"

The fact that you were born twice sheds special light on the day you have been celebrating as your birthday. It lets you see that the day of your physical birth was really your death day; for, while you came from your mother's womb with life in you, it was only human life, and that, as far as fulfilling your God-given purpose in this world, was the same as death. To be all that you should be, you had to be born again, and this time you have to be "born of God,"[88] as St. John has put it in that unforgettable prologue to his Gospel.

That brings you face-to-face with the mystery of two solidarities — one in sin, the other in sanctity; one in the man, Adam, the other in the Man-God, Jesus Christ. These are the solidarities that explain your two births: the first of which was a stillbirth, the second a very real resurrection.

Take no mere man's word for this. Truths so basic demand an infallible Teacher. So let the Holy Spirit make clear to you your manner of birth, your inherited traits, and the characteristics of your parents. The first truth He teaches is that you are a child of

[88] Cf. John 1:13.

Adam. Your father Adam could give you only what he had. Through him you received life of the body. But because your first father was the original sinner, he gave you a body in which was already sown the seed of death. Since it was into such a body that God had to breathe your soul, at your very conception you received a soul that was dead in sin. Such is the law of solidarity. Such, the legacy you received from your first parents. "Through one man," says the Holy Spirit by the pen of St. Paul, "sin entered the world, and through sin death." That man was your father Adam; that sin was Original Sin; that death is the death which has "spread to all men, because all have sinned."[89]

There is the fact: You were born dead, and dead you stayed so long as you remained incorporated in Adam the sinner. It was Christ by His Baptism who excorporated you from that Adam and that sin as He incorporated you into Himself and His sanctity. This second Adam, as He is called, brought you back to life and made you a "new creature,"[90] for when you came forth from the womb of Baptism, you were more than human: you were pulsing with the life of God, for you were "sharing," as St. Peter so daringly states it, "in the divine nature."[91] "You were born not of blood, nor of the will of the flesh, nor of the will of man, but of God."[92]

You were born of God.

Now you know your real birthday. Now you can understand why Louis IX, King of France, was so fond of signing himself "Louis of Poissy," for it was in the humble village of Poissy that this saintly monarch had been baptized. His mother, Blanche of Castile, had

[89] Rom. 5:12.
[90] 2 Cor. 5:17.
[91] 2 Pet. 1:4.
[92] John 1:13.

given him human life, had made him son of an earthly monarch, King Louis VIII, had given him hereditary title to the throne of France, which, at that time, was really the center of the civilized universe. But Louis IX had eyes for reality. He knew his real birthday, his real Mother, and his real Father. That is why he signed himself "Louis of Poissy," for he knew that it was there, at the baptismal font, that he had been called back from death, had been given life far superior to any that Blanche of Castile could give him, and had been made heir to a throne and a kingdom that would never pass away. The throne he inherited from his earthly father was overturned, brutally broken, and scornfully tossed aside by the Revolution of 1790. But, since about 1270, Louis IX has been enthroned where he has no fear of Jacobins, far less of the guillotine. Wise, indeed, was he to sign himself "Louis of Poissy," for that was really to sign himself "son of God."

You, too, have been born of God. You, too, are a child of the Omnipotent and the Eternal. Weigh it well, and you will be as happy and as wise as was "Louis of Poissy" and his later successor Louis XVI, who was very fond of telling how his father, the Dauphin, often showed him the parish register wherein his name and the date of his Baptism appeared among the names of the children of peasants and the dates of the days when they, like him, had been made children of God. It was a lesson in proper evaluation. It showed Louis wherein lay true liberty, real equality, and genuine fraternity. It told him that the baptized serf had equal right with baptized sovereign to look into the face of Almighty God and call Him "Father."

History records many illustrious dates in the life of Pope Pius XI.[93] He himself had the perfect right to name several days as

---

[93] Pius XI (1857-1939), Pope from 1922.

glorious ones. There were many days — more than with any pontiff before him, except Pius IX — when the world watched as he, surrounded by all the magnificence of St. Peter's on a day of canonization, elevated to the altar of God some heroic soul who would ever afterward be called "saint." The day he settled the Roman Question, the day he sent out his thunderous encyclical *Mit brennender Sorge*[94] blasting Hitler and his Nazism, and that day not so long after when he filled the civilized world with admiration because of his frontal attack on atheistic Communism in his letter *Divini Redemptoris*,[95] must have been memorable days for this fearless, forthright Pope. Yet, when asked to name the greatest day of his life, unhesitatingly he passed over all of these and named the day of his Baptism. That was the day on which he was made much more than the Vicar of Christ on earth. On that day, he had been raised from the dead, had been born of God, had been made heir to Heaven, had been made, in the unity of the Mystical Body, one with the very Son of God.

You, too, have had such a day.

Repetition of this truth is necessary. You cannot live as a true man unless you realize that you are "born of God."

∽

In Baptism, you die and rise with Christ

Perhaps Nicodemus will open your eyes. Do you recall the night he came to Christ? St. John tells you that this man was a "leader in the Jewish community."[96] Later you learn he was member of the

---

[94] To the Bishops of Germany: On the Church and the German Reich, March 14, 1937.

[95] March 19, 1937.

[96] John 3:1.

Sanhedrin. A more important and powerful man could hardly have come to Jesus. Nicodemus opened the conversation with an admission he could never afford to make in public. "Rabbi," he said, "we know that you have a mission from God to teach."[97] No other member of the Sanhedrin would have called Jesus "Rabbi" with any sincerity. No other leader of the people would have admitted that Christ had a mission from God, far less that it was a mission to teach. The sincerity, the earnestness, and the patent good will of this man moved God's only Son. Christ "seized the opportunity" to enlighten this influential Pharisee: "Truly, truly, I say to you, unless one is born anew, he cannot see the kingdom of God."[98]

To see the kingdom of God was the whole meaning of life for any real Jew — just as it is now for Jew and Gentile alike! Down through the years, the object of Nicodemus's study and the petition of his prayers had been to see the kingdom of God. Now he is face-to-face with One he recognizes as having come from God, and he is told that "unless he is born anew" — or, as the word may mean, unless his is born "from above" — "he cannot see the kingdom of God."

When he finally finds his voice, he asks in bewilderment, "But how can a man be born in his old age? Can he really enter his mother's womb a second time and have another birth?"[99]

The earnest but literal-minded Pharisee is forgetting his oneness with Adam and the essential distinction between body and soul. He is not thinking of the difference between physical life and spiritual life — between death that is death, and death that is only

[97] John 3:2.
[98] John 3:3 (Revised Standard Version).
[99] John 3:4.

a transition to another life. Perhaps his question was only another way of saying, "Good Master, go on. Tell me more. Tell me how I can be born again."

At any rate, Jesus answered, "Truly, truly, I say to you, unless one is born of water and the Spirit, he cannot enter the kingdom of God."[100]

There it is again: the intransigence of Christ, His refusal to compromise. He will insist on truth, even the plain truth, always. If Nicodemus or any other man is to enter the kingdom of God, it will be on God's terms, and no others! Seeing perplexity, pleading, and hunger for an explanation follow one another like waves across the countenance of this earnest Jew, Jesus goes on to say, "What is born of the flesh is flesh, and what is born of the Spirit is spirit."[101]

That should have opened the eyes of this Pharisee to the fact that Jesus was not talking of physical birth. Yet Christ still saw perplexity in those earnest, pleading eyes. Ever the kind teacher, Jesus will help the man over his difficulty. As He so often did, Christ now takes that which is at hand. A breeze had sprung up in the night. The Lord leans forward and says, "Do not be perplexed because I said to you, you must all of you be born anew." Then He takes His example: "The breeze blows at will, and you can hear its sound, but you do not know where it comes from or whither it goes." Nicodemus could not question that. The breeze was blowing around him right then. As he shook his head in acceptance of the facts, Jesus said, "Something like this takes place in everyone born of the Spirit."[102]

[100] John 3:5.
[101] John 3:6.
[102] John 3:7-8.

Nicodemus was still puzzled, but you need not be. Your meteorologists may give you quite a satisfactory explanation of the way of the winds, but unless they know much about your God, they will never tell you anything about the will of the winds. The breeze still blows at will. And that is the will of God. So, too, with your rebirth. It was accomplished by the will of God through "water and the Spirit." It was a death and a resurrection "in Christ Jesus."

If you know anything about the way Baptism was administered in the early Church, Christ's words, and John's words, and the words of St. Paul will enable you to see the veil of the Temple rent from top to bottom, hear the earth quake, and watch the great stone being rolled back from Christ's tomb.[103] For you will see both Calvary and the risen Christ; you will witness death and resurrection. How could it be otherwise when you know that it was only after three years of careful training that, in the early Church, the catechumens were allowed to don the long white robe that was to be their baptismal garment and that it was only on Easter Eve that they were allowed to wrap themselves in it? At such a time, how could your mind be on anything other than Christ's death and Resurrection?

When you know that those who were to be baptized were taken to a sunken pool, that they wrapped their long white garment around them in a manner vividly reminiscent of the way a shroud is wrapped around a corpse, and then walked down into that pool, which was so like a grave, until the waters reached over their heads, you cannot miss the symbolism of complete burial. When you know that they came forth on the other side of that pool as new creatures, born again, resurrected from the dead, you can

---

[103] Cf. Matt. 27:51, 28:2.

understand vividly that passage in Paul's letter to the Romans which begins, "Do you not know that all of us who have been baptized into union with Jesus Christ have been baptized into union with His death? Yes, we were buried in death with Him by means of Baptism, in order that, just as Christ was raised from the dead by the glorious power of the Father, so we may also conduct ourselves by a new principle of life."[104]

You, most likely, were not baptized that way, but your Baptism signified the same realities of death with Christ and resurrection in Him, so you can thrill to Paul's words: "If we have died with Christ, we believe we shall also live with Him. . . . The life that He lives is a life for God. Thus, too, you must consider yourselves dead to sin, but alive to God in Christ Jesus."[105]

A new principle of life — alive to God in Christ Jesus. That means only one thing: there has been a new creation! That is exactly what Paul told his Corinthians: "If any man is in Christ, he is a new creation."[106] That is what he repeated to his Galatians with a little different stress: "What really counts is not circumcision or its absence, but being a new creature."[107]

Centuries have rolled away since Christ spoke to Nicodemus and Paul wrote to his converts, but the truths told and the sacrament mentioned remain. Death in Christ and resurrection with Him go on. In all truth you have been made a "new creature," for by Baptism, *you were made Christ*.

That last statement usually makes people feel as bewildered as Nicodemus the night Jesus told him that he had to be born again.

---

[104] Rom. 6:3-5.
[105] Rom. 6:8, 10-11.
[106] 2 Cor. 5:17.
[107] Gal. 6:15.

But if you do not grasp that firmly and hold on to it, life can be nothing but a blank. So sit with Jesus by Jacob's well, and see if you cannot gain greater and clearer understanding of what it means to be baptized.

∞

In Baptism, you became Christ

It is nearly noon. The Lord is alone. He is tired and thirsty. The disciples have gone off to buy food in the tiny nearby Samaritan town of Sychar. As Jesus sits there in the noonday heat, He must have thought of His ancestor Jacob and that patriarch's well-loved son Joseph, for this was the place Jacob had given to Joseph, who was both type and figure of Jesus. But, if He was in reverie, He is suddenly awakened from it by a woman who had come from the town to draw water from the well.

Jesus looks at her and says, "Let me have a drink." She starts with real surprise. Her reply would both startle and surprise you if St. John did not explain that Jews have no dealings with Samaritans and that it was most unusual for a man to address a woman in public this way. She says, "How can you, a Jew, ask me, a Samaritan woman, for a drink?"[108]

Jesus again looks at her. What is it that wells up in the Sacred Heart at this moment? Is it divine pity for her and her sinfulness, divine hunger for her love, divine thirst that she fulfill the purpose for which she had been created — that she satisfy, in her way, the need of God? "If you understood God's gift," He says, and knew who it was who said to you, 'Let me have a drink,' you would have asked Him, and He would have given you living water."[109]

[108] John 4:7, 9.
[109] John 4:10.

Christ always spoke to provoke thought and promote inquiry. He had made men rational. He would have them save themselves by using the reason He had given them on the revelation He was making to them. You have seen this in the case of Nicodemus. You see it now in the case of this Samaritan adulteress. "Sir," the woman replies, "you have no means of drawing water, and the well is deep. Where, then, do you get the living water? Are you greater than our father Jacob, who gave us the well out of which he and his children and his flocks used to drink?"[110]

What a wealth of tragic irony lies in those words. To the Source of all life and the Creator of all water, this abandoned woman asks, "Where do you get living water?" To the Father of all men, the Good Shepherd who longs to guide one flock, she speaks of Jacob as father and makes mention of his children and his flocks. But, as with Nicodemus, Jesus will take the earthly words of this very earthly woman and change them into words glowing with eternal life. "Anyone who drinks of this water," He says, "will thirst again, but he who drinks of the water I will give him will never thirst." Christ sees the mocking light of incredulity flash in the woman's eyes. He sees the smile that starts at the corner of her passionate mouth. So He repeats His statement with greater emphasis and clearer truth. "No, the water I will give him will become in him a fountain of water welling up into eternal life."[111]

She did not understand what Jesus was saying. She missed this life-giving truth just as Nicodemus had missed a similar one. But you cannot miss it. You know the water Jesus meant. You have been to His well. You have quenched your thirst and need never thirst again, for you have been baptized.

[110] John 4:11-12.
[111] John 4:13-14.

Baptism is the lone well in this killing white desert we call the world. Without its waters, men blacken, swell, and die; their bones bleach to a glaring white under a scorching sun. But once life has been lifted from this inexhaustible deep, man tastes eternity, for he drinks in Him who is timeless, and man can walk the ways of this world without ever again knowing thirst.

It all seems unbelievable, but it must be believed. You have drunk these waters. By them *you were made Christ* — and Christ is God!

The senses are deceived here just as they are in the Eucharist. For although Baptism is a sacrament, and a sacrament is a visible sign, nevertheless, as far as the human eye can discern, you were not one whit changed after going to this well and drinking these waters.

Although sins have been remitted, a share in the life of God has been given, and God Himself — Father, Son, and Holy Spirit — had come to dwell within you, you appeared not one bit different. Although wonders greater far than those of creation had taken place within you, you looked exactly the same as before. You had been lifted to heights immeasurable to man, taken through that portal which is the gateway to God. You had been set breathing an atmosphere that is life eternal. You had been stamped with an image that neither time nor eternity can ever efface. From a child of Adam, you had been changed and made a child of God, with incontestable title to that heritage which holds "what eye hath not seen, nor ear heard, nor the heart of man conceived."[112] You had been given lien on Almighty God. Yet you looked exactly the same as when you were "dead in your sins."[113]

[112] 1 Cor. 2:9.
[113] Eph. 2:1.

With appearances so deceiving, what hope is there for vivid recognition of truth? How can this all-important religious reality be made tangible for you? How can you be brought to what will be an accurate and an irreversible appreciation of this "gift of God"?

Will it help, first of all, to show you that these "living waters" are really the waters that came from the side of the dead Christ when Longinus went looking for His heart with a lance?[114] Those are the only waters that really belong to God made man; those are the waters that form part of His sacred and all-saving humanity as much as His blood, His flesh, His whole frame. It is from Christ's death that you receive true life. It is from His stilled Heart that grace streams, and grace is a share in the very life of God. Truly, the waters of Baptism are tinged with His blood, for they are the life-giving waters that come from His pierced Sacred Heart. And you are one who was born from the lance-opened side of Christ!

The baptismal ceremony is often called a *christening*. That word is composed of the noun *Christ* and the suffix *en*, which means "to make." When you lighten a room, you make it light; when you whiten a wall, you make it white; when you brighten a metal, you make it bright. In like manner, when you were christened, *you were made Christ*.

Now you can see the egregious error so many make: they stress the negative aspect of this tremendous reality and neglect almost entirely the pulsing positive side. The child's catechism told you the full truth, but you have focused on only half of that truth. It said that Baptism blotted out Original Sin and any other actual sins you may have committed. That is true — true with the truth of God. But the catechism said more than that, and it is this more that is the positive side which merits heavier and heavier accent.

---

[114] Cf. John 19:34.

You are actually stressing death when talking or thinking about a sacrament that gives life.

When Christ called Lazarus to come forth, He did not command death to depart; He commanded life to return. When the widow of Naim once more held her boy in her arms, when the wife of Jairus once again pressed her daughter to her heart,[115] do you think either of these mothers could talk about death? *Life* throbbed on their every horizon. So should it throb on all yours — you who have been baptized, you who have been made alive in Christ Jesus, who have been born of God.

What would the father and mother of a stillborn child give to be able to set the tiny heart of their dead baby beating? What they cannot do was done for you by your Father, God, and your Mother, Holy Church. Stillborn supernaturally, you were warmed to life.

That clarifies St. Peter's daring description of grace as a "participation in the divine nature." That also tells you why you can be calm even if you have to look out on a world in chaos, and why you must carry yourself with majesty even if you are surrounded by all that is mean and degrading. You are a child of God. There throbs in you a life that was before all time and tides. You live with the life of God the Creator, God the Redeemer, God who is Sanctity and Sanctifier. What if the world thinks little of you? What if the teeming millions pass you by as a nonentity? You know that within you is He before whose throne the "four living creatures do not rest day or night saying, 'Holy, holy, holy, the Lord God Almighty, who was, and who is, and who is coming'" and before whom the twenty-four ancients cast their crowns saying, "Worthy art Thou, O Lord, our God to receive glory and honor and power, for Thou

---

[115] Cf. Mark 5:22-23, 39-42; Luke 7:11-15.

hast created all things And because of Thy will they were, and were created."[116]

You were raised from the dead. You are a new creature. *You were made Christ*.

You cannot remind yourself of that truth often enough; for, as St. Thomas of Aquinas[117] taught, it is from incorporation in Christ — this being made Christ — that all the other stupendous effects of Baptism naturally result. This intellectual giant insists that it was to this being made Christ that all the antecedent plans of God tended, and from it all subsequent divine benefits flow. For, from the moment you were made Christ, all that is His became yours. Yours is His Passion. Yours is His death. Yours is His Resurrection, His Ascension, His enthronement in Heaven.

"In the human body," says St. Thomas, "the members thereof take feeling and activity from the head. In the spiritual body, of which Christ is the Head, it is from Christ that the spiritual sense comes to the members; that is, the knowledge of the truth and that spiritual activity which is the fruit of grace. The baptized are enlightened by Christ into a knowledge of the truth, and the infusion of grace enables them to bring forth a harvest of good works."[118] He could say all that because St. Paul before him had said, "You are alive to God in Christ Jesus."[119]

No wonder Father Leo Trese said that "the greatest thing that could ever happen to anybody" is to be baptized. No wonder St. Augustine cried, "Let us congratulate ourselves. Let us break forth

---

[116] Apoc. 4:8-11 (RSV = Rev. 4:8-11).

[117] St. Thomas Aquinas (c. 1225-1274), Dominican philospher and theologian.

[118] *Summa Theologica*, III, Q. 69, art. 5.

[119] Rom. 6:11.

into thanksgiving; for we are become not only Christians, but Christ."[120]

Now you can appreciate Paul's cry of "I live, now not I, but Christ lives in me."[121] And you can evaluate properly the words of St. Leo the Great: "Recognize, O Christian, the dignity that is yours. Having been elevated to a participation of the divine nature, do not allow yourself to sink back into your former ignoble condition. Consider the Body of which you are a member, and have constantly before you the thought of Jesus, who is the Head of that Body. You have been drawn from squalid obscurity and established in the divine kingdom. Remember that Baptism has made you a dwelling place for the Holy Spirit."[122]

"Recognize, O Christian, the dignity that is yours." That dignity is towering. It is as high as God. But that dignity imposes obligation. Just as a tree can function only as a tree, an animal as an animal, a man as a man, so a Christian must function only *as Christ!*

Is that possible? St. Paul thought so, and, while under the direct inspiration of God the Holy Spirit, told his Galatians, Corinthians, and Philippians so. What else is meant by his command "Have this mind in you which was also in Christ Jesus"?[123] What is meant by his direct questioning of the Corinthians, "Do you not know that you are the temple of God and the Spirit of God dwells in you?"[124]

Yes, St. Paul thought it not only possible but imperative to think with the mind of Christ, to love with the heart of Christ,

[120] *Tract. in Joan.*
[121] Gal. 2:20.
[122] Sermon 21 on the Nativity.
[123] Phil. 2:5.
[124] 1 Cor. 3:16.

and to live to the Father with the life of Christ thanks to the Holy Spirit, who is in truth the Spirit of Christ. It is He who vivifies the Mystical Body of Christ, and it is of Him you have been reborn; for Christ's words to Nicodemus were, "Unless one is born again of water and *the Spirit* . . ." The soul of your soul is that Person who is the Substantial Love of the Father for the Son and the Son for the Father. The truth is you have been given "fellowship with the Father and with the Son in the one and the same Spirit."[125]

Now you see why Chesterton was inadequate. You need not say your name is Lazarus and you live. You can cry, "I have been made Christ, and I will never die." If big ideas make big people, what must your stature be if you can say with exact truth, "I have been made Christ by the Spirit of Christ who raised me from the dead."

∞

You must mature in Christ

All this requires thought, but the labor is light when the harvest is viewed. "Thus we attain to perfect manhood," said St. Paul, "to the mature proportions that befit Christ's complement."[126] That is what you want: maturity in Christ Jesus. That is what the world needs: Christians who are truly mature, having grown up in Jesus Christ. "Thus we shall no longer be children," Paul says, "tossed to and fro and carried about by every wind of doctrine, which wicked men devise with the ingenuity and cleverness that error suggests. Rather, by professing truth, let us grow up in every respect in love and bring about union with Christ who is the Head. . . . This, therefore, I say to you and assert in the Lord, that from now on, you are not to conduct yourselves as the Gentiles do,

---

[125] 1 John 1:3.
[126] Eph. 4:13.

in emptiness of their minds, with their understanding plunged in darkness, estranged, because of the ignorance that exists among them and the obstinacy of their hearts, from the life that God imparts. . . . You are to put off your old self. . . . Renew yourself constantly by spiritual considerations, and put on the new self, created after the image of God in the holiness and justice that come from truth."[127]

Throughout this chapter, your gaze has been focused really on one spot. It is the principle on which your entire life as a Christian, your destiny in time and eternity, rests — namely, on the *divine life communicated and received.* How accurately the saintly Dom Marmion spoke when he said, "Participation in the divine life constitutes the very basis of Christianity and the substance of all holiness."

You received divine life in Baptism. But that was only a beginning. That was your babyhood in sanctity, your infancy in Christ-likeness. Like all life, this divine life was to develop and grow. You were to mature as Christ Jesus. Have you been doing it? If not, the next step in this ever-steepening stairway will help you greatly, for it will show you that burning within you is that Flame of God you call the Holy Spirit.

---

[127] Eph. 4:14-24.

∽

Chapter Four

You are one who breathes by the fire of God's Spirit

Someone is sure to ask if the truths so far told about you will put bread on your table, put clothes on your back, or keep a roof over your head. The questioner will pose as a realist and plead with us to come to grips with life.

Christ, after a fast of forty days and forty nights, faced something similar. You know the identity of the one who suggested that He change stones into bread. You know the answer God gave him.[128] But perhaps a fiery friend of Christ will bring this matter to as sharp a focus, as he bas-reliefs the character of the questioner and interprets his question.

A priest, about to embrace the life of a solitary, once wrote to Leon Bloy[129] asking him for special prayers on the plea that he, the priest, did not possess the soul of a saint. This French realist, ever sensitive to truth and the God who made us for His glory, replied, "You say, 'I do not have the soul of a saint.' . . . Well, then, I answer you with certainty that I have the soul of a saint; that my fearful

[128] Cf. Matt. 4:2-4.
[129] Leon Bloy (1846-1917), Catholic convert and writer.

bourgeois of a landlord, my baker, my butcher, my grocer, all of whom may be horrible scoundrels, have the souls of saints, having all been called, as fully as you or I, as fully as St. Francis or St. Paul, to eternal life, and having been bought at the same price. . . . There is no man who is not potentially a saint, and sin or sins, even the blackest of them, are but accident that in no way alters the substance."

Bloy knew that "not by bread alone does man live,"[130] that clothes do not make the man or the woman, that "we have not here a lasting city."[131] So he comes to grips with life and details an experience that can be yours any day in the week, and almost any hour of the day. He says, "When I go to a café to read the petty and stupid newspapers, I look at the customers around me, I see their silly joy, I hear their foolish nonsense or their blasphemies, and I reflect that there I am, among immortal souls unaware of what they are, souls made to adore eternally the Holy Trinity, souls as precious as angelic spirits; and sometimes I weep. . . ."

As you ride home this day in a crowded bus or in the more crowded subway, look around you, and know that you are looking at more immortal souls, too many of whom are utterly unaware of what they are. Listen to their talk, and see if Bloy's summation is far off. Look at their faces — especially of those who smile and laugh; study their eyes, and you will see that, with too many of them, it is only the face that smiles or laughs, not the person, and most assuredly not the soul of the person; for they, too, are unaware of what they are.

Such an experience can reduce any sensitive soul to tears, for it is tragic.

[130] Matt. 4:4.
[131] Heb. 13:14.

In this same letter, this French mystic, who was ever at grips with life, exclaimed, "Ah! if people only knew how beautiful the soul is! But you know it, and it would be your duty to teach it to me if I did not know it myself. What sorry Christians we are! We have received the sacraments of Baptism, Confirmation, sometimes Holy Orders . . . and yet, with all that, we lack *character!*" Then, in typical Bloy fashion, he concludes, "There is a deceptive form of humility that resembles ingratitude. We have been made saints by our Lord Jesus Christ, and we dare not believe and say resolutely that we are saints! Ah! my dear friend, what beautiful and enrapturing words could be said by a preacher who would be truly filled with this thought!"[132]

To have an immortal soul! To be made to the image and likeness of God Himself! To be stamped with the very character of Christ — God's only Son — and not to know it! To have had the mind of God conceive you, the heart of God love you, the hand of God reach out, take you, and ingraft you into that Tree which is Christ! And to be wholly absorbed in bread, clothes, a room, and a roof!

Know thyself!

The trouble with the questioner, the "realist" mentioned at the beginning of the chapter, is that these truths frighten him. They put him on a height too appallingly high, and he is subject to vertigo.

Yet, nothing is nearer to his heart or yours; nor is there anything that can satiate your hungers or quench your thirsts or explain you to yourself with greater clarity than these same truths about your self and your soul.

[132] Leon Bloy, *Pilgrim of the Absolute* (New York: Pantheon Books, 1947), 223, 224.

∞

The modern world neglects the soul

Your world is a baffled world and one well calculated to confuse you. For it has taken those many marvelous modern inventions, which Leo XIII named "sparks of Divinity" and Pius XII called "manifestations of the Deity," and so twisted them from their proper purpose that they are now serving ends almost directly opposed to those they were supposed to serve. God allowed man to discover and invent these things so that, with them, man might harness the powers of Heaven and earth and have these, too, help him to the realization of those potentialities in his immortal soul which can make him more and more Godlike. But too often these inventions minister, both directly and indirectly, to the seven capital sins which sleep in every human and to the three concupiscences which will never die.[133]

Let us grip reality. Modern industry has raised the standard of your living to a great height, but what has it done to the standard of your life? Day in and day out, and often enough all the night through, it produces things that minister untiringly to the needs, the longings, and even the lusts of your body. But what does it produce that will minister to the ever-pressing needs, the yearnings, and the unyielding loves of your immortal soul? Material progress and financial prosperity have been achieved, but at the exorbitant cost of man's humanity and his peerless and utterly priceless personality.

Today the machine so dehumanizes and depersonalizes man that he comes to be looked upon — and too often looks upon

---

[133] The seven capital sins are pride, avarice, envy, wrath, lust, gluttony, and sloth. The three concupiscences are the lust of the eyes, the lust of the flesh, and the pride of life (cf. 1 John 2:16).

himself — as only another cog in the mammoth machine called Industrialism, and a cog that can very easily be replaced. The fact is universal and, at last, is being universally recognized. Takayama Iwao wrote, "The heavy burden of mechanical civilization, the hood of culture in print, the materialistic view of man, the idea of Almighty Science — through all these things man is losing what he is by nature. I am afraid the world is regressing rather than progressing." Can you question his analysis as you watch humanity swarming out of some giant factory at the end of a shift, or see it welling up out of some subway entrance as it hurries to work?

At such moments, it is hard to believe that these jammed midgets are the lords of God's visible creation. But the fault is not God's. It is the world's — that world for which God's Christ, on the night before He died, refused to pray.[134] But you must never forget that it is in that world that you live. It has been aptly described as "one huge body with an arterial system of roads, railways, airlines, and shipping lines; with a nervous system of telephone, telegraph, cables, and radio waves; the whole palpitating very restlessly."

Now, there is nothing wrong with such a body as a body. That arterial system and that nervous system can minister to God and all God's human children. But it is that "restless palpitation"; it is the "soul" of that body which is inimical to God and to you. It creates an atmosphere in which you must breathe. It shapes an environment in which you must live. But you well know that no one is completely immune to the effects of environment. Because of the speed of your modern life and living, you never reflect on the monstrous fact that, for the most part, your civilization is made up of an agglomeration of ready-made men and ready-made women. Count

[134] Cf. John 17:9.

the people you know who do not think ready-made thoughts, speak ready-made words, voice ready-made opinions, and even feel ready-made emotions. How many people do you know who do not follow ready-made political platforms, accept ready-made economic programs, and have as their life aim some ready-made financial goal? No wonder one witty Frenchman said, "These people do not think or speak — they simply echo."

Small wonder humans grow restless and resentful. The great wonder is that they do not recognize the cause of their restlessness and resentment. It lies in the wholesale denial of that very possession which differentiates them from all the rest of God's wondrous creation — their immortal souls. The denial is real enough, but goes unrecognized because it is not always put into words.

In a world afraid of truth, language is often used to cloak and conceal actuality; words are made into masks not only to hide ignorance but to cover the cold, clammy features of fear. To admit that you are the possessor of an immortal soul calls for courage; for it is an admission that carries with it the weighty burden of responsibility. It not only says that you are an individual who must answer for all your decisions and every one of your deeds, but that you are a shaper of a personal destiny that will endure forever.

That frightens a lone human — and rightly so! But no human need ever be alone. That is why this question of the soul merits such rapt attention. For it is no mere speculative matter. It is coming to grips with reality in a way that the man who thinks of nothing but bread, clothes, and a house never grasps it. Actually, it is a matter of far more practical importance even than air for your lungs. For its answer spells the difference between truth and falsity, between hope and despair, between happiness and misery, between true life and an existence of deceit and drudgery. More, it ultimately gives you the difference between sanity and madness, between humanity as God made it and that animality to which pseudo-scientists would reduce it.

If you do not possess an immortal soul, you have no grounds for hope, no reason for effort, no call for courage, and no demand for loyalty, and anything like sorrow, remorse, or repentance is completely senseless. If you are not the possessor of a soul that is immortal, then love, fidelity, justice, honesty, patriotism, and the like are mere catchwords, coined to lure the unthinking on to the accomplishment of something for the benefit of the ones who coined the catchwords.

But if you have an immortal soul, you not only have something to live for; you have Someone to die for! You can face all hazards, take all risks, ride all blows, and rise from every defeat, for no matter how bowed or bloody you may become, you can never be beaten! If you have an immortal soul, life is not so much a wearying warfare as a stirring challenge to the best that is in you, and, ultimately, it is found to be a divine romance!

And it can be proved to the hilt that you do have an immortal soul. But it demands a little time so that you can think, some silence in which you can reflect, and a touch of darkness so that you can see aright.

∽

You have an immortal soul

The first thing to reflect upon is that you are *more than matter*. You can come to grips with life by laying your hand on death. No one should be able to look on the body of a dead friend without realizing that man is more than matter. For nothing about the dead body, as a body, is missing; but it does not function any longer. Why? Because man is more than matter, more than flesh and blood, more than a mass of ganglia; because, while life can be found in a body, and manifested through a body, it is something essentially distinct from the body.

It is so painfully obvious that your patience may be strained as you are asked to apply one simple philosophic axiom: that actions are an infallible index to nature — that what one habitually does is a spotless mirror in which can be seen what one is. That is an axiom you apply a hundred and more times a day, for its application puts bread on the table, puts clothes on your back, and pays the rent. Yet, in the much more important concerns of life, the axiom is not always remembered.

You will shoo away the squirrel that might mess up your lawn with its digging or clog your rainspout by storing his acorns there, but you never do a thing to the oak that yearly messes up the entire front of your estate by dropping its acorns all over your lawn and letting its dry leaves fall all over your porch. If the animal gnaws one little hole in the side of your veranda, you will take measures to punish it in order to protect your property, but if the oak should drop a limb that ruins your roof, you do not reproach it with so much as a gesture! Why? Because you know the oak has only a vegetative soul; it can only grow and produce. But the squirrel has a sensitive soul; it can hear, see, and feel. That is why you shout to shoo it away or raise a stick to frighten it.

So far, so good. There is a difference between an animal and a vegetable. But how about man? Apply the same axiom to the same illustration. Suppose a boy made himself a nuisance by continually crossing your lawn and cutting his initials all over your front porch. What would you do? Would you bear with him as you do with the oak, or simply shoo him away as you do the animal? Never. For you recognize different natures from the different actions. Oaks do not frisk about on your lawn or store acorns in your drainpipe. Squirrels do not plan mischief or deliberately indulge in malice. Man, and man alone, is a responsible agent, for man, and man alone, can rationalize, since man, and man alone, has a soul that is more than matter. Hence, it is from man, and from man alone, that you can demand redress for making himself a nuisance at the front of your house.

Schemes, mischief, and malice are all abstractions and universal ideas. They are all nonmaterial. So the soul that conceives them must be of the same nature: it must be nonmaterial! If you want a silk purse, you must still have silk; a sow's ear will not do! If you have a thought, you must have a thinking faculty. If that thought is nonmaterial — or spiritual — it must be received in a faculty that is of like nature — nonmaterial, or spiritual. There must be proportion between cause and effect. You can bump into humans, but you will never bump into humanity. You can hug an affectionate person, but you will never throw your arms around affection. You can cheer a patriot, but you will never be able to cheer patriotism. You can never see enough of your beloved, but you will never set your eyes on love.

Love, patriotism, affection, and *humanity* are all abstractions. They live only in your mind and not in matter. Yet your mind handles these concepts as naturally as your eyes see color, your ears detect sound, and your hands feel pressure. Actions show you nature; nonmaterial, or spiritual, acts can come only from a nonmaterial, or spiritual, faculty. But handling abstract ideas cannot be called anything other than a nonmaterial, or spiritual, act.

Now, if your soul is nonmaterial, it is spiritual; for that is what is meant by nonmaterial. But if your soul is spiritual, it is simple, for a thing that is spiritual has no parts; it is a whole in itself. But if your soul is simple, it must be immortal; it must go on existing forever, for what can bring it to its dissolution or death? It cannot unravel like a ball of twine; it cannot fall apart like a broken-down machine; it cannot be separated from its principle of life as your body can, for it *is* life's principle! So it will live on as the angels live on; it will live on as God lives on. For it is spirit, and spirits do not die!

Indeed you can prove that you have a soul, and that it is immortal. It is almost as easy as showing there is a sun in a cloudless sky at noon, or stars at night! God Himself, when He walked our earth, proved to men that the Source of eternal life was in their midst. At the very beginning of His public life, when John the Baptist sent messengers to ascertain if He was the Christ, the anointed of God, and very God Himself, Jesus pointed to His works and told those messengers they were to return to John and report the things the Nazarene was doing: opening the eyes of the blind, unstopping the ears of the deaf, setting the lame and the halt walking aright, raising the very dead to life, and preaching the Good Tidings to the poor.[135] These were *actions* that could come only from a nature that was divine.

Then, St. John tells us that just before Christ's death in Jerusalem, the Jews surrounded Him and angrily demanded that He speak out. "How long will you keep us in suspense?" they asked. "If you are the Messiah, tell us outright." Jesus complied. "I told you," He said, "but you refuse to believe. The things I am doing in the name of my Father testify on my behalf." Then, as the Jews reached for stones to put Him to death, He argued, "Many a kindly deed have I performed under your eyes, with power from my Father; for which particular deed do you mean to stone me?" "Not for a kindly deed," the Jews retorted, "do we mean to stone you, but for blasphemy and because you, a man, make yourself God." Jesus reasoned with them, then climaxed His case with these words: "If I

---

[135] Cf. Matt. 11:2-5.

do not act as my Father does, then do not believe me; but if I do, then believe on the strength of my actions, even if you do not believe my words. Thus the truth will dawn on you, and you will understand that the Father is in me and I am in the Father." St. John ends that chapter with these words: "The result was that many believed in him there and then."[136]

If you did not have a spiritual, simple, immortal soul, you could not have understood this simple argument that the Man who wants you to come to grips with life provoked, nor could you have understood His unfounded demand. But now that you have taken this much time to think, you will understand Leon Bloy's indignation and his fiery impatience, which was really charity, since it was overflowing pity. To the unreflecting men who are concerned only with bread, clothes, and a roof, Bloy cries, "Souls do exist! You have been bought, paid for at a great price, St. Paul used to say. I should think so! It took nothing less than the blood of God! Such things we cannot understand. But what we do understand very well is that nothing in this world or in Hell would be able to pay for our souls. . . .

"Some saints have declared that if, by divine permission, one could see a soul as it really is, one would die on the spot as though one had been thrown into a furnace or a volcano. Yes, the soul of anyone, the soul of a bailiff, the soul of a concierge would consume us."

Then Bloy exclaims, "Ah! Lord, what a sorry people of God! What a strange and inconceivable people of God! An endless and universal procession, a torrent of torches more brilliant than the stars, and they do not even know what they are! . . . Blast furnaces large as worlds, but invisible, and not knowing themselves to be

[136] John 10:24-42.

furnaces. . . . Your souls! Ah! I am constantly thinking of those invisible roaring fires!"[137]

∞

You are composed of soul and body

Know yourself! Know your soul! Know it is a "roaring fire" a "blast furnace large as worlds." But pause a moment and realize that this blinding and beautiful creation, this invisible, immortal soul, is not you. No, it is only part of you — the more important part, as the child's catechism told you, but part nevertheless.

G. K. Chesterton once gave a formula for action that should prove most profitable for you. He said, "Stare at a familiar thing until it begins to look strange; then you'll be seeing it for the first time." Stare now at your soul; stare at yourself. Both already look strange enough; but before you really see them for the first time, they will look stranger yet.

You are not your soul. Nor are you your body. Then who are you? You are the *person* who possesses that soul and that body. You are the resultant responsible agent for that body and that soul which are wedded in an embrace which is *you*. Does that seem strange? Then stare! See that you are one of God's most marvelous creations, for you are not all spirit, nor are you all matter; you are not all angel, nor are you all animal. You are a composite that only Omniscience could conceive and only Omnipotence bring together and hold in place; for you are the resultant of the union of such completely disparate things as a material, corruptible body and a soul that is spirit, incorruptible and immortal.

That simple, familiar fact, when stared at and seen aright, is positively staggering; for while oil and water will not mix, they

[137] Bloy, *Pilgrim of the Absolute*, 225, 226, 227.

will emulsify; and while black and white are clashing contraries, they can be blended into gray; but spirit and matter — these are farther apart than any existing poles, yet in you they not only meet, but they unite and live in perfect harmony.

Stare at yourself until you see clearly what flat contradictions combine to make you. Death and life are diametrically opposed; yet you live in a body that dies and a soul that lives forever. Time is ever passing, eternity is a perpetual now; yet you are a meeting place for the passing and the ever perpetual. Heaven and earth are not only distinct; they are almost infinitely distant from one another; yet in you, Heaven begins on earth. Although you are kin to the angels by your intellect, you have passions that can pull you lower than any beast. Indeed, you are one whom only Omnipotent Omniscience could have made come true, for you are a perfect union of opposites.

Now, while it is true that you are not your body nor are you your soul, it is even more true that that body and that soul are yours! The point must be made in passing; for there have been those, and there are some even today, who consider the body a shameful thing. That is an insult to God, who made the body, and it is no glowing compliment to you, who must use it. For realize that your fleshy frame is no mere adjunct to your immortal soul; it is an essential part of you and the eternally predestinated complement of your utterly unique and immortal spirit. So long as you live on earth, your soul can function only in and through your body; and when you get to Heaven, and time is no more, that same fleshy body will have just as essential a part to play in your glorification of God as your spiritual soul. In fact, you will not really and fully be *yourself* until that body of yours is resurrected and glorified. So you can glory in your body not only inasmuch as it will one day be glorified, but because even now on earth, and in time, you can glorify God in it. "Are you not aware" asks St. Paul as the climax to his argument for sinlessness and his plea for spotless chastity, "that your bodies are members of Christ's Body? . . . Are you not aware that your body is the temple of the Holy Spirit? Him you have received from God. You are not your own masters. You have been bought, and at a price! So then, glorify God in your body!"[138]

Your body is a member of Christ's Body. Your body is a temple of the Holy Spirit. Your body is an instrument in which you can glorify God. Doesn't that make you stare at your hands, study your arms, and go to a mirror to scan your own face? This flesh you feed, wash, clothe, and put to rest — this corruptible thing that is ever dying and ever producing new life within it — is yours and yet not yours, for "you are not your own master." Your body as well as your soul "has been bought, and at a price!" It is not something to serve you alone, but something with which to give glory to God. It is holy!

But it is the soul that we must take more care of and right now give the closer consideration to. But since it is invisible, we will catch sight of it only by staring at the body. If you must say that your soul without its body is nothing but "a wandering perfection crying for completion," what must you say of your body without its soul? The best you can say is that it is a bit of blighted beauty — beauty because it comes from the hand of God, blighted because it lacks the breath of life.

∞

The Holy Spirit works in the Church
Michelangelo, the great painter and sculptor, when he had finished his statue of Moses, stepped back to survey his work. What

[138] Cf. 1 Cor. 6:15, 19-20.

met his eyes was so lifelike that he walked up to it, struck it on the knee, and said, "Speak!" Of course, the statue did not obey; for while Michelangelo could create, in the loose sense of that word, a body that was lifelike, he could not create, in the strict sense of the word, a soul that would elevate that marble and have it pulse with warm human life. But when God sculpted, something different took place. You read in the book of Genesis how God modeled in clay. When He finished His work, He did not step back to survey His mastery; He bent over the clay He had shaped and breathed into it the breath of life, and the "slime of earth"[139] stood up a living man, empowered to do what Michelangelo's Moses will never do: see, recognize, and speak to God.

The soul *elevates!* God's breath elevated cold clay to the towering height where it became the crown of God's visible creation.

The Soul of the Mystical Body does the same as the soul of your physical body; it, too, elevates. But, like the soul of your physical body, it, too, is invisible. You can learn of its presence and judge of its nature only from the actions of that Mystical Body.

Let us watch God in a somewhat parallel performance to His sculpting in clay and study the similarly astounding results of His actions. Let us look at the first public manifestation of the Mystical Body. It took place the day a mighty wind was heard in Jerusalem and fire fell from Heaven.[140] It is the first Pentecost, and God the Holy Spirit is seen as flame.

You have seen how a soul elevates the physical body of man so that clay might perform human actions. You are now going to see the Holy Spirit, the Soul of the Mystical Body, elevate human clay and have it perform actions that are far more than human. From

---

[139] Gen. 2:7.
[140] Cf. Acts 2:1-3.

this visible coming of the Holy Spirit, you are to learn just what His invisible presence means to *you*, for from the fall of flame upon the Apostles, you will see who it is that burns in you and by whom it is that you breathe the higher life.

The Mystical Body had been born. Like any newborn thing, it was both small and weak. Its members were few — the Apostles and disciples. Mary had been named its mother, and, in a sense, she was nursing it in the Cenacle,[141] when the Soul of this tiny body made Himself manifest by that rain of flame and the strong wind blowing. The infant Church instantly stirred with greater life, then moved out of doors and spoke fluently in diverse tongues. Then Peter, who had been named its visible head, told a dumfounded Jerusalem the truth about Jesus, and marvelous was the immediate growth of His Mystical Body.

If ever the function of a soul was made manifest, Pentecost is the day on which that was done. At creation you saw clay take on life and speak to God. At Pentecost you see a similar marvel. Men who, on Holy Thursday night and Good Friday afternoon, did not have stomach enough to act like men suddenly come forth on this Sunday morning and act as fearlessly as God. Men who, for fifty days, had been staying in the Cenacle, behind locked doors, "for fear of the Jews"[142] now come forth with courage enough not only to tell the truth fearlessly to the city of Jerusalem, but to flaunt it in the face of the very council and that Sanhedrin which had condemned Christ to death. The transformation is complete, and it would be completely bewildering if you did not know that the soul elevates; and that the Soul of the Mystical Body is the Holy Spirit.

[141] The upper room in which the Last Supper and the first Pentecost took place.

[142] John 20:19.

Bethlehem had witnessed the birth of the God-Man. Calvary had seen the coming into being of men who would very truly be men of God. But it was only at Pentecost that the world was granted the sight and allowed to hear this new being — the mystical Christ, God incarnated, as it were, in the flesh of Peter, James, John, Andrew, Philip, and the rest. And what a revelation it was! The man who quailed before the voice of a servant girl and denied with oaths that he knew the Nazarene is heard commanding the men of Israel to listen to his words, and those words pierced their very hearts: "Jesus of Nazareth was a man accredited to you by God. . . . You crucified and slew Him by the hands of wicked men. God has raised up this Jesus, and of that fact we are all witnesses. . . . Receiving from the Father the promised Holy Spirit, He has poured forth that which you see and hear. . . . Therefore, let all Israel know most assuredly that God has proved him both Lord and Christ this very Jesus whom you have crucified."[143]

That is not only a courageous speech; it is also a condemnatory one. Yet Peter so pierced the hearts of his hearers with it that about three thousand accepted his word, were baptized, and, like you at your Baptism, received as soul of their soul God the Holy Spirit, as they were thus incorporated in Christ's Mystical Body. Like you, they were set breathing by the God who burns.

You have learned that the soul elevates and that actions are an infallible index to nature. Watch the Soul of the Mystical Body in action as Peter and John come along a few days after Pentecost and cure a lame man who had asked them for an alms. It caused a sensation. A mighty crowd surged around the apostles as they stood in Solomon's Porch — that colonnade which ran along the east side of the Temple. Then the man who could not face a

---

[143] Acts 2:22-23, 32-33, 36.

single servant girl in the praetorium without denying Jesus thrice, turns to this mighty assembly and speaks out fearlessly: "Men of Israel, why do you marvel at this man, or why do you stare at us as though by any power or holiness of our own we had enabled him to walk? The God of Abraham, of Isaac, and of Jacob, the God of our fathers, has glorified his servant, Jesus, whom indeed you delivered up and disowned in the presence of Pilate, when he had decided to release Him. You, however, disowned the Holy and the Just One, and asked that a murderer be released to you; but you killed the Author of life, whom God has raised up from the dead."[144]

Again you see it was no conciliatory speech. Yet, although the police, the priests, and the Sadducees broke into this crowd and arrested Peter and John, the last line of the episode reads, "Many who had heard the message believed, and the number of the men grew to be about five thousand."[145] How the infant Mystical Body is growing, thanks to the actions of its Soul!

Farther on in that fourth chapter of the Acts, you learn what happened when Annas and Caiphas with "the rulers, elders, and scribes" held court and tried Peter and John; and you see how the soul elevates. For when these judges of Israel command the apostles to cease speaking in the name of Jesus, Peter and John answered, "Whether it is right in the sight of God to listen to you rather than to God, decide for yourselves. We cannot refrain from speaking of what we have seen and heard."[146] Imagine that defiance to the high priests, elders, and rulers of the people — and from Peter, the man who so often blundered!

[144] Acts 3:12-15.
[145] Acts 4:4.
[146] Acts 4:19-20.

In His physical body, Christ had been mighty in work as well as in word. In His Mystical Body, He is the same. "The apostles worked many signs and wonders among the people," St. Luke tells you. So great were these works that "the people used to carry the sick into the streets and lay them on beds and pallets so that, when Peter passed, his shadow at least might fall on some of them. Throngs came also from the towns near Jerusalem, bringing the sick and those troubled with unclean spirits, and they were all cured."[147]

How similar to what happened when Jesus began His public life in His physical body. St. Matthew relates how "Jesus toured the whole of Galilee, instructing the people in their synagogues and preaching the Good News of the kingdom, besides healing every disease and infirmity among His countrymen. The result was that the report about Him spread into every place in Syria. And all those suffering from various diseases were brought to Him, whether they were racked with pain, or possessed by demons, or epileptic, or paralyzed. And He cured them all."[148]

The parallels are perfect. What Jesus did through the members of His physical body at the outset of His public life, He does again through the members of His Mystical Body at the outset of that Body's public life. From every page of the Acts, it is evident that Jesus Christ continues to live on earth — that He, the Son of God and very God, prolongs His Incarnation in Peter, James, John, and the rest. Through them, He performs miracles as great as the ones He performed through the members of His physical body. Miracles are possible only to God, yet Peter's shadow occasions real miracles. Therefore, God is in the man who casts this shadow. It is the Spirit Jesus promised. It is God the Holy Spirit.

[147] Acts 5:12, 15-16.
[148] Matt. 4:23-24.

To realize that you breathe by the God who burns, you must study these parallels between the physical life and the mystical life of Jesus until you see in the visages of these one-time fishermen the very face of Christ and, in their gnarled fists, recognize the omnipotent hand of God. Then you may be able to scan your own countenance and see who you really are.

Note how the parallels stretch: jealousy, criticism, opposition, and open antagonism followed one another in rapid succession when Jesus walked and worked in that flesh He had assumed from Mary Immaculate. The same arise and follow one another in the same rapid succession as He now walks and works in the flesh He has assumed from the fishermen of Galilee. Look at what happened after the crowds came seeking to be touched by at least the shadow of Peter. In these opening chapters of the Acts, St. Luke, who gave you the charming biography of the infancy of the physical Christ, is giving you the challenging biography of the infancy of the mystical Jesus. In them you catch the flashes of that Flame which fell at Pentecost; for it is He who is the Soul of the Mystical Body, and like every other soul, He is present not only to the whole, but wholly present to each individual part.

∞

The Holy Spirit works in your own soul

As the crowds continued to come to hear Peter's words and see his marvelous works, "the high priest . . . and all who sided with him (that is, the party of the Sadducees) took action, as they were filled with jealousy. They seized the apostles and put them in the public prison. But during the night, an angel of the Lord opened the prison doors and let them out with the words, 'Go, stand in the Temple and declare to the people the full message of life.' On hearing this, the apostles went to the Temple about daybreak and began to teach. Meanwhile the chief priest and his party came and called together the Sanhedrin and all the elders of the Israelites. [What echoes that awakes of what happened to Jesus in His physical body!] They sent to the prison to have the apostles brought out. But when the officers came and failed to find them in prison, they returned and reported, 'We found the prison securely locked and the guards standing before the doors; but on opening them, we found no one inside.' When the officers of the Temple and the chief priests heard this report, they were very much perplexed about it as to how this thing could have happened. Someone, however, came and reported to them, 'Why, these men you put in prison are standing in the Temple and teaching the people.' "[149]

Now comes a line that will recall many a happening in the physical life of Jesus: "Then the officer went off with his men and brought them, but without violence because they feared they might be stoned by the people."[150] The people were on the side of the mystical Christ just as they had so often been on the side of the physical Jesus; and now, just as then, they strike fear into the hearts of the high priests and their servants. "Having brought the apostles, they placed them in the Sanhedrin. The high priest questioned them: 'We strictly charged you not to teach in this name, and here you have filled Jerusalem with your teaching. You are determined to make us responsible for this Man's death.' Peter and the apostles answered, 'One must obey God rather than men. The God of our fathers raised Jesus, whom you put to death, hanging Him on a gibbet. God exalted Him by His might to be Leader and Savior, to grant a change of heart and mind and forgiveness of sins

[149] Acts 5:17-25.
[150] Acts 5:26.

to Israel. And we are witnesses of these events, and so is the Holy Spirit, whom God has given to all who obey Him."[151]

"So is the Holy Spirit": what an enormous statement for any mere man to make! What a change in this man Peter! Brave he certainly is. But he always has been brave. Bold he is. Yet bold he always was. But he has now added something distinctly new. He is not the blusterer and blunderer he used to be. He is a person possessed of such assurance that his mere presence overawes. Even the Sanhedrin feels it. This is a new man, a new Peter. The explanation is the one Peter himself gives continually. Ever since the strong wind blew and those tongues of fire fell, Peter has not only spoken *of* the Holy Spirit, but most especially has spoken *by* the Holy Spirit. Peter was alive with a new life. His soul had a new Soul. And just as his rational soul manifested itself by his reasoning, this new Soul was manifesting itself by His revelations. It was the Spirit of Christ, the Holy Spirit, speaking and working through the fisherman who had obeyed Christ's command "not to depart from Jerusalem but to await what the Father had promised."[152]

The lifeless clay that was the body of the first man, Adam, the lifelike statue that Michelangelo made of Moses, the corpse of a loved friend — all teach you that the soul elevates. But it takes a transformed Peter whose life is a manifestation of Christ, to tell you who the Soul of the Mystical Body is and how high He elevates.

You know that all love is wont to go to excess. When that love is divine love, would you not expect it to go to excess divinely? The Gospels, by showing you God first as a newborn infant in a crib used for feeding cattle, then finally as a corpse on a Cross used

[151] Acts 5:27-32.
[152] Acts 1:4.

only for the worst of criminals, show you that your expectations are well founded. In the material body Christ took from Mary, divine love passed all bounds physically, sensibly, and empirically. In the Acts, and in the letters of the apostles, you see the same divine love still surpassing all bounds, but now it is in the Mystical Body Christ has taken from among men.

And in both the physical and mystical bodies you find the Spirit of Love, God the Holy Spirit, playing the dominant role. He overshadowed Mary at Nazareth, and nine months later, the result was seen at Bethlehem in that utterly unique creation of God: a human nature united hypostatically to the divine nature by the Second Person of the Blessed Trinity. The same Holy Spirit overshadows Mary, the Apostles, and the disciples in the Cenacle, and a few moments later the world sees another utterly unique creation of God: a body that belongs to the Second Person of the Blessed Trinity as truly as branches belong to a vine, and which is animated by the Blessed Trinity's Third Person, the Substantial Love of the Father for the Son and the Son for the Father — God the Holy Spirit.

If the rational soul elevated the clay that was to be Adam to the heights of being human, do you not see that this Soul of the Mystical Body who, as Pius XII says, is "essentially something infinite, uncreated: the Spirit of God," must elevate you to heights measureless leagues beyond the purely human? Can you escape the conclusion that, ever conscious though you may be of your finiteness, your creaturehood, and your humanity, once you have been made a member of Christ's Body, you not only can, but you must, use of yourself those startling words so often used by the early Fathers of the Church; you not only can, but you must, speak of yourself as "divinized," "deified," made somehow a "human-divine" being?

Now, if your nature has been elevated to supernature, what must the nature of your actions be? Rank imposes obligations; dignity begets duty. The higher the rank or dignity, the heavier the obligation or duty. What must be yours, who have been elevated to the towering dignity of being Christ's own member, who are vivified by Christ's own Spirit?

Instead of "plain living and high thinking," G. K. Chesterton demanded "plain thinking and high living." You have done some plain thinking in this chapter. See what high living is demanded of you in the next.

Chapter Five

❦

You are one whom God has called to rarest intimacy

If you were asked to name one of the most startling, mysterious, and utterly unique things on the face of the earth, what would your answer be? If you have been doing what Chesterton advised — staring at the familiar until it looks strange — you should not require much time for thought before pointing to *yourself* or naming the Mystical Body of Christ, which is the Holy Roman Catholic Church. For since no one will deny that Jesus Christ was utterly unique in human history, who can question your uniqueness who, in all truth, are a continuation of Jesus Christ in modern times?

❦

God called His Chosen People
to intimacy with Him

For an understanding and explanation of this startling phenomenon, you must turn to the Bible.

Begin at the beginning. Adam was unique. God made him so. And what intimacy he enjoyed with his Maker! In the cool of the evening, they walked together and talked together in that garden we call Paradise. But you know what happened to that intimacy!

Next look at Noah. He was unique, for God chose him to build that ark which was to be the means of keeping the human race from being completely washed away by that just judgment of God we call the Deluge. But the subsequent unity, peace, and intimacy is soon marred by man's building of Babel. Yet God always has a remnant. Abraham is unique, because he was called to father God's Chosen People.

Course down the history of this unique phenomenon called the Chosen People, and you will see there is nothing more startling or more mysterious in all time's annals. Go from Abraham, Isaac, and Jacob, through Joseph, and on to Moses. With this leader, come out of Egypt, cross the Red Sea, wander forty years in the desert; then, after the death of Moses, enter the Promised Land with Joshua. Go down through the judges and the kings. See the kingdom divided. Watch both Juda and Israel go into exile. Sit with Ezekiel by the waters of the Chobar puzzling over the mystery of it all and wondering what God will do next with this people with whom He has always been so intimate and who has so persistently bartered that intimacy for less than a mess of pottage.[153]

As you sit with Ezekiel, you will suddenly hear God speaking His mind, showing His heart, telling His determination to have a people He can call His own. "I will gather you from among the peoples," says God, "and assemble you out of the countries wherein you are scattered, and I will give you the land of Israel. . . . And I will give them one heart and will put a new spirit in them. And I will take away the stony heart out of their flesh, that they may walk in my commandments and keep my judgments and do them, and that they may be my people and I may be their God."[154]

[153] Cf. Gen. 25:29-33.
[154] Cf. Ezek. 11:17-20.

"They shall be my people, and I will be their God": that is the refrain that rings out again and again. You hear it not only with Ezekiel but with that contemporary of his, Jeremiah. To this mighty prophet, God once said, "Behold, the days shall come and I will make a new covenant with the house of Israel and the house of Juda — not according to the covenant which I made with their fathers, in the days when I took them by the hand to bring them out of the land of Egypt, the covenant which they made void. But this shall be the covenant that I will make with the house of Israel after these days, saith the Lord: I will put my law within them, and I will write it in their heart: and I will be their God, and they shall be my people."[155]

The bewildering history that followed on God's choice shows both how unfaithful man can be and how determined God is. It was well summed up in that parable about the vinedressers which Jesus told the high priests and the elders — the council of the nation. He told them of the "landowner who planted a vineyard, set up a fence about it, dug a wine-vat in it, and built a tower; he then leased it out to vinedressers and went abroad. When the harvest season drew near, he sent his agents to the vinedressers to receive his share of the vintage. But the vinedressers seized his agents, beat one of them, killed another, and stoned a third. So he sent another group of agents, more numerous than the first; but they treated them in the same way. Finally, he sent to them his own son, saying, 'They will respect my son.' But when the vinedressers saw his son, they said among themselves, 'This is the heir; come, let us kill him and seize upon his inheritance.' So they laid hold of him, drove him out of the vineyard, and killed him."[156]

[155] Cf. Jer. 31:31-33.
[156] Matt. 21:33-39.

Not a pleasant story in any circumstances. But most especially not a pleasant story for the hearers to whom it was directly addressed. These high priests and elders knew Scripture. In the words falling from the lips of Jesus, they could hear clearly the voice of Isaiah as he sang his song about how his good friend had a vineyard which he fenced in, cleared of stones, planted with a choice vine, built a tower in the middle, and set up a winepress. He then waited for the grapes to grow. But it yielded him only wild grapes. Isaiah's "friend" then asks that question which rings out with such poignancy every year in Good Friday's moving Liturgy. It is that piercing line in which God asks, "What is there that I ought to do more to my vineyard, that I have not done to it?"[157]

This council of the nation knew that Isaiah had gone on to say, "I will show you what I will do to my vineyard. I will take away the hedge thereof, and it shall be wasted: I will break down the wall thereof, and it shall be trodden down. And I will make it desolate."[158] That is why they are so ready with a reply when Jesus asks, "When the owner of the vineyard returns, what will he do to those vinedressers?" They answer, "He will put these wretches to a wretched death. And besides, he will lease the vineyard out to other vinedressers, who will give him his due share of the vintage at its proper season."[159]

How that answer must have stuck in their throats! For they knew that God was the landowner who planted a vineyard. They knew that they, the Chosen People, were that vineyard, for Isaiah had been most explicit, saying, "For the vineyard of the Lord of hosts is the house of Israel; and the man of Juda his pleasant

---

[157] Isa. 5:4.
[158] Isa. 5:5.
[159] Matt. 21:40-41.

plant."[160] Jeremiah had been no less explicit: "I planted thee a chosen vineyard, all true seed."[161] They well knew that the fence God had set about them was the law of Moses and that special Providence He had always extended to the Jews. The winepress in their midst was the altar of holocausts, and the tower, Jerusalem's Temple. They also knew that the agents Jesus mentioned were the prophets of God whom they had stoned and killed.

But Jesus would leave them in no doubt. Looking them in the eye, He said, "I tell you: the kingdom of God will be taken away from you and turned over to a nation that will produce the fruits expected of it."[162]

∞

God calls you to even greater intimacy

You belong to that nation. You are one from whom Almighty God expects plentiful fruits. For you are one who has been chosen by God just as surely as was Abram, Noah, Joseph, Moses, or Joshua; just as surely as the patriarchs, prophets, judges, and kings of Israel — and chosen, be it said with awe, *for greater intimacy!* They were but God's vineyard; you are a branch of that Vine who is His only Son. God wrote His law in the hearts of the Jews but you, as St. Paul says, "are the epistle of Christ," one that has been written "not with ink but with the Spirit of the living God."[163] God would give His Chosen People a heart of flesh, but to you He would give His very Spirit of Love to be your "quickening spirit," your very Soul! If they were called to rare intimacy — and who

[160] Isa. 5:7.
[161] Jer. 2:21.
[162] Matt. 21:43.
[163] 2 Cor. 3:3.

can doubt it? — what shall be said of your call whom God the Father made a member in the Body possessed by God the Son, and who has been gifted and graced by Father and Son with that Bond who is their love and their loving?

God's fiery determination to have a people He could call "His own" has been evidenced to you in every covenant He made with the Jews, for no matter who the mediator was, the sacred pact always closed with the words: "and they shall be my people, and I will be their God."[164]

But what deference God shows to man's free will! He had dowered man with liberty. He will never take back that gift. He will invite and even call. But He will force no man to accept. To date, man's response has been none too gracious and none too generous. Yet we know that God's determination is to know final fulfillment, for St. John, at the close of the book of Revelation, shares with us his vision of the "new Heaven and the new earth" and allows us to hear the voice from the throne exclaiming, "How wonderful! God's dwelling place is among men; he shall make His home among them. They shall be His people, and God Himself shall abide in their midst."[165]

That is the future that not only explains all past history for you, but tells you very exactly just what is going on at present. God is building His "new Jerusalem"; He is fashioning His "new Heaven" and His "new earth"; He is shaping a people He can call His very own, and *you* are one of them!

The blindness of many modern historians is equaled and occasionally surpassed only by the ignorance of commentators on current events. Although they see precisely what is happening, they

[164] Cf. Jer. 24:7.
[165] Apoc. 21:1, 3 (RSV = Rev. 21:1, 3).

have no idea of exactly what is going on; or in the events that pass before their eyes, they never note the strong hand of God.

You are a child of this very confused century, but you need never be the least bit confused. All you need to do is realize that the tempo of modern times, which lately has been elevated higher than the speed of sound, means only that the hammer of God is falling faster, the marble *moves* beneath His chisel, and the statue is all but stepping forth from the cold stone. In all truth, the city of God is being built rapidly, and the people of God are crowding in!

That is why it can be said that in all mankind's long history, there was never a more glorious time in which to be alive, for God is nearer now than you know! If Moses, in what was very like his last will and testament, could say, "No other nation is so great; no other nation has gods that draw near it, as our God draws near to us,"[166] what must you say of yourself and your fellow Catholics who this day form the Mystical Body of Christ, with God's only Son as your Head and the Blessed Trinity's Third Person as your Soul?

How almost infinitely distant was God from His Chosen People under the Old Covenant when compared with the divine intimacy granted you under the New! They heard His voice from a burning bush; you have seen His Word, clothed in your own flesh, walking your own dusty earth. They received two tablets of stone that held ten stern commands, and they were given these amid the thunder and lightning of Sinai; you have been given a Law of Love. It came to you from a human heart that had broken out of love, but which was, nonetheless, the Sacred Heart of God. They had a "cloud by day and a pillar of fire by night";[167] you have Emmanuel — God with you! They fed on manna and quail, and

---

[166] Deut. 4:7.
[167] Cf. Num. 14:14.

drank water that gushed from a rock, but they died; you eat the Living Bread that came down from Heaven — and you will live forever. They had the Ark of the Covenant, which was made of purest gold, but it held only a vessel of manna, the tables of the Law, and Aaron's rod; you have Jesus Christ in person — Body and Blood, Soul and Divinity — tenting in your tabernacle under the guise of a tiny white Host. They had promises; you have fulfillment. They looked on symbols, and shadows; you look on substance. They had men of God who were truly His messengers; but you have God Himself and Him whom He sent — His only Son — plus the Holy Spirit. They had the Temple of God, which had a Holy of Holies; but you *are* God's temple and are to be holy with God's own sanctity.

This last is the reality that proves beyond all doubt or quibble that the most startling and marvelous thing on the face of the earth at this moment is the Holy Roman Catholic Church — the Mystical Body of Christ, God's Chosen People, of which *you* are one! For to be holy with God's own holiness is very truly "something out of this world."

⚭

God calls you to be perfect

The Church does not ask you to be saintly as John the Baptist or John the Beloved were saintly; nor to be as angelic as Michael, Gabriel, and Raphael are angelic. She does not tell you to take the spotless Mother of God as your ultimate model or your final norm. She goes farther. Up above the angels and archangels, beyond the thrones, dominations, principalities, and powers, into realms higher far than those occupied by the virtues, cherubim, and flaming seraphim, she tells you, "Look, and take as your exemplar Almighty God Himself." You have heard Paul speaking to his Ephesians and saying, "Follow God's example, as his very dear children, and let your conduct be guided by love." Think not for a second that that can be watered down. Paul's demand is explicit. It is the love God Himself has manifested that is to be your guide and your gauge. "Be guided by love," he says, "as Christ also loved us and delivered Himself for us as an offering to God, a sacrifice that has an agreeable fragrance."[168] And what was Paul doing but echoing the Master who had said, "Be perfect as your heavenly Father is perfect"?[169]

Yes, the impossible is demanded of you. You, who cannot keep the Ten Commandments of God nor the Six Precepts of the Church — the minimum demanded of your creaturehood and your Catholicity — for any length of time without grace from God; you, who cannot successfully resist a real temptation — be it to pride or sensuality — unless God aids you; you, who cannot make a perfect act of love of God — and consequently a proper act of love of self — without help from Heaven; you are asked to be "perfect as God is perfect." And this command comes from the lips of Divine Wisdom and Infinite Truth.

What, then, is the answer? You know how difficult it is to be perfectly human; how, then, can you ever be perfectly divine? Is God demanding the impossible? Yes — even though one of the fundamental principles of Catholic moral theology is "No one is held to the impossible." The seeming contradiction is resolved by recalling that Gabriel told Mary, "Nothing is impossible with God";[170] that Paul said of himself, "I can do all things in Him who strengthens me";[171] and that Christ said to you, "Behold I am with

[168] Eph. 5:1-2.
[169] Matt. 5:48.
[170] Luke 1:37.
[171] Phil. 4:13.

you all days."[172] Hence you can tell yourself that you can be as perfect as your heavenly Father is perfect because you have that Father's Son as your Head and that Father's Spirit as your Soul. You can be perfect because God has called you to rarest intimacy.

There is the answer to what seemed unanswerable: You have been *deified*. And if you really knew yourself, you would see that there is something natural in this transformation, something normal in this surprising elevation. For "you shall be as gods"[173] was what Satan said to your first parents, as he lured them to disobey God. At those words, something deep in human nature stirred. Note well it was not concupiscence; not any proneness to evil. For there was none in your first parents! But there was something in these words of Satan that made the temptation sound like an invitation to human nature to reach out and take what was, in some way, its due.

Despite God's explicit command and His threat of death, Adam and Eve disobeyed Him. From the very beginning of the human race, then, there throbbed in man a desire to be more than human. It was what might be called a connatural desire; it was — and it still is — a desire for deification. From that mad moment in Eden to this present madder moment in your own times, that desire has driven mankind. Perhaps now, as never before, it is seen working most feverishly. For the state has been deified; human reason has been deified; the collective will has been deified; and now it is massed humanity that the Communists would make a god.

The desire is legitimate. It derives from God Himself. But it must be properly directed! God made you for Himself in a deeper, truer, more intimate sense than is usually recognized. When you

[172] Matt. 28:20.
[173] Gen. 3:5.

come to know yourself fully, you will have acquired a surprisingly accurate knowledge of all mankind. Then you will realize that in every man, woman, and child, there is an innate craving, an imperious necessity of nature for union with God — the closest possible union; nothing short of an actual deification.

Back in the twelfth century, St. Bernard of Clairvaux[174] once described you as a "soul panting with a desert-thirst for God." It is gratifying to find Hermann Hesse, in the twentieth century, saying much the same thing, even though he is describing modern man without God. He depicts him as a wolf roving restlessly in "the endless and loveless desert that is Western Civilization," hideously crying his hunger and thirst for Eternity.

Man, to be man, must have contact with God. It is a necessity of his nature, a demand made by his essential insufficiency. But to be fully man, the human must be deified. What, on the lips of Satan, was a temptation and a deceit, is, on the lips of God, not only an invitation, but a challenge and something of a divine command. "Follow me," said Christ. "Be ye perfect as your Heavenly Father is perfect." This deification, then, is not something to which only the most spiritually daring may aspire; it is a duty the most earthly of us must accomplish. And it is possible in and through Christ Jesus, for God became man so that we men might become like unto God.

It is His Incarnation that explains your deification, for it paved the way for your incorporation in Him who, besides being the Son of Man, is the only-begotten Son of God. His Incarnation is the only thing that will ever, or can ever, explain you to yourself. St. Augustine expressed it well when he said, "He is come down so that we may ascend upward, and while remaining in His own

---

[174] St. Bernard (1090-1153), abbot of Clairvaux.

Nature, He is made to partake of our nature; we meantime remaining in our nature are made to be partakers even of His Nature; with this difference: that His participation in our nature does not lessen His Divine Nature, but our participation in His Nature marvelously betters our nature."[175]

Do you believe that? Do you really believe that you have been called to be like God? St. John Chrysostom reminds you that you give wholehearted credence to something far more unbelievable — God's becoming man! "If you hesitate to believe that so great a boon [as union with God, or deification] should be bestowed on you," says this man of the "golden tongue," "realize that the abasement of the Divine Word in the Incarnation is a marvel far greater than your elevation." And St. Cyril of Alexandria exclaims, "To say that you cannot be one with God except by union of will is untrue. For above that union is another more sublime and far superior, which is wrought by the communication of the Divinity to man who, while keeping his own nature, is, so to speak, transformed into God, just as iron plunged into fire becomes fiery, and while remaining iron is changed into fire. . . . Union with God cannot exist otherwise than by participation with the Holy Spirit, diffusing in us the sanctification proper to Himself, imprinting and engraving on our souls the divine likeness."[176]

∝

God invites you to oneness with Him

St. Bernard of Clairvaux clarified it more when he took as his text: "Let Him kiss me with the kiss of His mouth"[177] and explained

---

[175] *Epistle 140 ad Honoratum.*

[176] St. Cyril (d. 444; Patriarch of Alexandria), *In Joan.*

[177] Song of Sol. 1:1 (RSV = Song of Sol. 1:2).

the deepest drive in man — a drive about which your present-day depth psychologists know so little. He told his monks that what the human soul desires in this "Kiss of God" is the infusion of the Holy Spirit, for it is the Holy Spirit who can transform the soul and bring it to supreme happiness.

"The Son reveals Himself and the Father to whom He pleases," says the saint. "But the revelation is made by a Kiss, that is, by the Holy Spirit, as the Apostle bears witness when he says, 'But to us God has revealed them by His Spirit. . . .' By this revelation, the Holy Spirit not only communicates the light of knowledge, but kindles in the soul the flames of love. Hence the words of St. Paul: 'The charity of God is shed abroad in our hearts by the Holy Spirit who is given to us.' "

Knowledge and love — how St. Bernard insisted on these two! By his insistence, he was giving his monks the anatomy of their souls. Bernard showed how both faculties could be filled by being kissed with the "Kiss of His mouth" — God the Holy Spirit. Then he proved himself a real psychologist by adding, "If you are a slave, you will fear the face of the Lord. If you are a hireling, you will hope that He will hire you. If you are a disciple, you will attend to the instructions of your Master. If you are a son, you will honor your Father. But if you are a lover, you will ask your Beloved for a kiss!"

What a climax! And how expertly defended: "In the human soul," says Bernard, "love holds the first place among all the affections." Then he describes the kind of love *you* should have: "She loves with an ardent love who is so inebriated with love that she loses sight of the Majesty of her Beloved. What! She dares to ask for a kiss from Him who 'looketh upon the earth and maketh it tremble!' Is she drunk? Obviously! And fully drunk!"[178]

[178] Serm. VII, 3.

You, a soul thirsting for God, are to quench that thirst by becoming "God-intoxicated." That is the language St. Bernard used back in the twelfth century as he commented on the Song of Songs, which Solomon had written ten centuries before Christ. That is the language used today by men who have seen truth and know what mankind must have if it is to be mankind!

Do you feel that you are one "intoxicated with God"? You should, for you have been "kissed with the Kiss of His mouth" at Baptism and Confirmation. You should, for you breathe by the God who burns.

If you have not reached this point of inebriation, it may be because you have not yielded yourself to that Spirit of love who has been given to you as gift. He dwells in you to deify you by making you a partaker in the divine nature, so that you may know the union with God that merges into that stupendous unity Christ prayed for at His Last Supper and then went out and died so that it might be achieved.

Ferdinand Prat, S.J., in his book *Theology of St. Paul*, writes that "the mystery par excellence is the design conceived by God from all eternity, but revealed only in the Gospel, to save all men without distinction of race, identifying them with His beloved Son in the unity of the Mystical Body."

Paul tells you that this unity spells unity with the very Trinity, since it brings you to the Father, in the Son, through the Holy Spirit. That is the degree of intimacy to which you have been called!

Take as addressed to you the words Paul penned to his Ephesians: "You, too, after you had heard the message of truth, the Good News proclaiming your salvation, and had believed in it, in Him you have been sealed with the promised Holy Spirit, who is the first installment of our inheritance. The final purpose of thus being sealed is our redemption as God's possession to the praise of His glory."[179]

"It follows that you are no longer foreigners and guests; no, you are fellow citizens with the saints, and members of God's household. You are an edifice built on the foundation of the Apostles and prophets with Christ Jesus Himself as the chief cornerstone. In Him the whole structure is being closely fitted together by the Spirit to become God's temple consecrated to the Lord. In Him you, too, are being fitted by the Spirit into the edifice to become God's dwelling place."[180] At this moment, the Holy Spirit is working in you, to fit you for the intimacy God decreed and desires: oneness with Himself through the same Holy Spirit!

One with God: of course it is breathtaking — and frightening. But it is a truth that scares you into adoring gratitude to God and a real reverence for yourself and all your fellowmen.

You need hardly be told that this oneness is organic, not numerical. You do not become God; you become one with God. You become an independent cell that maintains its own individual life, while contributing to the total life of the organism that is Christ's Mystical Body. Unity is not sameness. Your oneness with God is real, but it never bespeaks equality, nor does it even destroy distinguishability. Unity in any and every living being supposes diversity; hence, oneness with God will always admit distinctness.

The distinctness is there; so is the *unity.* Your individuality remains, but it does not prevent closest intimacy with God! Branches as branches are nothing unless they are in the vine; and members as members are nothing unless they are in the body; likewise Christians as Christians are nothing unless they are in Christ

[179] Eph. 1:13-14.
[180] Eph. 2:19-22.

Jesus, abiding in Him as He abides in them, according to those words He addressed to them the night before He died.[181]

Now, the essential point in all this is that your happiness lies in your intimacy with God. But your intimacy with God lies in your oneness with Christ, for there is only one way to God: the Man, Christ Jesus. He said so Himself, and He cannot deceive.[182] You were made one with Him by Baptism, and that oneness was deepened by Confirmation. Hence, in all truth, Christ is the source of your real life.

∞

The soul unifies all members of the body

Lay firm hold on this seemingly elusive truth by staring at your own body and soul. In your body, as you read this page, there are billions on billions of individual cells, each leading its own individual life and, in time, dying its own individual death; yet your body is a unit. So unity and diversity are not contradictory. Second, in the body, through which you read this page, there is not a single cell that was there when you first learned to read; yet it is the same body. Physiologists tell you that your body is renewed completely every seven years. Yet you say it is always the same body. In fact, you will insist that the body you take to the tomb is identical with the one you had at birth, and you will not be wrong; even though your physiologists are scientifically right.

How can we explain such unity amid such diversity, and such identity amid such constant change? The answer is — *your soul.*

The one same soul that God created and infused into the matter prepared by your parents has vivified each and every one of the

[181] Cf. John 15:2-7.
[182] John 14:6.

countless cells that have gone to make up your body down the years, uniting them so as to make one body, identifying them so as to make each of them yours.

You have already learned that the soul *elevates*. You now learn two other functions of your one principle of life: it unifies and identifies. What is true of your human soul in its relation to your physical body is true likewise of the Holy Spirit in His relation to Christ's Mystical Body: He not only elevates; He unifies and identifies. At this moment, as you read this line, there are hundreds of millions of individual cells in Christ's Mystical Body. Each is living its own individual life. Each will die its own individual death. Yet each is united with every other one of those hundreds of millions, and each and all are identified with Jesus Christ thanks to God the Holy Spirit.

Who but God could count the myriad billions on billions of cells that have been in this *one* Body of Christ since He first said "Come, follow me" to some fishermen by Galilee's lake and thus began to prepare the matter that one day would be informed by His Holy Spirit? From every nation, race, and culture they have come; from every generation of men and women; from every civilization from that of the then-crumbling Greco-Roman world to your own Western World — and they have all been made one in Christ Jesus, thanks to God the Holy Spirit.

The next important thing to learn is that it is the *person* who acts, just as it is the person who suffers. That means that it is not your eye that reads this page of print; it is *you*. It will not be your hand that will turn this page when you have read it; it will be you.

This axiom, when applied to Christ's Mystical Body, not only clears away countless difficulties but clarifies life's purpose and fills all living with the greatest joy. To learn that you are dealing with strict fact, let us turn to the Gospel for an episode in the early part of Christ's physical Passion, and then to the Acts for an episode in the early part of His mystical Passion. These two accounts not only prove that it is the person who acts and suffers, and that you have been called to rarest intimacy with Almighty God, but they also show what your actions and your sufferings today can mean to God's only and eternal Son.

The first scene is in the house of Annas. It is late at night. Jesus of Nazareth, just taken prisoner in the Garden of Gethsemani, is being pushed into a hall where the father-in-law of Caiphas will question Him about His disciples and His doctrine. This is contrary to all Jewish law, which never required a defendant to testify against himself. Jesus reminds them of this by asking, " 'Why do you question me? Question those who heard what I said. You see, they know what I said.' No sooner had Jesus said this than one of the guards who stood by gave Him a blow on the face and said, 'Is this the way you answer the chief priest?' Jesus protested. 'If I was wrong in speaking this way,' He said to him, 'then prove me wrong; but if I was right, then why do you strike me?' "[183]

Remember those words — "Why do you strike me?" — as you turn now to the ninth chapter of the Acts and read how Saul of Tarsus, a man who had been "ravaging the Church" in and around Jerusalem, goes to the high priest "breathing threats of death against the disciples of the Lord," and obtains from him "letters to the synagogues at Damascus, so that if he found any men or women belonging to the Way, he might bring them in bonds to Jerusalem."[184]

Saul set off for Damascus. But as he was approaching that city "a light from the sky flashed round about him, and falling to the

---

[183] John 18:21-23.
[184] Acts 9:1-2.

ground, he heard a voice saying to him, 'Saul, Saul, why do you persecute me?' 'Who are You, Lord?' he asked. Jesus replied, 'I am Jesus, whom you are persecuting.' "[185]

The parallel is perfect. The fist of a soldier fell on the face of Christ; it struck a physical member of the body Jesus had taken from Mary. The Person who owned that body cried, "Why do you strike me?" The angry zeal of Saul struck Christians, the mystical members of the same Jesus. The Person who owns those mystical members and that Mystical Body feels those blows and cries out, "Why do you persecute me?"

The identification is obvious. Jesus of Nazareth possesses the Mystical Body just as truly, just as intimately, just as personally, as He possessed the physical body in which He lived, suffered, died, and redeemed. You cannot fail to see, then, that He will live, suffer, die, and save through those men and women who are His mystical members; for the unity and the identity are as evident as your own unity and identity, and they are achieved the same way: through the soul. Could you or anyone else conceive a more conclusive demonstration that it is the person who acts and suffers than that given when Saul asks, "Who are You, Lord?" and receives the reply: "I am Jesus, whom you are persecuting"?

Since Jesus is one with His Mystical Body, He could have sundered the heavens any of the days you have lived and asked countless members of various courts exactly what He asked of that lawless court in the house of Annas, and what He asked of Saul on the road to Damascus. To that court in Hungary which tried and condemned the drugged Cardinal Mindszenty,[186] could He not

---

[185] Acts 9:3-5.

[186] József Mindszenty (1892-1975), Hungarian cardinal who was persecuted and imprisoned by Hungary's Communist regime.

have said, "Why do you strike me?" Could He not ask any of those barbarous Peoples' Courts of China: "Why do you strike me?"

His members are being struck; He feels the blows. Indeed He would be justified in crying out. So would you, if you were to exclaim, "What intimacy I am allowed with my God! What value there can be in all my acts and all my sufferings if I live in Christ Jesus!"

∞

You can be "filled with the Holy Spirit"

You can be "God-intoxicated," for you can be "filled with the Holy Spirit"[187] as truly as was St. Stephen or St. Paul, for the soul in any body is fully in the whole and fully in each part. That is to say, your human soul is in your toe as well as in the tip of your ear; in your hand as well as in your heart; in your lungs as well as in your head. Your soul is not only in your entire body, but is entirely in every single member of your body. It has to be so, for such is the nature of the spiritual.

But what is true of your physical body and its soul is just as true about Christ's Mystical Body and its soul. Hence, God the Holy Spirit is not only in the entire Mystical Body, but is entirely in each member of that Body. He is in you just as entirely as He was in St. Stephen or St. Paul, of whom Scripture says they were "filled with the Holy Spirit."

But that irrefutable proof presents a mountainous problem. If the Holy Spirit is entirely present in each member of Christ's Mystical Body, why isn't the world filled with Stephens and Pauls? If this Spirit of God burns and breathes in all of us, why aren't we "all life, all fire, and all love"?

[187] Acts 7:55, 13:9.

The answer is: We should be. But the explanation of that answer brings relief even as it provides you with a real spur.

Teresa of Avila[188] once described a soul as "a capacity for God and nothing else." That is a perfect description. It not only tells you just who should fill your soul, but it perfectly solves your difficulty, for the accent is on *capacity*. You can be filled literally "to capacity" with God — to *your* capacity. I, too, can be filled to my capacity with God. Yet neither of us will be as full as was St. Stephen or St. Paul, for, like stars, capacity differs from capacity.

Yet the fact remains: you can be, and you should be, "filled with the Holy Spirit" and thus become a "God-intoxicated" individual. If you do not become so, it will not be God's fault, for the wind is yet blowing and the flames fall just as truly as they did that day in the Cenacle in Jerusalem.

In his monumental encyclical *Mystici Corporis*, Pius XII has touched on every phase of the intimacy to which you have been called, and on every function of the Soul of the Mystical Body. In a single sentence, the Pontiff tells you that it is the Holy Spirit who unifies, identifies, and is not only totally present in the whole Body, but totally present in each member of that Body. "To this Spirit of Christ," says the Pontiff, "as to an invisible principle, is to be ascribed the fact that all the parts of the body are joined one with another and with their exalted Head; for He is entire in the Head, entire in the Body, and entire in each of the members." That is why the Pope could add, "The Church, then, no less than each of her holy members can make this thought of the Apostle their own: 'And I live, now not I, but Christ liveth in me.' "

If you are a holy member — and what rational being would be other than holy when he or she realizes that the very holiness of

---

[188] St. Teresa of Avila (1515-1582), Carmelite nun and mystic.

God is the Soul of their soul? — you not only live with the life of Christ, but you allow Christ to live fully in you. Then you can think the very thoughts of God, for you will have the mind of Christ.[189]

[189] Cf. 1 Cor. 2:16.

Chapter Six

You are one who can think the thoughts of God

The Power of Positive Thinking was the title Norman Vincent Peale gave to a book that became something of a rage in the middle of the twentieth century. But its popularity, far from being an index or surety for the wealth of thought contained in the book, was in reality a disturbing revelation of the poverty of thinking done by the book buyers. For the truly judicious could not read far into the book without seeing that of the three terms used in the title, the first was the only honest one.

The book was not about thinking and far less about positive thinking. It was all about power. Very definitely its author had the cart before the horse; for the object of all thinking, be it positive or negative, is truth, not power — just as the basic consideration for faith is verity, not vigor. The author of the book reversed all that. His concern was not with thinking, but with autosuggestion. His purpose was power, not peace of soul. Actually, his ultimate was behavior rather than belief, although one may credit him with being unconscious of his real drive and very well meaning in his effort.

Of course, as with all error, his was not without its modicum of truth. An optimistic faith will invigorate! But let it be faith, that is, an intellectual conviction based on revelation, and not what Dr. Peale advocated: a conditioned reflex — and one conditioned by yourself through autosuggestion. The book abounded with exhortations such as: "Ten times a day repeat these dynamic words"; "Ten times a day practice the following affirmation." As you can see, that is not banishing unbelief by any spiritual penetration into truth; that is banishing it by a species of brainwashing. That technique will never lead you on to a knowledge of self. It is calculated only to maintain self-deception. No wonder one very thoughtful critic, Ulrich Sonnemann, summed up the book as a mixing of "untrue theology with a just as untrue psychology."

The Power of Positive Thinking, its error, and even its popularity stirred memories of another book that, ten years earlier, had been just as popular, and just as erroneous. Is it a mere coincidence that this other book — entitled *On Being a Real Person* — came from the pen of one who, like Dr. Peale, held a New York City pulpit from which he also preached this optimistic "faith," which has as the first article in its creed: "Believe in yourself" — and which gives very little theological grounds for such a belief?

Harry Emerson Fosdick's *On Being a Real Person* failed to live up to the promise of its title because of the same fundamental error as in the other book: groundless faith. In *On Being a Real Person*, Dr. Fosdick seemed headed in the right direction, but just at the end, he refused to take the last logical step that would have brought him and his reader face-to-face with the one Character who can enable any human to be a real person: the incarnate Son of God.

Both of these divines spoke about faith. In the closing chapters of *On Being a Real Person*, there is much about "the constructive use of the faith-faculty." And the author does not leave you in the dark or in doubt about his concept of "faith" and this "faculty." He says that faith is something "as inherent in your constitution as affection"; therefore, it is not something you get but something you already have. It is "a capacity to believe in persons, ideas, or causes, and confide ourselves to them." Consequently, you can see the function of this "faith-faculty": it gives you "focus" and is a "source of integration," for it can give you a "strong one-directional drive." The author then concluded that if such a drive once took possession of you, and you made the total self-commitment it demands, you would become a real person.

Here again, error has its kernel of truth. You see the error clearly enough: you have no specific "faith-faculty." You make an act of faith with your intellect spurred on by your will. You assent to the verity in a revealed truth because of the veracity in the One revealing. The "habit" of faith is not a possession you have from your nature; it is a specific gift from your God.

Once you receive this gift, what this author says is not without its force, for you then can be said to have a "capacity to believe in a Person, His ideas, and His cause, and even to confide yourself to them." In very truth, it is faith that gives your life focus and is the "source of integration." But it is a faith based on truest theology, and the integration is made along the lines of soundest psychology. You have a Person: Jesus Christ. He gives you a cause: the spread of His kingdom, His conquest of souls. To Him and for them, you can make a total self-commitment, which will give your life a "strong one-directional drive" for the glory of God. Possessed by such a drive, you will become a very real person, for you will become the person God made you to be. But you will become that only in and through the Person of His Son, Jesus Christ.

To give Dr. Fosdick his due, we must remember that he did speak of "shoulders stronger than your own" being under every load you carried, and a "Mind wiser than your own" being behind it. Undoubtedly he meant God, although he did not name Him. But you know with the certainty of faith that Omnipotence shoulders every burden with you and that Omniscience planned or simply permitted that you be so burdened. You know that you can have power. And you are certain that you can always think positively, for you know that you can think the very thoughts of God, since in all truth you can have the mind of Jesus Christ.[190]

∞

You must have the mind of Christ

The two popular Protestant divines were very close to truth. They had almost hit on what the modern existential-analytical school takes to be a new discovery — namely, that you become what you know yourself to be. That you should "become what you are" is not a new truth, but it *is* truth and therefore unalterable. Had Drs. Fosdick and Peale really known who you are, they might have been more successful in their prescriptions for helping you to become yourself. But you, who know yourself to be a Christian, know full well that you are to become Christ. Further, since it is true that you are what your thoughts are, you know you will never become what you should be unless you have the mind of Christ and, with it, think the thoughts of God.

Through lips that a seraph had cleansed by fire, God once said to His people, "My thoughts are not your thoughts; nor your ways my ways. . . . For as the heavens are exalted above the earth, so are my ways exalted above your ways, and my thoughts above your thoughts."[191] If God were to speak to His "Chosen People" today, would He have to repeat those words? You can answer that

[190] Cf. 1 Cor. 2:16.
[191] Isa. 55:8-9.

question with finality. All you need to do is look at your own thoughts and examine your own particular ways. If they are as different and as distant from God's as heaven is from earth, it is high time you listened to the same prophet of the fire-cleansed lips as he says, "Seek ye the Lord while He may be found; call upon Him while He is near."[192]

There, in a single sentence, you are told what has been wrong with man from the beginning, and what is wrong with so many men today. They did not, and many still do not call upon God while He is near — and He is always nearer than can be expressed. They did not, and many still do not, seek Him while He can be found, and no seeker need ever fail to find Him; for He is the "Obvious Invisible" staring out at you from everything that is.

Yes, from everything and everyone. For if Leon Bloy could rightly say that Napoleon Bonaparte was "the Face of God in the darkness" why cannot you discern the features of "the most beautiful of the sons of men"[193] in the deeper dark that has held a Hitler, a Stalin, and a Mussolini? If Bloy could see that "this strange being called Napoleon could never make a gesture without unconsciously betraying the Three Persons of the Trinity," why is it that you do not see your God in everything from the "birds of the air" and the "flowers of the field"[194] to disasters the size of the Deluge and visitations as obviously God-sent as were the Ten Plagues of Egypt or the brimstone that fell on Gomorrah?

In the beginning, man did not think the thoughts of God; Paradise was lost. Today men do not have the mind of Christ; Paradise is not being regained, and your civilization is something

[192] Isa. 55:6.
[193] Ps. 45:2.
[194] Matt. 6:26, 28.

of a shambles. It is inevitable, for thoughts rule the world. The thoughts ruling your era are no more the thoughts of God than were the thoughts that ruled the Chosen People when Zion was captive in Babylon and Jerusalem without the smoke of sacrifice. That being true, you can see how imperative it is that you have the mind of Christ.

Hilaire Belloc's statement that "a man is his mind" should set you examining not only your habitual thoughts, but your very habits of thinking; for it is the habit that is all-important. It was right here that both of the authors mentioned at the beginning of this chapter had something positive to offer, for according to them, if on examination you were to find that you have the habit of riveting your attention on the things you lack, your inadequacies, your imperfect qualities and definite limitations, you would immediately realize that you are on the wrong track and would instantly switch over to stressing the positive, of placing strong emphasis on your real possessions, your good qualities, your actual abilities, and the definite virtues you have acquired. Then you would soon find that this kind of thinking would make you much more optimistic and a better person to live with.

∞

You yourself form your habits of thought

But all that, helpful enough as far as it goes, does not go nearly far enough; for you were not born simply to be a nice person to live with. You were called into being to become like God!

So, flimsy as may have been the application by the two authors, the principle they were using is as solid as granite: you acquire your habits of thought. Hence, it is you who actually make your own mind, fashion your own psychological self, and shape your social personality.

At birth, you were the most helpless being imaginable. If you had not been watched over and constantly cared for by a loving mother or a devoted nurse, you would never have survived. Yet, from the first moment of your existence, in the infallible eyes of God, you were of infinite worth because of the tremendous potentialities dormant in your immortal soul.

The vital principle that set your tiny body squirming was dowered with faculties that, if properly developed, would one day allow you to reach out and take God into your own possession. Within you was the indestructible image of that creative (and ever-creating) Trinity that is God. The spiritual substance that gave life to that flesh of yours was to function, in time, through a memory, an intellect, and a will — three powers that, when properly used, would enable you to be so like God that you would be able not only to think His thoughts, but to love what He loves, and hence be very like Him. Has that time arrived yet for you?

You have grown up physically. As the years went on, you have managed to mature to some extent emotionally; and formal education has given you enough mental development to allow you to pass as a cultured person. But what of your spiritual soul? Has there been a corresponding growth and a parallel development in it? Or must you, like so many others, confess that, in a world ruled by law, you are an anomaly — that, while all nature follows God's plan and grows, you have frustrated Omnipotence?

Stunted growth, arrested adolescence, and immaturity are alarmingly present in the emotional and mental realms, but they are nothing compared with what one finds in the spiritual world. In a civilization called Christian, if development had been at all normal, Christ — the mature Christ, the Good Shepherd and the Good Samaritan, the Christ who went about doing good, the Christ no one could convict of sin — would be seen all around you. But what is the actuality? Dwarfs where only giants should walk. God's plan for humans looks like a blueprint that is seldom consulted. He wills *saints!*

Since "a man is his mind," you have an infallible gauge wherewith to measure your Christianity (and that of anyone else). It is the mind of Christ. You are what your thoughts are. Therefore, you can estimate your Godlikeness with perfect accuracy by finding out if you habitually think the thoughts of God. To know your spiritual height with exactness, stand beside Him who said, "I do always the things that please the Father."[195]

In nature, growth and increase are the normal condition of every living thing. In supernature, however, arrested development and stunted growth seem almost universal. But the most frightening part of it all is that people seem unconcerned about their failure to "grow up in Him who is the Head — even Christ."[196]

If saplings in their orchards fail to show an increase from year to year, how quickly people seek the cause and try to secure a remedy. If a child shows the slightest sign of not developing normally, how soon the pediatrician is consulted. But for your soul, for the only growth that matters eternally, for your maturing into Christ, what lack of concern!

Can you account for this unconcern for the "one thing necessary"?[197] Can you tell why you are not as tall today as Mary's Son and why the talents entrusted to you at Baptism have not been doubled? The reason is obvious: You have not consciously cultivated the habit of thinking the thoughts of God by having the mind of Christ.

[195] Cf. John 8:29.
[196] Eph. 4:15 (Douay version).
[197] Luke 10:42.

You know that perfection is a matter of habit, that habit is a matter of conscious repetition, and that conscious repetition depends on deliberate thought and firm determination. You acquired the habit of walking, thinking, and talking by repeated acts. Now, what is so patently true in the realm of nature is every bit as true in the realm of grace. You must cultivate the habit of walking with God, talking to God, and thinking like God if you are to mature as Christ. Baptism, with its breathless endowment, was only birth. The newly born must grow! It takes years for him to attain his full stature. So, too, with your soul. It will take time for you to grow in the likeness of Christ. But all the time you must grow!

∞

God wants you to love
Him as only you can

Leon Bloy once said, "We become nothing; not even a blockhead." This statement occurs in *The Ungrateful Beggar* — who was Bloy himself. As usual, this genius immediately clarified his idea: "If a man is not the greatest artist in the world before he has ever drawn a line, he will never become such."

With that thrust, Bloy laid bare exactly what it is that has filled countless mental institutions and strewn the world with human wrecks. It is the refusal to assess properly one's liabilities as well as one's assets.

That is why certain people conceive an utterly unrealizable ambition; then, goaded on by it, stretch themselves far beyond their reach and their grasp. Of course they lose their balance and fall into depths from which, oftentimes, there is no rising. These people do not know themselves. They do not accept themselves as God has made them with all their very real assets — and their equally real liabilities.

"We become nothing; not even a blockhead." Consequently, in order to stay sane, you must know not only your abilities, but also your liabilities. To become holy, you must accept both gratefully from God.

Christ told you this truth in parable form more than once. He, the Infallible One, has cautioned you not to begin to build a tower until you are sure you have enough bricks and mortar — not to set out for war against a foe who is far your superior.[198] Christ was really saying, "Never attempt the impossible!" And let it be stated apodictically: there are many, many goals that are absolutely impossible for certain individual humans — and meant to be so by the God who gave them their limitations as well as their assets.

But there is one goal no one need ever miss, for it is one that God has made possible for every human He has created. That goal is sanctity. And sanctity is very much a matter of having the mind of Christ, for that will mean thinking the thoughts of God and then doing His all-holy will.

Yet a caution must be issued. As has been said, you have your limitations in the supernatural order just as truly as you have them in the natural. Get to know them, and you will never overreach! Einsteins are rare in the natural order; so are Joans of Arc[199] in the supernatural. An Edison comes once in every three or four lifetimes; so does a Curé of Ars.[200] If you have not been called to become a *great* saint — a Dominic,[201] a Bernard, or an Ignatius of

---

[198] Luke 14:28-32.

[199] St. Joan of Arc (1412-1431), French heroine who led the French army against English invaders.

[200] The Curé of Ars, or St. John Vianney (1786-1859), patron saint of parish priests.

[201] St. Dominic (1170-1221), founder of the Dominican Order.

Loyola[202] — you have undeniably been called to become a saint, and that is greatness enough for any man, woman, or child.

Time will make you acquainted with your supernatural limitations, just as it did, and yet does, with your natural ones. It is highly probable that you will never be able to pray as did Teresa of Avila, Catherine of Siena,[203] or Gemma Galgani.[204] Yet, so long as you have a mind and a will, you can always do your particular kind of praying, and that, indeed, is the only kind by which you can praise your God! Perhaps it already seems quite evident to you that you will never be able to love God as did the Poor Man of Assisi[205] and bear in your body the five wounds of the Christ; or love Him as did St. Bernard, that man of Clairvaux who loved the Crucified so ardently that one day Christ unfixed Himself from a Cross in order to hug His loving monk. Perhaps you already know that you will never be so aflame with love for God that your body, like that of St. Francis Xavier,[206] will not be able to hold the fire.

But so long as you live, you will be able to love your God exactly as He wishes to be loved by *you*. Perhaps the pithiest and best advice that can be given on this point is: Pray as *you* can; don't try to pray as you can't! Love your God as *you* can; don't try to love Him with somebody else's heart! Live with your loving God as *you* can.

Paul put this whole matter clearly to the Corinthians. He wrote, "Now, concerning spiritual gifts, brothers, I would not have

[202] St. Ignatius of Loyola (c. 1491-1556), founder of the Jesuits.

[203] St. Catherine of Siena (1347-1380), Dominican tertiary.

[204] St. Gemma Galgani (1878-1903), Italian stigmatist.

[205] St. Francis of Assisi (c. 1182-1226), stigmatist and founder of the Franciscan Order.

[206] St. Francis Xavier (1506-1552), Jesuit missionary known as the Apostle of the Indies.

you ignorant. . . . There is a distribution of gifts, but the same Spirit distributes them. There is a distribution of ministrations, but it is the same Lord to whom we minister. There is a distribution of activities, but it is the same God who activates them all in everyone. The manifestation of the Spirit is given to each individual for the common good. For example, to one is imparted the ability to speak with wisdom, to another with knowledge under the guidance of the same Spirit, to another by the same Spirit is imparted wonder-working confidence, to another gifts of healing by the one Spirit, to another the performance of miracles, to another inspired preaching, to another the discernment of spirits, to another the ability to speak in various languages, to another the ability to interpret them. But it is one and the same Spirit who is active in all these gifts, which He distributes just as He wishes."[207]

That last line awakens echoes of the voice of Christ the night He spoke with Nicodemus and told him the "breeze blows at will."[208] But Paul's point was to show that there is unity amid all this variety and that it is achieved by this Spirit, who distributes the various gifts "just as He wishes."

He continues, "For example, just as the body is a unit, although it has many members, and all the members of the body, many though they are, form but one body, so, too, is the Christ. . . . The body, I repeat, is not formed of one but of many members. Suppose the foot should say, 'Because I am not a hand, I am no part of the body,' is it, for all that, no part of the body? And suppose the ear should say, 'Because I am not an eye, I am no part of the body,' is it, for all that, no part of the body? If the whole body were eye, where would the hearing be? If the whole body were hearing, where

[207] 1 Cor. 12:1, 4-11.
[208] John 3:8.

would the sense of smell be? But, as it is, God has put the members, every last one of them, in the body, as He wished. Now, if they were all one member, where would the body be? But, as it is, there are certainly many members, but a unified body. The eye cannot say to the hand, 'I have no need of you,' nor the head to the feet, 'I have no need of you.' . . .

"You are Christ's body and individually its members. And God has established in His Church some in the first rank — namely, Apostles; others in the second rank — namely, fervent preachers; and still others in the third rank — namely, teachers. After that come wonder-workers, then those with the gifts of healing, then assistants, administrators, and those that speak a variety of languages.

"Are all of us Apostles? Are all of us inspired preachers? Are all of us teachers? Are all of us wonder-workers? Do all of us have the gifts of healing? Do all of us speak in languages? Do all of us act as interpreters?

"Be eager always to have the gift that is more precious than all the others. I am now going to point out to you the way by far the most excellent."[209]

That last gift, "more precious than all the others," is one you have, yet one you must always cultivate. It is something given by God yet brought to perfection by man when he labors to acquire the habit. It is the gift of love. You hardly need to be told that you grow in love by loving. You can read Paul's famous thirteenth chapter in this same first letter to the Corinthians by yourself and learn the habit you must acquire. But it is the last line in his twelfth chapter that highlights again the ultimate purpose of this book, which is to show you "the most excellent way." This is only

[209] 1 Cor. 12:12, 14-21, 27-31.

another way of saying, as the Douay version puts it, "Let this mind be in you which was also in Christ Jesus."[210]

But what does it mean to have the mind of Christ? Exactly what the words signify. You are to think as Christ thought, have the ideals Christ had, use the principles Christ used, and live the truths Christ lived. When you have to judge an event, estimate the worth of person, or evaluate principles, you are to use Christ's gauge and Christ's standards. Although kings imprison men like John the Baptist, you are to tell the crowds what manner of man the imprisoned is. When modern pharisees thank God that they are not like other men, have the trumpet sounded as they give what they call alms, and strain out the gnat even as they swallow the camel,[211] you are to point to humble publicans, generous widows, and honest, uncompromising, and selfless children. When the "righteous" would stone some poor woman taken in adultery, you are to do what you can to save her life. The pattern is clear, for the Gospels are anything but cloudy. And the beauty of it is that it is all so modern!

Your day rings with calls for "integration." Could anything be found that will so completely knot all things into one for you as will the mind of Christ? Jesus, in literal truth, was a Man of one idea. That idea was the will of the Father.

Hence, if you wish to become the integrated person your day demands, if you wish to have peace of soul and happiness of heart and to attain life's only genuine success — sanctity — you will begin now to cultivate that virtue which was the cardinal virtue of Christ's life, the very core of His character. Theologians name it *pietas*. In actual life, it is a loving child's reverential regard for

[210] Phil. 2:5.
[211] Cf. Luke 18:11; Matt. 6:2, 23:23.

everything connected with his father. That was the virtue which integrated Christ's life. That is the virtue which will integrate yours and make you, in all truth, a Christian; for it gives you the mind of Christ in the fullest sense of that word *mind*, since it also takes in His Heart!

∞

Worldliness opposes the mind of Christ

But do not think that this will be easily obtained. Against your acquisition of this mind of Christ is arrayed that triple entente of deadly enemies: the world, the flesh, and the Devil, each of which will exert itself to the utmost to keep you from ever having the mind of Christ. Underestimate none of them, but keep special guard against the first. The world is a spirit as inescapable as the atmosphere, and just as all-pervasive. For the world of men, God gladly died. For the world of matter, God, after exerting His omnipotence to bring it into being, goes on exerting all His wondrous powers for its preservation in what is called His unfailing Providence. But for the spirit of the world, or worldliness, God would not utter so much as a single short prayer. And that is your chief enemy — more dangerous than the Devil, with whom it is allied; more deceptive and far slyer than your ever-sly flesh.

Have you already been taken in by it? Has it already prevented you from having the mind of Christ?

Your present-day capitalistic world is immersed in matter. Its leaders, far from being God-centered, or even man-centered, are only machine-centered. Instead of a theocracy, or even a democracy under God, you live in what is only a technocracy. The apotheosis of method and technique, so universal in your day, can mean death for the heart and mind of man, the destruction of his very soul. For such an apotheosis could take place only in a culture that is sensate — one that denies all spiritual values. And such a culture is yours. It is pragmatic to the core; and its pragmatism begins and ends in material production.

In such an atmosphere you can make a living, but you can never live life that is truly human — unless you acquire the habit of thinking with the mind of Christ! Without His mind, your soul will be smothered in a world filled with smoke.

∽

The Holy Spirit enables you to have the mind of Christ

"Now, we have received not the spirit of the world," says St. Paul, "but the Spirit imparted by God."[212] That Spirit is the Spirit of Christ — the promised Paraclete — the Holy Spirit, the Third Person of the Blessed Trinity, consubstantial with the Father and the Son. Thanks to that Spirit, Paul was enabled to recognize the gifts bestowed on him by God. Thanks to the same Spirit, you can do the same. Thanks to that Spirit, Paul could say, "We have the mind of Christ." Thanks to the same Spirit, you can make the same proud boast; for this is the Spirit petitioned by the Son, sent by the Father, "to be with you for all time to come"; this is the "Spirit of Truth" whom "the world is incapable of receiving,"[213] but whom you have received first at Baptism, then more fully at Confirmation; this is the Spirit who dwells in you and works in you to transform you into a "new creature";[214] and because this Spirit "fathoms all things, even the depths of God,"[215] He can empower

---

[212] 1 Cor. 2:12.
[213] John 14:16-17.
[214] 2 Cor. 5:17.
[215] 1 Cor. 2:10.

you to think the thoughts of God and enable you to have the mind of Christ.

If you are to be a Christian, you must yield yourself completely to the Fire of God, the Holy Spirit. For that is precisely what Christ did as man. If you read the life of Christ as portrayed in the Gospels, you will note how the Trinity is ever locked in unity. The Father's will was the Son's "passionless passion," but He followed it only under the dominance of the Holy Spirit.

This Third Person of the Blessed Trinity all but ruled the earthly life of the Trinity's Second Person, a life that was dedicated to the reparation of the outraged dignity of the Father, the First Person. It was the Holy Spirit who overshadowed Mary so that the Eternal Word might take flesh in time. It was the Holy Spirit who poured the fullness of sanctifying grace into the human soul of the God-Man, elevating it to the supernatural level and empowering it to act supernaturally. At the Baptism of Christ, John the Baptist saw "the Spirit coming down in the shape of a dove from Heaven" and resting on Him. St. Matthew tells you that the heavens opened, and a voice rang out saying, "This is my Son, the beloved, with whom I am well pleased."[216] So by Jordan's muddy bank, the eternal Trinity manifested Itself in Its entirety in the voice, the dove, and the Man. Matthew follows that revelation with: "Then Jesus was led by the Spirit into the desert to be put to the test by the Devil."[217]

St. Luke tells you it was the same Holy Spirit who led Jesus out of the desert and set Him to the work of His public life.[218] During that public life, how much in evidence the Holy Spirit was! Again

[216] Matt. 3:17.
[217] Matt. 4:1.
[218] Luke 4:14.

and again, Jesus drove devils out of possessed persons. His enemies accused Him of doing so by Beelzebub, the prince of devils. Jesus refuted the charge vigorously and climaxed His case by giving testimony to the Holy Spirit, saying, "But if I drive out demons by the Spirit of God, then evidently the kingdom of God has now made its way to you."[219] Was it not when "prompted by the Spirit" that Jesus exulted and said, "I praise you, Father, Lord of Heaven and earth, for hiding these things from wise and prudent men and revealing them to little ones"?[220]

So you can course through the entire public life and see that Jesus was ever under the dominance of this Spirit, who abides in you for the same purpose: that He may so dominate you that the Father will be able to say of you, a Christian, what He has already said of His Christ. But the climax, which comes as something of a surprise even to the most learned, is given by St. Paul when, in his letter to the Hebrews, he tells you that the Crucifixion, Christ's chief work on earth, was offered "through His eternal Spirit."[221]

Obviously Christ acted always under the promptings of the Holy Spirit and, as Dom Marmion has said in his book *Christ the Life of the Soul*, was "infinitely docile to such promptings."[222]

What is to keep you from being the same? Does not every dictate of reason and demand of decency prompt you to similar docility? Since you are His member, are you not obliged to follow the lead of your Head? It is the very same Spirit who worked in Christ who works in you. But He must have your cooperation! "Whoever

---

[219] Matt. 12:28.

[220] Luke 10:21.

[221] Heb. 9:14.

[222] Columba Marmion, *Christ the Life of the Soul* (St. Louis, Missouri: Herder, 1935).

are led by the Spirit of God, they are the sons of God. Now, you have not received a spirit of bondage so that you are again in fear, but you have received a spirit of adoption as sons, in virtue of which you cry, 'Abba, Father!' The Spirit Himself joins His testimony to that of our spirit that we are the children of God."[223]

Fear not, then, if this Spirit should lead you into the desert to be tempted. Yield yourself to His promptings, and you will come out of every desert as did the Christ — magnificently triumphant. Allow this Spirit to rule your life, and you will have a faith that will never falter, a hope that will never disappoint — far less die — and a love that will flame higher and higher until you are lost in the living Flame who is Love. "This hope does not disappoint," says St. Paul, "because God's love is poured forth in our hearts by the Holy Spirit who has been given us."[224]

How dear you are to God — and how intimate to the entire Trinity!

On the night before He died, Jesus said, "I will ask the Father, and He will grant you another Advocate to be with you for all time to come."[225] That was Christ's promise to His Apostles and to His Church. That was His promise to you! For He who is the Soul of the Church, which is Christ's Mystical Body, is your Soul; for you are Christ's member, and as you have already learned, the Soul is present fully in the whole and fully in each part. You have all the fire that is God the Holy Spirit flaming within you. He is there for the identical purpose He is in the Church: to vitalize, to vigorize! The Son asked the Father on your behalf, and the Father sent the Holy Spirit to you to be with you for all time to come!

[223] Rom. 8:14-16.
[224] Rom. 5:5.
[225] John 14:16.

Once the waters of Baptism flowed and you were born again, the Holy Spirit took up an entirely new presence in your soul, for He took on an entirely new function. He had been *sent* to you to bring you closer to your Creator; He had been sent to fashion newer bonds of friendship between you and your Maker; He had been sent to create in you an affinity for the infinite, to give you a taste for the divine, and endow you with what is called a "connaturalness" for the things of God. In short, He had been sent to give you the mind of Christ.

But what a price was paid so that you might be so endowed — and paid by the entire Trinity! The Father had to send the Son to Bethlehem, Egypt, Nazareth, Gethsemani, and Golgotha. The Son had to be born in a cattle cave and die on a criminal's Cross, for this indwelling of the Holy Spirit in your immortal soul is the splendidly perfect fruit of Jesus' redeeming.

But never forget that God is purest act. Therefore He is ever acting. The Holy Spirit, then, never ceases to work within you, so that you may ever grow in the likeness of Christ.

Cling to that truth. God the Holy Spirit is within you to make you become like God the Son so that you may ever please God the Father.

On this truth, which has been called "the central and most consoling truth of our Faith" the saintly Father Olier,[226] founder of the Sulpicians, based his whole system of spirituality. In his *Catechism for an Interior Life*, he asks, "Who deserves the name of Christian?" And he answers, "He who is possessed by the Spirit of Christ." Then he explains that it is God the Holy Spirit who "makes us live both interiorly and exteriorly like Jesus Christ." He assures you that the Holy Spirit is "there in the soul with the

---

[226] Jean-Jacques Olier (1608-1657).

Father and the Son, and infuses the same dispositions, the same sentiments, the same virtues of Jesus Christ."

Now when you read St. Paul's "Let this mind be in you which was also in Christ," you know that he is telling you to listen to the Holy Spirit who dwells in your soul.

∞

You can learn how to grow in the likeness of Christ

But it is St. Thomas Aquinas who again tells you that you must make it a *habit* and then quietly insists that habits are the result of repeated acts. He is again drawing out the perfect parallel between the natural and the supernatural. He tells you that your body grows in vigor just so long as you exercise it properly; that your mind grows in mastery just so long as you exercise it on more and more difficult problems; and that your will grows in strength just so long as you exercise it in acts of firm determination. His analogy is inescapable: your soul will grow in the likeness of Christ just so long as you exercise it steadily under the promptings of the Holy Spirit, using His grace, His virtues, and His gifts to cultivate the habit of having the mind of Christ and using it to think the thoughts of God. And this you can do even though you live in a world inimical to Jesus.

An American poet, Clifford J. Laube, put it thus in what he called a "Cry Out of Babylon":

> We are the sad inheritors of haste,
> Sons of distraction, fervered from the start.
> With desolation is our hope made waste
> Because no man has quiet in his heart.
>
> Yet through the din of these disordered years
> Truth's Bride, still unenslaved and unenticed,

Utters her old entreaty, touched with tears:
"Put first things first. Think with the Mind of Christ."

Think with the Mind of Christ? This rule is hard;
Yes, doubly hard amid this hellish grind
Of wheels and words. But oh, the rich reward:
To be a cell in the Supernal Mind![227]

You can have that reward today. And it is a reward you need never lose, for it is something wholly and truly spiritual.

Your body, vigorous as it may be, will one day reach the peak of its performance. After that, it will gradually decline; for it will be unable to repair the losses sustained in daily living. The process of dissolution will have set in. What is true of your physical powers is true also of your natural spiritual strengths. Your intellect will one day lose its brilliance, for the brain cells on which it depends for its activity will suffer deterioration. Since your will, in its functioning, depends on your intellect, it, too, will decline.

But so long as life lasts, the spiritual energies of your supernatural soul can go on increasing day by day, moment by moment, for you can always go on growing in grace and thus becoming more and more like Christ. Death can find you at your supernatural strongest.

Unlike natural life, the life given you at your rebirth, the life as member of Christ's Mystical Body, should never know diminution, far less taste death. Thanks to prayer, the Sacraments, and the Sacrifice of the Mass, it can and should increase steadily in strength and beauty.

The further you penetrate into this marvel and mystery which is yourself, the closer you come to your God. Each advance in

[227] *Crags* (Richmond Hill, New York: Monastine Press, 1938).

clearer knowledge of who you are has been an advance in clearer knowledge of Him who is. Heed, then, the words of that fire-cleansed Isaiah as he bids you climb yet higher. Fear not the height, for here you will breathe your native atmosphere, for very truly here is your home. "Come," says the prophet, "let us climb up to the Lord's mountain peak, to the house where the God of Jacob dwells; He shall teach us the right way; we will walk in the paths He has chosen. . . . Let us walk together in the path where the Lord shows us light."[228]

[228] Isa. 2:3, 5.

Chapter Seven

∽

You are one who can be as free as God

In his first published article, Jacques Maritain, in the vein that made his godfather, Leon Bloy, famous, wrote, "It seems that in our times truth is too strong for souls, and that they are able to feed only on diminished truth."

With those words, the then-young philosopher told a truth that was vivid and vital both for his times and for your own. Yet, because of the words he used, he told it untruthfully. For no truth can ever be too strong for any soul. A soul is a capacity for God, and God is infinite, eternal, ever-living Truth. Hence, no soul will ever bend under the pressure or possession of truth — even if that Truth is infinite. Souls are strong — in their own way, as strong as God. But about the persons who possess souls, the story is different. Many a truth can be of such strength as literally to shatter them.

The truth you have been learning about yourself may have already staggered you, but it has been food and drink to your thirsting and ever-hungry soul. In one word, St. Augustine described that soul of yours perfectly. *Irrequietem*, he called it. But how to translate that? "Restless" is too colorless and weak. "Insatiable" would be nearer actuality, yet it might prove deceptive, for your soul can, and will, know a rest, which will be pure, perfect bliss when it has laid hold on complete Truth, pure Love, and perfect Beauty.

To anyone who knows your human soul, that is but a platitude. If it cannot be said to be as old as the sun, it certainly is a few centuries older than today's sunrise. Yet psychologists and psychiatrists are just making the discovery that deep in you is a dynamism driving you toward the Infinite. They are calling it "an effective impulse carrying man to the Divine." How very old the new!

∞

Your soul hungers for God

Yet, when Pius XII faced the scientists present for the Fifth International Congress of Psychotherapy and Clinical Psychiatry on April 13, 1953, he urged them to study this "drive." "It pertains to the technique of your science," he said, "to clarify the questions of the existence, the structure, and the mode of action of this dynamism." Then, with what may well have been sly humor, the Pontiff added, "If its outcome proves to be positive, it should not be declared irreconcilable with reason or faith. This would only show that, even in its deepest roots, *esse ab alio* [to have received being from another, or to be a creature] also implies *esse ad alium* [to be impelled toward that other, or toward the Creator] and that St. Augustine's words: 'Thou hast made us for Thyself, O Lord, and our heart shall not rest until it rests in Thee' find a new confirmation in the very depths of man's psychic being. Even if there were question of a dynamism involving all men, peoples, epochs, and cultures, what a help, and what an invaluable help, this would be for the search after God and the affirmation of His existence."

His Holiness knew this dynamism exists. He knew its structure and its mode of action, for he knew himself. He was fully aware that he had what St. Augustine called a *pondus*, which is rightly translated as "a gravitational pull" toward God.

Strenuously St. Thomas taught that the mind of man has a "natural movement" toward truth, and the will of man, a "natural movement" toward good. Pius XII was one individual who had followed both of those "natural movements" until he stood before the world not only as one of the most learned men of recent times, but also as one of the most saintly.

Thomas Aquinas had watched the intellect and the will of man much as your research students of today watch their every experiment. He then drew his conclusions. He went from the actions he had watched to the nature of the agent he had seen acting. He noted that man will pursue one science until he is master of it. But then, instead of knowing that repose we call satisfaction and bliss, his mind is more restless than ever. His conquest of one specific set of truths has but whetted his natural appetite for more truth.

The saint then realized that the human mind is constituted with a measureless capacity for knowledge. He performed the same experiment, as it were, and came to the same conclusion about the human will, or, as you call it, the heart. That has a measureless capacity for love. Thomas drew the only allowable conclusion — namely, the mind of man would know rest only when it had gained possession of all truth, and the human heart would know happiness and perfect contentment only when it could hold as its own not this good or that good, but all Goodness.

This means, as you readily recognize, that you and every other human must not only find God; you must possess Him. You must be able to have Him and hold Him as your very own, for He alone can satisfy your hungry heart, since He is Love in all its goodness; and He alone can quiet your ever-questing mind, since He is Truth in all its fullness.

You can no more escape this "gravitational pull" of your soul toward God, than can a compass needle avoid pointing to the north. By your very nature, because you are a creature, you are pulled toward God. Indeed you have an "effective impulse carrying you toward the Divine." You are instinct with an upward yearning toward Him who is eternal, almighty, immense, and immutable, toward Him who is Truth untarnished, Beauty undying, Love ever enduring and utterly unfailing.

Now, all that is true of you as man. Think, then, what a drive toward God you have once you have been reborn of "water and the Spirit"[229] and stamped with that absolutely indelible character of Christ. Think how you are pulled toward love and truth once you have been made His member and have the Spirit of truth and the Spirit of love as Soul of your soul.

Father Pius-Raymond Régamey, O.P., found this attraction to God to be a pull not only to the north, as a compass needle, but to the east, west, and south as well. In his book *The Cross and the Christian*, he says, "Our attraction to God is fourfold: by the very nature of the soul, in virtue of our baptismal character, through the effects of sanctifying and actual grace, and by the action of all the virtues grace engenders in us."[230]

∞

Your soul is your essence

This truth, which is exactly as old as man, is of paramount importance to you if you are ever to understand yourself. That is why Pius XII, in that memorable address to the Fifth International

[229] John 3:5.

[230] Pius-Raymond Régamey, *The Cross and the Christian* (St. Louis, Missouri: Herder, 1954).

Congress of Psychotherapy and Clinical Psychiatry could say so sincerely, "The Church looks with satisfaction at the new paths opened by psychiatry in this postwar period. . . ." For, as he added, it is capable of achieving precious results for medicine, for the knowledge of the soul in general, for the religious dispositions of man, and for their development." His Holiness commended the mobilization of science for the conquest of mental illness and insisted that it was welcomed by the Church, for she realizes that the recovery of the spirit from a mental illness is like "the first step toward gaining him for Christ; for it affords him the possibility of becoming for the first time a conscious and active member of His Mystical Body, or of returning to such active membership from an atrophied, inert condition."

Because psychiatry has some truth, the Church, "the pillar and ground of truth," has respect for it. But because the Church is the pillar and ground of truth, she must warn this very young science about certain pitfalls. So the Pope went on to tell the group that their concentration on particular psychic dynamisms must never blind them to the obvious fact that the "existential" man in his inmost structure is identified with the "essential" man. What the Pope was saying to these scientists is that while you, as a person, may have deep psychic dynamisms, those deep dynamisms are not you; that while these "drives" actually exist in the soul and function there, they are not the soul; that while you really have an innate impulse that turns you toward God, that "push" or "pull," deep and powerful though it be, will never of itself bring you to God. You must do that. For you, the person, are the master of all these drives.

"What constitutes man," the Pope said, "is principally the soul, the substantial form of his nature." Picture the faces of those scientists as they heard this Thomistic terminology. Men who shy from the very word *soul* were listening to a man who showed deep knowledge of their own science use that term, not only with no apology, but with an assurance that showed he took it for granted that the term would be both universally accepted and warmly welcomed, since it is so manifestly correct. His Holiness went on to say, "From it [that is, from this soul, which he called the substantial form of man's nature] flows all the vital activity of man. In it are rooted all the psychic dynamisms with their own proper structure and their organic law. It is the soul that nature charges with the government of all man's energies, insofar as these have not acquired their final determination. Given this ontological and psychological fact, it follows that it would be a departure from reality to attempt, in theory or in practice, to entrust the determining role of the whole to one particular factor, for example, to one of the elementary psychic dynamisms, and thus install a secondary power at the helm.

"These psychic dynamisms may be in the soul, in man. They are not, however, the soul nor the man. They are energies of considerable intensity perhaps, but nature has entrusted their direction to the center-post, to the spiritual soul endowed with intellect and will, which is normally capable of governing these energies. That these energies may exercise pressure upon one activity does not necessarily signify that they compel it. To deprive the soul of its central place would be to deny an ontological and psychic reality."

That truth would explain to psychologists many persons who have heretofore puzzled them completely, and account for certain phenomena they could not satisfactorily understand before. But the youngest student of fundamental Scholastic psychology will recognize that the Pope has merely enunciated in slightly different words a thesis that is hundreds and hundreds of years old: man's will can be influenced; it can never be forced. That truth became axiomatic centuries before Freud. You most likely heard it expressed as "You can lead a horse to water, but you cannot make him drink."

Pius XII brought his whole talk to focus when he said, "Original Sin did not take away from man the possibility or the obligation of directing his own actions through his soul. It cannot be alleged that the psychic troubles and disorders which disturb the normal functionings of the psychic being represent what usually happens."

How psychiatrists need ever to be conscious of that: the abnormal is not the usual, far less the universal!

∞

You face the danger of failing to be human

"The moral struggle to remain on the right path," the Pope continued, "does not prove that it is impossible to follow that path, nor does it authorize any drawing back." Then, going to the heart of the real danger, he said, "One should be slow to lower man in the concrete, together with his personal character, to the level of the brute."

That last line is for *you* — as well as for every psychologist, psychiatrist, and modern scientist. For the ever-disturbing fact is that you, who have been made to reach to the Divine, can actually fail to be human.

Nothing else in God's visible creation can fail as you can fail. A stone must ever be a stone, and a star, a star. "A rose by any other name would smell as sweet,"[231] but it could beget only other roses. Willows cannot fail to be willows any more than dogs can fail to be

---

[231] William Shakespeare, *Romeo and Juliet*, Act 2, scene 2, line 43.

dogs. But humans can, and humans often do, fail to be human. And, strange as it may appear, it is because of their highest gift that visible creation's highest creatures can fall lower than any other creature and fail to be themselves. Because man can choose, man can be less than man. Because this rational animal has been endowed by God with something that is truly godly, he can be more brutish and animal than any of the brute animals. That godly gift is free will.

It may come as a blow — and a stunning blow — to be told that you, blessed though you are with human nature, can perform actions that are not human. Yet it is a basic and all-important truth. Open any manual in moral theology, and on its first pages you will find a fascinating — but, at the same time, humbling — treatise on "human acts." The first fundamental distinction you will meet is rendered unforgettable in Latin since it is something of a play on words. You will learn that there is a vital, fundamental, and eternally important difference between acts which are that "of a human" and acts which are only that "of a man." The first requires advertence of the intellect, exercise of the will, and freedom of choice. In other words, it must be a *deliberate* act. The other is an act placed by one who is not paying attention to what he is doing, who has neither his mind nor his will on his deed.

Father Walter Farrell, O.P., put it this way: "When we catch ourselves up now and then, and ask in astonishment, 'Why in the world did I do that?' only to find that there is no answer to the *why* of the question, we are right in concluding that we need sleep, or a vacation, or a visit to a doctor. For while a human being has certainly placed the act, he has not acted humanly.

"Practically, we have a whole set of phrases to express the difference between a human action and one that is not human. A servant explains, 'I'm sorry, I didn't mean that'; and of course the apology has to be accepted, even though the coffee spilled on us is, unlike most coffee, incredibly hot. A man whose foot has been trampled in a subway crowd says what he says because he is 'angry, not himself.' We are 'beside ourselves' with indignation, "absent-minded, forgetful, cross, hysterical, or terror-stricken,' and of course our actions are not human."[232] Unquestionably, though, they are the actions of a human being.

Reflection on this distinction shows you what it costs to be human. You are the only creature on earth who can be held to account for his deeds, for you are the only one on earth who can choose between right and wrong — the only one who can be moral or immoral. Mark Twain was more than witty when he said, "Man is the only animal who can blush — or ever needs to,"[233] just as he was tragically exact when he said, "Man is a rational animal — in definition more often than in daily life." By those characteristically clever remarks, he shows the distinct difference between human acts and acts that are merely those of a man.

Because this distinction has never been sufficiently realized, your world is filled with false philosophies that inevitably inculcate hideous immoralities. Because human beings can fail to be human; because man is a walking paradox; because he is a being who unites such opposites as spirit and matter, is capable of such extremes as love and hate, nobility and meanness, sanctity and sin; because he goes through life ever under the inexorable laws of nature regarding his physical body, yet possesses a faculty in his soul that enables him to withhold obedience from nature's ultimate Lawgiver, some would-be thinkers have grown frightened

[232] Walter Farrell, A Companion to the Summa (New York: Sheed and Ward, 1939), Vol. 2, 4.

[233] Mark Twain, Following the Equator, ch. 36.

and have taken refuge in what can rightly be called "escapism." Fearing the responsibility entailed in being free, they have denied their own freedom. Frightened by the price demanded to be human, they flee the very privilege of paying that price. Intimidated by the heights to which their minds and hearts impelled them, they pull down God's masterpiece and make of man an animal, a machine, or a mere process, by denying him his distinctive prerogative of free will.

Now the climbing gets sheer. The mountain of God to which Isaiah invited you is high. You are striving to learn who you are. You will succeed only when you see that your God is liberty and that you are *free*.

His Holiness Pius XII said you were an *esse ab alio* and an *esse ad alium*. Ultimately that means exactly what was printed on the first page Father McNabb tore from the catechism: You are from God and you are for God. But that would be stating sublime truth too simply for the intelligentsia of your day who seem to think that what is profound should never be stated briefly or too clearly. Frequently they tempt one to think that the lavish richness of their technical terms is but a smokescreen hiding dire poverty of ideas.

Since World War II, existentialism has held a place far forward on the stage. But it will never hold that place long, nor will it command the audience's full attention. The existentialists want to study man in the concrete. They want to fix their gaze on the existing individual. That is exactly what they should do! But they must be philosophers enough to answer that first and fundamental question: Where did this existing individual get his existence and his individuality? Not from himself. Ultimately, not from his parents, for they, too, were but the effects of some causes that preexisted them. The existentialists must be philosophers enough not to stop thinking until they have found the ultimate and only valid explanation of the existence of their concrete existing individual or of any other concrete individual who exists.

If they do that, they will come face-to-face with the First Cause who is Himself uncaused, with that First Being who alone is Necessary Being, with that Primal Existence from whom all other existence is derived. They will discover that the existence of their concrete existing individual is something borrowed; that it is something which He who is Self-Subsisting Being lent them; and they will awaken to the humbling and exalting realization that He Who Is allows them to be.

∞

God made you from nothing

After that first conclusion, they should be able to reach the next one: everything that exists, if it is to continue in existence, must cling to Him who has lent it its existence. That is an obvious and inescapable conclusion. Yet the sharpest of these philosphers — as many another man — let the completely obvious escape them. With all the force of its being, every creature must cling to the Creator, if it is to remain in being, simply because each was made from *nothing*.

In the earliest pages of this book, you saw how wrong it was to define creation as "the production of something out of nothing." There, forceful insistence was made that the definition be completed; and heavy stress was laid on the fact that you are from God, just as is every other creature, for creation is an act that God alone can perform. But now let Frank Sheed show you there is a proper accent to be placed on the first part of this definition.

In his book *Theology and Sanity*, Frank Sheed tells how he can never forget the first time he heard himself saying that God had made him, and all other things that exist, *out of nothing:* "I had known it, like any other Catholic, from childhood; but I had never properly taken it in. I had said it a thousand times, but I had never heard what I was saying. In the sudden realization of this particular truth there is something quite peculiarly shattering. There are truths of religion immeasurably mightier in themselves, and the realization of any one of them might well make the heart miss a beat. But this one goes to the very essence of what we are, and goes there almost with the effect of annihilation. Indeed it is a kind of annihilation. God uses no material in our making; we are made of nothing. At least self-sufficiency is annihilated, and all those customary ways that the illusion of self-sufficiency has made for us.

"The first effect of realizing that one is made of nothing is a kind of panic-stricken insecurity. One looks around for some more stable thing to clutch, and in this matter none of the beings of our experience are any more stable than we, for at the origin of them all is the same truth: all are made of nothing. But the panic and the insecurity are merely instinctive and transient. A mental habit has been annihilated, but a way toward a sounder mental habit is at last clear. For although we are made of nothing, we are made into something; and since what we are made *of* does not count for us, we are forced to a more intense concentration upon the God we are made *by*."

Now, there is an instance of positive thinking — even of the habit of positive thinking. And it shows you what power can be generated from the faith that makes one think thus positively. Were you to define creation inadequately, and describe yourself as one who was "produced from nothing," you would have reason for pessimism and even despondency when you thought of your origin. But when you think positively, and define correctly, you get a lift that takes you to the heights: to know that God is your Maker. . . . But go along with Frank Sheed on this ascent.

"What follows," he says, "is very simple, but revolutionary. If a carpenter makes a chair, he can leave it and the chair will not cease to be. For the material he used in its making has a quality called rigidity, by which it will retain its nature as a chair. The maker has left the chair, but it can still rely for continuance in existence upon the material he used, the wood. Similarly, if the Maker of the Universe left it, the Universe too would have to rely for continuance in existence on the material He used — nothing. In short, the truth that God used no material in our making carries with it the not-sufficiently-realized truth that God continues to hold us in being, and that unless He did so we should simply cease to be.

"This is the truth about the Universe as a whole and about every part of it. Material beings — the human body, for instance — are made up of atoms, and these again of electrons and protons, and these again of who knows what; but whatever may be the ultimate constituents of matter, God made them out of nothing, so that they and the beings so imposingly built up of them exist only because He keeps them in existence. Spiritual beings — the human soul, for instance — have no constituent parts. Yet they do not escape this universal law. They are created by God of nothing, and could not survive an instant without His conserving power. We are held above the surface of our native nothingness solely by God's continuing will to hold us so. 'In Him we live and move and have our being.' "[234]

Let the existentialists think those thoughts, and they will see that their beloved "existence" is nothing but a cry of the utterly helpless for divine aid. In the very center of their being, every

---

[234] Frank Sheed, *Theology and Sanity* (New York: Sheed and Ward, 1946), 5, 6; Acts 17:28.

created existence is but an indigence! Every creature on earth — and you are one of them! — is but a beggar with empty hands held out to God so that they might receive from Him their next moment of existence.

Now you have a firmer grasp on the terms Pius XII used about you, saying you were an *esse ab alio* and an *esse ad alium*. The word *esse* represents you; the words *alio* and *alium* refer to God; the prepositions in between — *ab* and *ad* — tell you the whole story of your life as it should be lived. They say that you, like the very stars of heaven, are to trace a circle, to swing in an orbit that has God as its beginning and God as its end. They say that you, in your deepest essence, bespeak a relation to God — no accidental or adventitious relation such as color to your cheek, but something as substantial and constitutional as marrow to your bones. It is a real relation, no mere fiction of the mind — an everlasting and indestructible relation, for as long as you are you, and God is God, you will be as dependent on Him as actual song is on the actual singer. Finally, it is a total relation, one that affects not only your mind, your will, and your soul, but every last atom in your body, every least mode or modality in your being.

Frank Sheed is helping you up the mountain of God. He has swung you far out over an abyss. Let him haul you up to the firm footing of the rock of religion. He has shown you why you can be called a "religious animal" with, perhaps, truer grounds than you can be called a "rational animal"; for religion is really a relation of man to God, and you are an essential, substantial, total relation.

∞

All creation teaches you to glorify God

Look out now on the world and learn why you live; learn that you are to obey; learn from the least thing in existence how easy it is for you, the highest thing in visible creation, to glorify your God. Your universe is ever at prayer, is ever intent upon the praise of its Maker. Betelgeuse, that giant star in the shoulder of Orion, that tiny bee buried and busy in the calix of the humblest of flowers, and everything else that you can see in the universe is crying to God for its next moment in being and is bowing down to God by its present moment of existence. There is humility and obedience.

The book you hold in your hand, the light by which you read it, the chair in which you sit, or the lounge on which you lie — each is but a conformity to God's will, an act of obedience to His commanding *fiat*, and this not only in its deepest essence, mind you, but throughout its entire structure. There is nothing that exists which is not a limitless submission to Almighty God; for it is an ontological relation to the Only Absolute; it is dependence and homage.

Look at your universe, and hear it as one loud, answering "Here I am" to God the Creator's call. Your Rocky Mountains are honoring your God just by being the Rocky Mountains. Their red, rusty thrust skyward is adoration. The ceaseless surge of the Atlantic as well as the rhythmic tides of the Pacific are but repeated acts of docility to God the Maker. Everything that is, just by accepting its being, is cult and religion. But be ever conscious of the fact that you, and you alone, because of your mind and free will, can give your God a praise, a docility, a humility, and an obedience, can give Him a glory that is called *formal*. That is the religion, the cult, and the reverence that makes Him glad!

Let the universe teach you how easy it is to serve your God. Just by being, you are obeying! You are a submission to God's will that has taken flesh and blood. Your every heartbeat and your every breath are acts of humility and of obedience. Make each of them a formal act of glory to God by simply being what you are, and being that joyously, gratefully, big-heartedly, and even exultingly. Take your being just as it is, and love it just because it has pleased God to make it as it is, and your very existence will be an act of love to Him who gave it to you out of love.

In the myriad distractions of modern existence, it is comforting to recall a magnificent passage from St. Augustine's commentary on the last verse of Psalm 34, which Fathers Kleist and Lilly rendered in rhythmic prose as "My theme, then, shall your justice be; upon my lips shall never die your praise." Augustine takes that verse and asks the question that will immediately leap to the mind of all who are rationalistic or literal: "Who can spend the whole day, let alone his whole life, praising God?" The saint answers, "I'll show you how," and then enunciates that simplest yet best of all rules: "Whatever you do, do well, and you have praised God." He then began to specify: "When you sing a hymn, you praise God. . . . When you leave off singing and seek refreshments, once again you praise God, provided you use temperance and do not become drunk. Even by sleep you praise God, provided you do not rise therefrom to do evil. Are you a businessman? Do not cheat, and you have praised God. Is farming your occupation? Then do not raise any strife, and you have praised God. In the simple performance of your everyday works you can praise God and thus spend a lifetime in His service."

It may come as a surprise to you that even by an act of man, you can praise God. But do not miss the point that there is praise and praise of God and you are to give Him that praise which becomes formal glory. That means your acts are to be human acts — those that come from a deliberate choice. Otherwise you serve God only as a man and not as a human; and you have already learned what a world of difference there is between acting humanly and acting only as a man.

Father Gerald Vann, O.P., titled one of his best books *Morals Makyth Man*.[235] But do not think that he is contradicting Hilaire Belloc, who so strongly insisted that "man is his mind." And do not ever forget that you are what your thoughts are. Father Vann's title is but a more exact rendition of Belloc's truth, and an exegesis, as it were, of the relation between character and habitual concepts. When Belloc says, "Man is his mind," he is using the word *mind* in the same sense and with the same full meaning that St. Augustine uses the Latin word *mens*, for, like Augustine, Belloc means much more than mere thinking or the faculty for thinking. Both really refer to the whole soul. For thoughts that are not dynamic, concepts that never generate action, and ideas that never lead on to deeds are among the most sterile and foolish actions the "rational animal" can perform. If the will of man does not come into play in some fashion, the man has not acted humanly.

Jacques Maritain's definition of a man as "an animal who feeds on transcendentals" has place here since the transcendental notions of *being, truth,* and *good* are convertible. What is, is true; what is and what is true, is also good. Therefore, if the mind is merely seeking a truth and finds it, then the will, recognizing the goodness and beauty in the truth discovered, will love it. That is why you can say that if the will does not enter into the act somehow, the act has not been human.

Still, it is not logical or even ontological truth that concerns you right now; it is moral truth.

The seeming clash of opinion between Belloc and Vann, two twentieth-century thinkers, reminds one forcibly of what looked like a similar clash of opinion between St. Bernard and William of

---

[235] Gerald Vann, *Morals Makyth Man* (London: Longmans, Green and Co., 1938).

St. Thierry[236] who, back in the twelfth century, sought to discover precisely where, in you, lies the image of God. These two Cistercians will enable you to see yourself as you have never seen yourself before, because they will open your eyes to your own Godlikeness.

∞

You are great because you are made in God's image and likeness

Just as Frank Sheed said many times that he "was made by God out of nothing," yet never heard himself once, you most likely have said you were "made to the image and likeness of God" many times without once knowing whether you were talking about two things or only one; and if about two, where they differed and where they were to be found in you.

Have you ever realized that this description of you as "an image and likeness of God" bespeaks the continual presence in you of Him who is divine? Stand before a mirror. If the mirror is all it should be, it holds an image of you that is truly lifelike, for it gives back any movement you make. But how long will that image stay in that mirror, and how long will it remain lifelike? The answer to that simple question ought to have you ready to do what Moses did when he saw a bush burning but not being consumed: prepare to worship.

Your lifelike image in the mirror was made by you inasmuch as you brought it into being by coming before that glass. It will stay in being only so long as you stay before that mirror. You are made to the image and likeness of God. You mirror the Almighty. That is the richest and fullest, just as it is the fundamental, meaning of

---

[236] William of St. Thierry (c. 1085-1148), theologian and mystical writer.

your existence. You are a mirror into which God is ever looking and from which His image and likeness shine out upon the world. But just as the image you make in the glass lives only so long as you are present, so you live only so long as God shines into you and out of you.

What reverence you should have for the universe and everything in it! For the universe itself is God's looking glass; every particle in it mirrors forth something of His perfection. But only in man will you find His image and likeness, so only to man should go your highest respect and reverence.

The two Cistercians St. Bernard and William of St. Thierry started out just as you did. They wanted to know themselves! "Know thyself" led them to the discovery of their greatness.

That is your first big surprise, for you know that these men, being Cistercians, were dedicated to humility. They lived the Rule of St. Benedict to the very letter, and the heart of that rule is the famous seventh chapter, which is given over totally to twelve degrees of humility. But your surprise vanishes when you hear St. Bernard define humility as "truth." The honest man is the humble man; and the truly humble man is one whose heart is ever singing as Mary Immaculate sang — *Magnificat* — because, like her, he knows, in all honesty, that God has made him great.

Setting out from the identical point — the command "Know thyself" — these two Cistercians pursued independent studies. They climbed the same mountain, but took different routes. Yet they both arrived at the peak that says that man is great, and his greatness lies in the fact that he is made to the image and likeness of God.

The first and fundamental truth the humble St. Bernard will teach you is that you are a "noble creature," and that not only are you a noble creature but, of all the visible creatures Omnipotence has placed on earth, you are the noblest. Bernard says you are so exalted a creature that you are capable of bearing in your being something of the very majesty of God.

Too long and too often has modern man failed to recognize his own surpassing dignity, or even to know precisely in what it consists. It does not lie in any accomplishment, no matter how stupendous; nor in any discovery, scientific or economic, be it ever so universally beneficial. Man's true dignity lies in his being, not in his doing or his having. It lies in being what nothing else on earth can ever be.

Habituated, as you are, to weights and measures, and to evaluating everything by statistics, pricing and prizing everything — even human beings — by quantity, you often allow yourself, foolishly, to feel dwarfed in the presence of what is materially immense. That is profoundly erroneous. For while the material universe is stupendous, it has nothing in it to compare with your greatness. For while all other things in creation show forth God, they do so but faintly. They bear what are rightly called but vestiges of His glory. But you, deep in the substance of your spiritual soul, carry His very image and likeness. That is why nothing under the sun equals you, far less surpasses you, in greatness.

Clement of Alexandria and Tertullian[237] are both credited with having said: "He who sees his brother sees God." Bernard of Clairvaux and William of St. Thierry will exegete that saying for you as they study the two words found in the first page of your catechism and on the first page of Scripture: "Let us make man to our image and likeness."[238]

[237] Clement of Alexandria (c. 150-c. 215), theologian; Tertullian (c. 160-c. 225), African Church Father.
[238] Gen. 1:26.

Are those two words synonyms describing the one reality? Or do they indicate two different actualities? If the latter, where, in you, are they to be found? Like Father Vann, St. Bernard finds them in your will. Like Hilaire Belloc, William of St. Thierry says in your mind. But let it be noted that he uses the word in the Augustinian sense; and for Augustine, *mind* was a synonym for *soul*.

In the tenth book of his *Confessions*, Augustine made a fascinating analysis of man's memory. Among many other things, he shows that it is this faculty that enables man to know he has a mind, and that he is really a man. But he goes much further than that. He proves that it is this same faculty that enables man to find his God — and find Him within himself! It is at the end of this analysis that the saint uttered his oft-quoted cry: "Late have I loved Thee, O Beauty so ancient and so new; late have I loved Thee! For behold Thou wert within me, and I outside. . . . Thou wert with me, and I was not with Thee."[239]

Because they know neither who they are nor what they are, millions must confess with Augustine, "Thou wert with me, and I was not with Thee." That ignorance is the real root of their unrest and the source of their unhappiness. They do not know that they were made to the image and likeness of God; or knowing it, they have no idea where within them is the mirror that holds that divine image and likeness.

Augustine and William of St. Thierry tell you this mirror is in your memory. But to understand that, you will have to know that in his tract *On the Trinity*, Augustine studied countless creatures that in some way reflect the unity and trinity of God. Yet it was only when he recalled his own analysis of man's memory, and from it went on to a fuller analysis of man's soul (which he called *mind*),

[239] Frank Sheed's translation.

that he found what he wanted. For in the one human soul, he found three distinct faculties: memory, intellect, and will, none of which was really distinct from the soul. Hence, he had a distinct trinity in an absolute unity. He had his image and likeness of God.

Taking Augustine as his guide, William of St. Thierry went on to construct an anatomy of your soul that will show you how very like the triune God you are. According to this monk, at the summit of your mind (*mind* is his term for your soul) is a secret point where resides the latent remembrance of your God, especially of His goodness and His power. This is your *memory*. As you see, he is truly Augustinian inasmuch as he is not talking about any actual recollection of God brought about by the exercise of this faculty, but of the ontological fact that within you is a power that at any moment, and at every moment, will enable you to recognize God within you. According to William, then, here, in this faculty called the *memory*, lies the most deeply graven trait of God's image, for it is the analogue of God *the Father*.

In the Trinity, you know, it is the Father who generates the Son, and from the Father and Son, as from one principle, proceeds the Holy Spirit. In your mind, as William of St. Thierry saw it, your memory generates reason, and from your memory and reason proceeds your will. In other words, your memory contains in itself the term toward which you should tend — God; your reason, alerted by this memory, immediately recognizes that it is to Him you ought to tend; your will, stirred by this memory and reason, immediately tends. That is how this monk talked when treating of the nature and dignity of love.

You can see, then, that your soul is something to stand in awe of. It is a burning bush! God is there! From this monk's lesson in your soul's anatomy, you learn on what you may legitimately exercise your wondrous faculties. If your intellect is born, as it were, of a memory of God, its function is indicated by its origin. The whole reason of its being is to tell you that you should tend to God. If your will is the product of that memory and that intelligence, it can tend toward only that which the memory contains and to which the intelligence testifies it should tend.

There you are as God made you, and as you should ever be: an intellect that knows *nothing* but God, a will that tends to *nothing* but God, because of a memory whence both proceed, which is filled with *nothing* but the remembrance of God. Thus, were it not for sin, you would be ever perfectly God-conscious, ever mirroring forth the splendor of the Trinity. But what Adam did in Paradise, and you have too often done since, so covers over this image of God within you that you can recognize yourself now as nothing better than an image that is tarnished and a likeness that has been lost.

Thus you would have remained — a shattered mirror — were it not for Jesus Christ, who took a physical body so that you might one day be joined to His Mystical Body and therein refurbish the image that was tarnished and regain the likeness that was lost.

The theory of Augustine and William may not be perfectly exact, but who is there who would dare say it is completely untrue? To think of your soul as one substance with three faculties, and these as analogous to Father, Son, and Holy Spirit, will fill you with the respect you should have for yourself, even as it will remind you of your life's work: to bring out that image by using the grace merited for you by Jesus Christ, and thus become like unto God.

ჯ

You have three human freedoms

Now let Bernard of Clairvaux show you that you are as free as God by proving that you have a liberty that can never be lost and two freedoms that can be regained.

Bernard, like others, centers everything in your will. But he does something really unique: he distinguishes the *image* of God in you from God's *likeness*. He teaches that as long as you exist (and never forget that you are an immortal) you will bear the image of God within your free will, for there it is impressed ineradicably — so much so, that whether you spend your eternity with God in Heaven, or apart from God in Hell, you will always remain one who mirrors forth the image of God. But the same is not true of God's likeness. That you can lose. That was already lost for you even before you were conceived, with the result that you came from your mother's womb bearing the image of God but not carrying His actual likeness.

This is truly a psychoanalysis! It will tell you more about yourself, your conflicts and complexes, your drives, fixations, obsessions, compulsions, and even your hallucinations than any expert in psychiatry could ever tell you. For Bernard goes deeper than any of your modern depth psychologists, and much further than any present-day psychoanalyst. He uncovers the root and exposes it fully; your modern scientists at most touch only some of the shoots.

Following that imperious command "Know thyself," Bernard came up against the undeniable fact that he — like you and every other human — was really a gnawing hunger for happiness. But, unlike so very many humans, Bernard saw that to appease this hunger, man had to choose between the various objects that presented themselves as possible sources of happiness. But choice, he realized, bespeaks freedom from force or necessity.

To prove that you have a free will would be worse than carrying sand to the shore or water to the sea. But to give you Bernard's analysis of your free will may well be like bringing rain to a land parched by drought or sending sunlight into a world drenched in darkness.

Your world is full of misery. Undoubtedly you yourself have often been perfectly miserable. Your present-day psychiatrists seek to account for it by going back to babyhood and even to birth; yes, and even beyond, by searching into the psyche of your parents. Bernard was wiser. He sought not only the cause of this man's or that man's misery, but the source of human misery itself.

That took him back not to birth, but to creation; not to any man's immediate parents, but to mankind's first parents. He saw that Adam, as he came from the hands of God, was happy; that Eve, before she disobeyed, was equally happy. He immediately saw that since she disobeyed and got Adam to follow her lead, neither he nor she, nor any of their descendants, save Christ and His immaculate Mother, have been as happy.

The first conclusion was obvious: unhappiness is connected with sin. But sin is a matter of choice, and choice ultimately rests in the will.

Many a man has been puzzled by this Fall of Adam. They ask *how* one so endowed could ever sin. Bernard went deeper; he asked *why* he sinned. The answer is found in infallible Scripture. Genesis tells you that Adam sinned for the same reason Lucifer sinned. Basically, it is the only reason anyone, be he angel or man, will ever sin. Lucifer and his legions and Adam and his children sinned, and modern men and women go on sinning just to be *like unto* God.

That was clue for Bernard of Clairvaux and, thanks to him, should be more than a clue for you. Every sinner, in his sin, is seeking happiness. Actually, then, he is seeking God! But, obviously, he is seeking Him in the wrong way and in the wrong place. The fact is that he has made a wrong choice, but that he made a choice is very right. In other words, every sinner is on the right road, but he is going in the wrong direction. He is seeking to be like unto

God, but has chosen that which alone can make him unlike the sinless almighty One.

The process, then, is not paradoxical; it eventuates in a flat contradiction. But that contradiction can clarify life and living for you; its clash will show you the real ultimates of your existence. This striving to be like unto God created Hell; yet you can now gain Heaven only by striving for that one end and striving successfully. Following an urge, a drive, to be like unto God, the first man fell into mankind's Original Sin; yet you can now attain sanctity by following that same urge. By allowing his grasp to exceed his reach, Adam lost his balance, and plunged himself and all his progeny into an abyss; yet it is now only by grasping what lies beyond your reach that you, or any other child of Adam, can climb to the heights of happiness where man is supposed to dwell. You simply must become like unto God or fail to be the human being God made you to be.

Bernard studied that contradiction thoroughly. It did not baffle him as it might many another man, who would see in the statement that it is necessary to become like unto God nothing but blasphemy. Bernard knew that God had said, "Let us make man to our image and likeness." He knew that God's only Son had asked, "Is it not written in your law, 'I said you are gods'?"[240] He knew that God the Holy Spirit speaking through St. John had said, "Dearly beloved, we are now the sons of God; and it hath not yet appeared what we shall be. We know that when He shall appear, we shall be like to Him."[241]

Bernard could course through Scripture from Genesis to Revelation and prove that the purpose of creation, re-creation, and

[240] John 10:34.
[241] 1 John 3:2.

glorification are one. They are to make men like unto God. But it was this truth that set him pondering, and should set you doing the same. If men are made to the image and likeness of Him who is Supreme Happiness, how is it that so many millions of men are so supremely unhappy? Can a mirror so distort an image as to make it appear the opposite of what it reflects? That was the question that set the Abbot of Clairvaux seeking the exact location of this image and likeness of God and studying precisely in what they consist.

Briefly, the results of his search are these: Adam was happy before his Fall and, being happy, was like unto God, who is Supreme Happiness. Since that Fall, no man, save Christ and His Mother, has known the same happiness, for no man has been so like unto God. Therefore, it was freedom from sin and freedom from sin's consequences that made Adam like unto God and happy. Hence, Bernard concluded that the words *image* and *likeness* in Genesis are not synonyms; they represent distinct realities. For man can lose his likeness to God by losing his freedom from sin and his freedom from sin's consequences (that is, freedom from the miseries of this life and the eternal miseries of the life to come), yet retain the image of God by still remaining free from constraint or necessity.

To St. Bernard, it was obvious that, before his Fall, Adam enjoyed three freedoms: a freedom *to choose*, which is the very essence of free will; freedom *to choose aright*, that is, to avoid sin; and, finally, the freedom *to carry out his choice*, and thus enjoy the friendship of God. But after his Fall, Adam enjoyed only one freedom — that basic freedom to choose. Bernard surmised, then, that if he had been right in concluding that the likeness to God consisted in the two freedoms Adam had lost by sinning, the image of God might lie in that first and fundamental freedom — the freedom of choice.

That was the surmise that led him to the conclusion that this freedom of choice or, as it is called today, "freedom from necessity or constraint," was utterly inalienable and immutable, as indestructible as man's soul, and as inamissible as that soul's existence. For the just who adhere to good, the sinners who consent to evil, and the damned who are confirmed in evil forever, each lay hold on their objects just as efficaciously as does God, by His eternal and immutable will, lay hold on His own perfection and beatitude.

An astounding conclusion! But reason it out with this very reasonable monk. "Freedom from necessity," he says, "belongs to all reasonable creatures, whether good or bad, equally and indifferently with God. Nor is this freedom lost or diminished by sin or by misery, nor is it any greater in the righteous than in the unrighteous, or more complete in angels than it is in men."

Those statements call for proof. Bernard proves them. "For just as the human will," he argues, "when grace turns it toward good, becomes thereby freely good, and makes the man free in doing good, that is to say, leads him on to will it, and does not force him to it in spite of himself, so also does the consent of the will, when spontaneously turned aside to evil, no less makes a man free and spontaneous in doing evil, since he is brought to it by his will, and not by any coercion."

Bernard had mentioned angels in the same breath with men, so his argument goes on: "As the angels in Heaven, and indeed God Himself, remain good freely, that is to say, by their own will, and not by any extrinsic necessity, so in just the same way, the Devil fell headlong into evil and remains there freely, that is to say, in virtue of a voluntary movement and not by any external compulsion."[242]

[242] *De Gratia et Libero Arbitrio*, ch. 4.

Were you to question the validity of that argument, you would be implicitly denying free will to God, beatifying angels without any merit on their part, and damning devils eternally without its being their due. Bernard concludes this part of his analysis of your free will by saying, "Freedom of will subsists, therefore, even when thought is enslaved, and as fully in the wicked as in the good, although in the latter in a better ordered state; it remains also as complete, after its own mode, in the creature as in the Creator."

To claim that there is free will in Hell just as well as in Heaven, and that the creature enjoys it as completely, after its own mode, as does the Creator, jolts many a mind. But all Bernard is saying is that even when you are not actually using it, you still possess a free will; although you are not always in the act of choosing, you are never without the ability or the faculty to make a free choice. If you have followed his thought thus far, you see why Bernard calls you a *nobilis creatura*. Following him further, you will see why he names you a being with the capacity to share in the very majesty of God.

⚮

You can share in God's wisdom and power

Bernard saw that you not only share in that fundamental freedom of God which is the very essence of your free will — namely, the freedom from necessity — but that you can share in God's wisdom and power as well. This is the heart of the saint's analysis. Freedom to choose he named *liberum arbitrium*, because, before man can choose, he must act as "arbiter" between the many possible choices that can be made. This is your share in God's free will. But to choose aright, you need a share in God's wisdom; so Bernard very aptly named this freedom to choose aright *liberum consilium* — for it is the heart of a wise "counselor" to lead one to

175

the right choice. But after you have chosen, and chosen aright, you need the freedom to carry out your choice and acquire possession of the thing you have chosen — and thus know happiness. The saint quite rightly named this freedom *liberum complacitum* — and taught that it is really a share in God's omnipotence, for you need power to carry out your choice and thus obtain joy.

Look into your own personal experiences. You are always free to choose. But, as you well know, you are not always able to choose aright. The past tells you that you have not always done so, although unquestionably you were always trying to do so. And perhaps even the present tells you that when you have chosen, and chosen aright, there are occasions when you still lack the strength to carry out the right choice. That experience is universal. Ovid, back in the days of Rome, expressed it for us all in his *Metamorphoses* when he said, "Clearly do I perceive the better thing, and with all my soul I approve it; but alas, it is the less good that I follow."

But you have better than this pagan poet to support you in your experience and to substantiate St. Bernard in his analysis. It was the great St. Paul, that flame of love for Christ Crucified, who openly confessed to the Romans, "The will, indeed, is present to me; but to accomplish that which is good, I find not. For the good that I will, I do not; but the evil which I will not, that I do."[243] Paul had the freedom to choose; and, to some extent, even the freedom to choose aright (since he saw the good); but did not have, as he confesses, the freedom to carry out his choice, the ability to do the good!

Now Bernard makes synthesis out of his analysis. "I think," he says, "that in these three freedoms consist the very image and likeness of the Creator, in whose image and likeness we have been

[243] Rom. 7:18-19.

made: the image consisting in free will, and a twofold likeness consisting in the other two freedoms. Perhaps this is the reason why free will alone never suffers any weakening or diminution of itself, because it is principally in the free will that the essence of the eternal and unchangeable Divinity is represented as in a perfect image. For, although the free will had a beginning, it will have no end; neither will it receive any increase or growth from justice or glory, nor suffer any loss from sin or misery. What, save Eternity itself, could bear a greater likeness to eternity? Now, in the other two freedoms, since they can be, not only partially diminished, but even totally lost, we can find a sort of accidental likeness to the divine wisdom and power added to the image of God which consist in free will alone."[244]

You are, and you always will be, great, because you are an image of God. Even the souls in Hell are great, yet they are anything but happy. In point of fact, it is their greatness, their possession of the image of God, that heightens their misery, because they have lost their likeness to God.

∞

You must live in Christ Jesus

You must recover your lost liberties and thus recapture your lost likeness. Your share in God's liberty will not make you happy. You must share also in His wisdom and His power.

That brings you face-to-face again with Jesus Christ, who is "the power of God and the wisdom of God."[245] And that brings you face-to-face again with the necessity of living in Christ Jesus and being always conscious of the fact that you are His member.

[244] *De Gratia et Libero Arbitrio*, ch. 9.
[245] 1 Cor. 1:24.

Finally, that brings you face-to-face with the imperious demand of your elevated nature: to have not only the mind of Christ, but the very will of the God-Man.

St. Augustine gave a peerless plan for life in the words: "Live in the Word." They mean exactly what St. Paul meant when he said, "For me, to live is Christ."[246] They show the goal that Bernard of Clairvaux set for each of his monks. In the second to last of that long, unfinished series of sermons on the Song of Songs, the saint paints the portrait of a vital member of Christ's Mystical Body — your portrait! — when he strokes again and again with vivid color and strong, sharp line the one word *Verbo*, which means Christ, the Word of God. Here is his description of you as you should be: you should be "clinging to the Word with all your strength; living in the Word; allowing yourself to be governed by the Word; conceiving from the Word what you are to bring forth for the Word."

Why do all these saints insist that you, a being of this century, should live in the Word of God — Christ Jesus? Because, strictly speaking, there is only one Image of God: His only-begotten Son. You are *made* to the image; He *is* the Image. So you see that to live in and by the Son is really a demand of your very nature, which, of course, becomes more imperious once that nature has been elevated to a supernature. And you have already seen that such a life is made possible through the Holy Spirit. You are a very real relation to the triune God. "Become what you are."

St. Bernard's conclusion after analyzing your free will is: "Man, therefore, has great need for Christ, the power of God and the wisdom of God, who, because He is wisdom, re-infuses true wisdom into man for the restoring of the *liberum consilium* [freedom to choose aright], and who, because He is power, restores the full

---

[246] Phil. 1:21.

power to repair in man the *liberum complacitum* [freedom to carry out the choice]." Then comes the promise of happiness, the kind that is rightly called bliss. Bernard says that if you live in Christ, and let Him, by His wisdom and power, work in you, then "becoming perfectly good by the gift of true wisdom, you will no longer sin, and becoming fully happy by the other gift, you will no longer be subject to suffering."

Is that too large a promise? In one sense, yes. Bernard realized that. So he immediately added, "Such perfection is not to be attained until the next life, when both freedoms, which are now lost, will be restored fully to the free will. . . . For the present, while we are still in this body of death and in this wicked world, let it suffice not to obey sin, by resisting concupiscence through *liberum consilium*, and by means of the *liberum complacitum* not to fear adversities for the sake of justice. . . . In this present life, we must learn by *liberum consilium* not to abuse free will, so that one day we may fully enjoy the *liberum complacitum*. Thus do we repair in ourselves the likeness of God. . . ."[247]

⚮

You can enjoy these freedoms even now

That you will not enjoy both these freedoms in their fullness until you are one with Christ in the bosom of the Father is true enough; but that you can acquire what is very close to the perfection of both even in this life is evidenced by the lives of the men to whom you have been listening. Bernard, Augustine, Paul, and countless other saints lived in Christ Jesus and allowed His mind and will to work in them. You will have these three freedoms (in what is just short of their plenitude) if you take and keep the

---

[247] *De Gratia et Libero Arbitrio,* ch. 9.

resolve "Live in the Word." You will be free from sin and free from the morbid fear of the consequences of sin — the adversities of this life — if you will walk ever conscious of who you are: a member of Jesus!

Christ said, "The truth shall make you free."[248] He also said, "I am the Truth."[249] He is the fullest truth about yourself — for you are Christ! Therefore, you can be free — and "free with that freedom," as St. Paul put it, "wherewith Christ has made you free."[250] Very specifically, that is freedom from sin, as the same apostle tells you in his letter to the Romans.[251]

Augustine has something very personal and consoling to say to you at this juncture. "This renewal [of the image and likeness of God within you]," he writes, "does not take place in the single moment of conversion as does the renewal at Baptism, when in a single moment every sin, be it ever so small, is instantly remitted. But, as it is one thing to be free from fever, and another to grow strong again from the infirmity which the fever produced; and again, one thing to pluck from the body a weapon that had been thrust into it, and another to heal the wound thereby made; so the first step, as in any cure, is to remove the cause of the infirmity, and this is done by the forgiving of all sins [in Baptism]; then, as in any cure, the second step is to heal the infirmity itself, and this takes place gradually by making progress in the renewal of that image [unto which you were made]."

Augustine is saying: Be of good cheer: justification is instantaneous, but sanctification is a very gradual growth! You did not

[248] John 8:32.
[249] John 14:6.
[250] Gal. 4:31.
[251] Cf. Rom. 6:22.

attain your present stature the moment you came from your mother's womb; neither will you become as tall as Christ overnight. Patience is required, but persistence even more. You can be free with these three freedoms right now, and you can even continue to grow in ever-greater liberty, for you have one freedom by nature, another by grace, and these two can lead you to the fullness of the third, which will be enjoyed in Heaven. But even on earth you can taste that fullness, for as St. Bernard says, "To contemplatives it is given, at rare moments, and for a short space of time, to enjoy the *liberum complacitum* — the freedom proper to Heaven."

Do you ask if you are to be a contemplative? You were born such! But the trouble is you too often contemplate the wrong things and the wrong person. You are "bent over," as St. Bernard put it, and you contemplate the things of earth and look upon your inferior self. Your one work in life is to "straighten up" and contemplate Him whose image you are and whose likeness you can recover. That is something possible to you, for you are one who can stand as straight as God!

Chapter Eight

∽

You are one who can
stand as straight as Christ

A few chapters back, you learned that you walk aright when your every step has definite meaning; that you live aright when your every moment contributes to your becoming; that you think aright when your every thought concludes somehow to the consciousness of who you are. That was a profound and a profitable lesson. You have just climbed the mountain of God. On its height you will learn how to put that previous lesson into practice.

Pius XII, through psychologists and psychiatrists, told you that you have a master faculty: free will; St. Bernard, St. Augustine, and William of St. Thierry showed you that in this master faculty lies the image and likeness of God. The Abbot of Clairvaux clarified life's issues by proving that happiness consists in the possession of three freedoms.

Pause here and study yourself as never before. Pore over this liberty which God has given you until you know both Him and yourself ever so much more intimately.

Liberty is a word and a gift that has been abused not only from the beginning of time, but from the very beginning of creation. Its careless use today accents the wisdom in the words uttered by

Confucius five centuries before Christ came. When asked what would be his first act if he were elected emperor of China, that sage unhesitatingly replied: "I should begin by fixing the meaning of words."

Bishop Fulton J. Sheen saw the need for fixing the meaning of the word *liberty* long before he was made a bishop and pointed out that there were three "liberties" that were then current and common concepts: the "liberty" to do what you *must* — a "liberty" then enjoyed by those who lived under the dictators Stalin, Hitler, and Mussolini; next, the "liberty" to do what you *liked* — a "liberty" exercised by those who had been taught, and tried to believe, that they had no real will or freedom; finally, there was the only true liberty — the liberty to do what you *ought.*

Loose thinking, of which there is so much in your world, has led many to regard *liberty* and *ought* as contradictions. Much modern writing and speech has labored to make them mean that. So you see how wise Confucius was. A little reflection will show you how exact Bishop Sheen is. For, as Father Vann insists, "morals maketh man." How can you be moral unless you do what you ought? How can you do what you ought unless you exercise your liberty?

It was Chesterton who said that if a good man could not be bad, he was not a very good man. Chesterton could have gone even farther and said that he was no man at all; for, as you have already learned, the only truly human acts are acts of morality — acts that spring from a deliberation and a choice, acts that are sired by free will. All other acts by human beings are really animal acts.

Disciples of Pavlov may know much about "conditioned reflexes," but would they ever understand or appreciate the truth in that sentence which has been cut into the marble above the entrance to the courthouse at Worcester, Massachusetts: "Obedience to law is the greatest liberty"?

Liberty demands much study. The first realization to sink into your being is that *responsibility* is written large in the eyes of every newborn child. Once Baptism's waters have flowed over that child's head, the writing becomes larger, for those waters weight everyone they touch with responsibility for the very *welfare of God!*

That frightens. But take courage; it is a fright that can be very salutary. You, as a baptized person, are responsible for the welfare of God, for you are to contribute to the success or the failure of God's only Son. Since *responsibility* connotes liberty, you see that you must have a liberty like God's own liberty, and since you have been made a member of Jesus Christ, that is precisely the kind of liberty you will enjoy if you actualize that determination you took to live in Christ Jesus.

Your presence on earth is a gift God has made to mankind to enable it to straighten its back and lift its head. That is something you learn from St. Bernard, who teaches that you, who were born "bent," live to acquire rectitude and to help all other men do the same. *Rectitude* and *responsibility* are the *R*s taught by the Abbot of Clairvaux.

∞

The truth will set you free

In a world such as yours, there is an imperative need to "fix the meaning of words," especially the meaning of the word *freedom*. Many a battle cry has been raised in its name that, at best, was ambiguous; and many a war has been waged for its sake that later was found to have been fought for a very false cause. Jesus Christ fixed the meaning of that word for you when He said, "The truth shall make you free."

That tremendous text will live for you only when you see it in its context. John the Beloved opens his eighth chapter with the vivid and most instructive account of how the scribes and Pharisees tried to trap Jesus by bringing Him a woman who had just been caught in adultery. Moses had commanded that such a woman be stoned to death. The scribes and Pharisees gloated over the fact that they could now place Jesus on the horns of a painful dilemma. If He set aside the Law in this woman's regard, they would have definite grounds to show that He disdained the sacrosanct code their God-chosen leader had given them. If he sided with the Law, they would point to Him as heartless and inhuman. Jesus bent over and wrote in the dust. After a time, He straightened up and spoke of that freedom which alone of all freedoms shows man to be a true son of God. He calmly said, "If there be one among you free from sin, let him be the first to throw a stone at her."[252]

It appears that there were no free men in that assembly of scribes and Pharisees, for John reports that "on hearing this, they stole away, one by one, beginning with the older men."[253]

When Jesus looks up and finds Himself alone with the woman, He gives a directive you must follow if you are to be your real self, know genuine happiness, and enjoy true freedom. He says, "Go, and from now on, sin no more."[254]

The next incident in that chapter shows Jesus again trying to straighten out and straighten up some very badly "bent" Pharisees. He tells them that He is the "light of the world" and adds, "He that follows me shall not walk in the dark, but have the light of life."[255] They challenge Him and say His testimony is not valid since it is self-testimony. Jesus refutes that charge with a revelation that

[252] John 8:7.
[253] John 8:9.
[254] John 8:11.
[255] John 8:12.

should have sent them to their knees in silent adoration. He told them that He was not a single witness, that He was not alone, that He and the Father were the Witnesses who were testifying to the truth. They say to Him, "Where is your Father?" He replies, "If you knew me, you would also know my Father."[256]

Seeing incredulity in the cunning faces before Him, Jesus uttered a blood-chilling prophecy, albeit a conditional one: "If you do not believe that I am He, you must die in your sins."[257] It was a terrifying statement. They immediately asked, "Who are you, anyway?"[258] It was a question torn from them by terror, for these Jews realized ever so much more vividly than does many a modern man, just what it means to "die in your sins." The patient and humble Son of God answers these stubborn men, "When you have lifted up the Son of Man, then at last you will understand that I am He."[259] Jesus was telling these men not only that He was God, but that they were going to crucify God!

St. John tells you that "as He delivered this discourse, many believed in Him."[260] It was to these that Jesus spoke, saying, "If you make my teaching your rule of life, you are truly my disciples; then you will know the truth, and the truth will make you free."[261]

It is surprising to learn that these men bridled at Christ's mention of freedom as something they did not already possess. But it gives you clear insight into their pride. "Descendants of Abraham are we," they angrily tell our Lord, indignantly adding, "and have

[256] John 8:19.
[257] John 8:24.
[258] John 8:25.
[259] John 8:28.
[260] John 8:30.
[261] Cf. John 8:31-32.

never been any man's slaves. What do you mean by saying, 'You will become free'?"[262]

Again the humility of God is manifest as Jesus replies, "I must be frank with you. I tell you, everyone who commits sin is a slave of sin." In that line, God tells you what constitutes real slavery, and in what true liberty consists. Then He adds a comment that reduces all living to one fixed objective. He says, "Now, a slave does not stay in the household forever." Of course not, for the master is always master and can rid himself of any slave. But no father can ever free himself from any son! So Jesus pointedly adds, "A son does stay forever. Consequently, if the Son should make you free, you will be free in reality."[263]

His audience did not accept even that. But you, who live long years after the Son of Man was lifted up; who do not have to ask Jesus, "Who are you, anyway?"; who have been made free "with that freedom wherewith the Son of God has made you free,"[264] must study that which alone can strip you of your Christ-won and Christ-bestowed freedom. You must study sin.

∞

You must see the truth about sin

Christ's great ancestor David intimates in one of his psalms that few know what sin is. He seems to say that it is something of a mystery. "Who can understand sin?"[265] he asks. Of course you can define it, and when you commit it, your conscience lets you know. But have you ever plumbed the heinousness of it?

[262] John 8:33.
[263] John 8:34-36.
[264] Gal. 4:31.
[265] Ps. 18:13 (RSV = Ps. 19:12).

The ancients had an axiom: "*Ab assuetis nulla fit passio,*" which means that the commonplace leaves you cold. You moderns have a simile closely allied to that axiom. It is a simile that fills the judicious with fear for the future of man, even as it plunges him into sorrow for the plight of God. Yet it is a simile that leaves the thoughtless millions unconcerned and thus bears out the truth of the ancients' axiom. That simile speaks of things being "as common as sin, and sin being as common as dirt."

Sad to say, that simile is founded on fact. Sin is common, distressingly and disastrously common. Some comfort, however, can be drawn from the distinction theologians always make between *formal* sin and sin that is only *material*. That is a distinction which reminds you of one made earlier between acts that are human and acts that are only those of a man, for it stresses the difference between deliberate acts and those that are performed with mind and will on something else. These theologians are insisting that sin, to be sin, must come from the will, for no one truly offends God save those who *intend* to offend Him.

So you see, Socrates had some reason to say, "Sin is ignorance," and that Christ was speaking deep truth when He mounted the Cross praying, "Father, forgive them; for they know not what they do."[266] Sin is something of a mystery. Yet Socrates was not fully right. All sin is not ignorance. But today, you cannot deny there is too great an ignorance of sin.

Do *you* know what sin is? Do you really know what it is in a *member of Christ?* Do you realize it should never be in one who is in Christ Jesus?

Of course not! For if you once fully realized who you are, who God is, and what sin is, it would be impossible for you to live and

[266] Luke 23:34.

189

yet sin. Indeed sin is ignorance! It is ignorance of your dignity, of God's transcendence, and of the hideous malice in a deliberate offense against Infinity. But you have been mounting this stairway that leads to God just to get rid of that ignorance. You have taken your stand on this pedestal that rises higher and ever higher, and boarded this ship that plunges on toward that horizon beyond all horizons, just to know who you are. And you have been learning that you can never know that until you know your God.

You have been told by experts that you are a real relation to God Almighty. You are in perfect position to see, then, that sin is just the opposite. It is a "going away from God" — hence, a denial of your very nature and, consequently, must mean death. But perhaps that is too swift. You are on the height that shows you "like to God" because of liberty. While you stand here, you are told that you can be as straight as Christ. Then in the next breath, you are urged to look at what can make you so unlike God, and which should never be found in anyone who is in Christ Jesus. That would be truly disconcerting had you not been taken to this height and held here for the specific purpose of inducing vertigo. That cannot be done unless you look down.

To put yourself in a whirl, look at these facts about yourself: St. Bernard of Clairvaux says you were born "bent"; that you are a creature who is "curved," one who is really "twisted." For you, who were made to the image and likeness of God, came into this world bearing the image but without the likeness. Yet you, who were born "bent," have the obligation of standing as straight as Christ, for Baptism made you a member in His Body. In other words, you who were born in sin, and who will ever be sinful, can never be your true self until you are without sin.

That clash of seeming contradictions is enough to set anyone reeling who does not know himself. It will do the same to you unless you are possessed by the truth about yourself, your God, and sin. That verb *possessed* is used purposefully. For it is one thing to possess a truth and quite another to be possessed by that truth. You must be possessed by the truth that you are Christ's member if you are ever to enjoy the liberty that will make you like unto God. For to be a member of Christ is to be truly a son of God. But to be a son of God is to stand as straight as Christ. To stand as straight as Christ, however, one has to be as free as Christ was free. To be as free as that, one must be ready to look the whole world in the face and fearlessly hurl Christ's challenge: "Which of you can prove me guilty of sin?"[267]

∽

Sinlessness is possible for you

Can you hurl that challenge today to a world that is filled with sin? Can you stand before your fellowmen, who say that sin is as common as dirt, and boldly ask, "Which of you can prove me guilty of sin?" If you have been living conscious of who you are, if you have been living in Christ Jesus — thinking His thoughts, aiming at His goals, working with His will, determined to win His victory — you can, for sin will have been as far from you as it was from Him.

Sin is as common as dirt in your modern world because too many have given only a notional assent to liberty, and, consequently, an unconscious but very real assent to slavery. Sin is as common as dirt because too many call themselves Christians without ever realizing that that means to *be* Christ. "Live in the Word" has no other signification. Membership in His Mystical Body has no more basic demand. Sin is as common as dirt today simply because

[267] John 8:46.

too many who possess truth have never once been really possessed by Him who is Truth!

Realize now, if you never realized it before, that God gave you liberty precisely so that you might stand as straight as Christ. But no one will ever stand that straight unless he uses liberty as Christ did. He used it to do what He *ought:* to be obedient to God the Father, "obedient unto death."[268] The straightness demanded of you is moral, not physical; it has to do with your free will, not with your bodily frame; it means sinlessness, for that, in its positive aspect, is the highest liberty. You ought to be sinless because Christ was sinless, and you are His member. You can be sinless because you have been made free "with that freedom wherewith Christ has made you free." But it is up to you to use that freedom! It does not work of itself. It is a divine gift that demands human cooperation.

Let no one tell you that sinlessness is impossible. Let no one cite Scripture, quoting Proverbs to the effect that "the just man falls seven times a day,"[269] intimating, of course, that you are far from such justice. At worst, that text can only mean that the just man falls into minor faults and imperfections. At best, it refers to temporal adversities, and not to sin at all. Should anyone cite John the Beloved, who in the first chapter of his first letter writes, "If we should say that we are not guilty of sin, we deceive ourselves, and the light of truth is not in us,"[270] quote for them the very first verse of the second chapter. John says, "My little children, I write this letter to keep you from sin," then add the sixth verse of the third chapter: "No one who abides in Him sins."

---

[268] Phil. 2:8.
[269] Prov. 24:16.
[270] 1 John 1:8.

Martin Luther, John Calvin, and a few like them have taught that it is utterly impossible for you, or any other human, to stand as straight as Christ. According to them, your nature is such that you simply must sin. That is such a defamation of both God and man that the Council of Trent thundered anathemas against it. And why not? If you were necessitated, by the very nature that God has given you, to fall, you would be glorifying your Maker by being down! If your will is so "bent" that you could never straighten up, you should be rewarded for being crooked! That is how absurd heretical doctrines can be. No wonder Trent thundered. Common sense should tell everyone that the sin you must commit is no sin at all.

You do not have to sin by nature; and certainly by your supernature you can be, you should be, and you will be free from sin if you will only live in Christ Jesus. That means living conscious of your dignity as His member! But for such a liberty, you must pay the price. It will cost you exactly what John Philpot Curran claimed that political liberty demands: eternal vigilance.[271] But it is well worth that price; for with it you buy a share in the "power of God and the wisdom of God"; you barter yourself and your selfishness for a share in the sinlessness of God's only Son; you actually become what you were made to be! But neither you nor any other human will be that vigilant until both you and they really come to know what sin is.

∞

Sin causes all evil and suffering
In the very first exercise of his famed *Spiritual Exercises*, Ignatius of Loyola has you so focus on sin that you are forced to recognize

---

[271] Speech on the Right of Election of Lord Mayor of Dublin, July 10, 1790.

its essential hideousness and hatefulness. He makes you stare at the effects produced by the single sin of the angels, then at those produced by the single sin of our first parents, and finally, at the result of dying with a single mortal sin on one's soul. He has the retreatant repeat this exercise three distinct times. Meditation becomes contemplation; contemplation becomes humiliation, which leads to intense detestation of sin.

Have you ever reflected on the fact that every horror in the long and horror-filled history of man, from the murder of Abel by his brother Cain, down to the wholesale slaughters of the entire populations of cities by a single bomb blast in your own day, is directly attributable to the single sin of disobedience committed by Adam in the Garden of Paradise? Have you ever realized that mankind, from a race of titans who should have walked on to life everlasting with the ever-living God, was changed into a "caravan on its way to death" simply because the first man did not use his liberty to do what he ought? Since no effect can be greater than its cause, the tidal wave of misery that engulfs all humankind ought to tell you something of the nature of sin — one single sin!

Adam's one no to God changed all creation, frustrated the original plan of Omnipotence, and filled all earth with death. The veritable sea of suffering that swirls its angry waters sooner or later about every son of Adam and daughter of Eve was "created" by that *fiat* spoken by your first parents to the Tempter — one single sin of disobedience!

Adam, in reaching for that forbidden fruit, brought into existence every hospital in your present-day world; every orphanage, insane asylum, and every home for the aged, the poor, and the incurables. Adam's hand fashioned every coffin mankind has used and dug every grave that will ever cover a human corpse. Every single heartache and every single heartbreak of humankind — from the first felt by Eve when she held in her arms the cold corpse of Abel, her own flesh and blood, and for the first time realized that "the wages of sin are death,"[272] down to the latest heartbroken daughter of Eve who weeps by a cradle that has been turned into a coffin — is directly traceable to that first misuse of liberty.

Misery was born, sickness and suffering came into being, and death itself was brought about by the refusal of the first man ever made to the image and likeness of God to use his liberty to obey. Those actualities will help you see sin.

The twentieth century witnessed two wars of worldwide extent and watched a long-drawn-out, cruel cold war. If you have been thinking as St. Ignatius of Loyola would have you think, you know that Adam was the "warmonger." For had he not said no to God back at the dawn of creation, mankind would never have known war. Terrible indeed is this liberty of man!

If you wish to know sin, make all this personal. If your mother wastes away from tuberculosis, tell yourself that God never planned thus; sin did it. If your father, at the peak of his powers, is struck dawn by a lightning-like heart attack, say sin did it; God never planned thus. If you have to watch your little child's limbs shrivel from a debilitating disease, recognize Adam's hand in it all, not the hand of God. If you should be forced to watch a cancer gnaw away at a sister or brother, know that sin sired that disease, not your Maker. Sickness, suffering, and death are from sin — not from your ever-sinless God.

St. Ignatius often speaks in his *Exercises* of "savoring" a truth. He is one man of God who would have you use every God-given power to come to such an intimate knowledge of a truth that you can say not only that you possess it, but that you are possessed by it.

[272] Rom. 6:23.

He would have you not only look at sin, but hear, taste, touch, and even smell it. He would have you contemplate it by the three faculties of your soul and then go on to experience it, as it were, through your five senses. He would have you know its hideousness more exactly than you know the back of your hand. That is why he takes you down into Hell and has you see, hear, smell, touch, and even taste Satan. He would have you know sin in its essence.

Perhaps it was before God said, "Let there be light" that this Light-Bearer, destined to serve before the throne of God in eternal happiness and glory, hollowed every depth in Hell by his single sin of pride-filled disobedience.

Who can count the dawns and the days since that defiant "I will not serve" of Lucifer? Throughout them all, he and his legions have known nothing but hate, unimaginable unhappiness, misery, and suffering. When the world's last sun has burned out, Hell's fires will still burn on, and the one refusal to use liberty aright will keep Lucifer and his legions in those flames which Christ called "unquenchable."[273]

You and your generation have been horrified by Hitler's gas chambers and the furnaces of Dachau. But what were they compared with that chamber and those fires called Hell! God tells you through St. Mark that souls there will be "salted with fire."[274] Can you imagine what that means? *Salted* must mean steeped, saturated, permeated through and through by fire! And one single sin of thought kindled those "unquenchable fires." Are you ready to cry with David, "Who can understand sin?" and have it mean, "What a mystery of horror is this thing which — God of mercy, forgive us — is as 'common as dirt'; this thing called sin!"

[273] Matt. 3:12.
[274] Mark 9:49.

Ignatius knows what it takes to win a real assent. He realizes how slowly humans become possessed by a truth. The horrors of Hell and the hideous history of man, which in his *Exercises* he would have you experience intimately, are not enough to alert you to the nature of sin. So Ignatius brings it closer to home as he has you ponder a tragic possibility. The saint would have you meditate long on the fact that it is possible for a soul who has served God religiously for a whole lifetime, to close that life with a single mortal sin, and die without repenting. As you see, it is not highly probable that a sincere soul would thus close its life; but the saint is teaching you the nature of sin, and this horror-filled possibility highlights that nature superbly.

God's mercy is such that He has made forgiveness almost too easy. Pardon comes so readily that few rightly measure the length, depth, height, and breadth of this thing called sin. Because absolution is gained so promptly, you may sometimes forget that certain sins *are* mortal — that they merit *eternal* punishment. Ignatius shows you that the single sin of an angel sparked the everlasting fires of Hell; that the single sin of a man caused every twinge of pain that humans will ever know. He now pulls you up sharply with the truth that it is not sin that sends one to Hell, but *unrepented* sin. Hence, the possibility he paints pulses with life; for who is there who cannot see that one sin can damn a soul eternally — that last sin committed before death's finger stops the heart that has not beat out its sincere contrition? It will always be true that one sin can send a soul to Hell — *your* soul; the soul even of the saintly!

Suppose St. Romuald,[275] the founder of the Camaldolese monks, had actually lived as long as the old biographies claimed: one

---

[275] St. Romuald (c. 950-1027).

hundred and twenty years. As a very young boy, Romuald had seen his own father kill a man. The young boy resolved to expiate that deed by being a monk in the truest sense of that word, the word *monk* coming from the Greek word *monos*, which means "alone."

A true monk, then, is one who lives for and with God alone. Every breath of his body, every beat of his heart, all the day long, all his life long, is directed to the praise of God alone. With resolute will, day in and day out, the monk denies his inferior self so that he may ever assert his higher self; he dies deliberately to all that is of the earth so that, as far as possible, he may ever walk with God alone. Thanks to such stern asceticism, he makes his sense appetites perfectly subject to his reason, and his reason ever completely subject to the will of God. He stands, then, as straight as Christ, and like Him, labors ever to do the things that please the Father. Romuald was that kind of a monk.

Think of the amount of merit such a monk amasses in a single year, to say nothing of a hundred years. Grant, now, that Romuald lived every year of the full century credited to him as a perfect monk.

But suppose that on the night he died, Satan deceived him even as he succeeded in deceiving Eve in Paradise. Such a thing is possible! Suppose this saintly old monk sinned mortally and then died in his sin. That mountain of merit he had amassed in the century of suffering, sacrifice, and sanctity would be blotted out as finally as if it had never been. The glory those hard monastic years had won would have to be denied Romuald by a God who is all-loving and all-just. The sin of a single moment would not only have washed away a century of holiness, but would have damned a man to misery unimaginable for ages unending.

Do you begin to savor sin? Do you begin to sense the weight of that which the world regards so lightly? The pressure of sin, for those who are truly sensitive and sensible brings on a sweat of blood. It did that to Christ.[276] It does that to true Christians.

∞

You must recognize what sin does to God

But even if you have fully tasted what it does to man, you are only beginning to savor sin. Ignatius is not done with it — or with you, yet. He now makes you perceive what it has done to God.

The Son of the Father, co-equal with Him in all things, became man. That is Bethlehem, and it is beautiful to the point of pain, for despite the loneliness, poverty, and closed doors, it is the warm, radiant splendor of God's love. But this Son of God became man in order to become *sin*. As St. Paul says, "He was made sin for us."[277] That is Calvary — and it is incarnated horror!

Until you have seen human spittle on a divine face, you have not looked at sin. Unless you have seen blunt spikes tear their way through omnipotent hands and render them still, you have not seen sin. Until you have looked and seen the sinless son of God writhing in agony, a "worm and no man,"[278] gazed with open eyes on "the most beautiful of the sons of men,"[279] and seen Him become only "bruises and sores and bleeding wounds,"[280] you have never looked on sin. Until you have seen the only Son of God as "a leper and one struck by God"[281] and realized that "from the sole of the foot to the top of the head there is no soundness in

[276] Cf. Luke 22:44.
[277] 2 Cor. 5:21.
[278] Ps. 21:7 (RSV = Ps. 22:6).
[279] Ps. 44:3 (RSV = Ps. 45:2).
[280] Isa. 1:6 (Revised Standard Version).
[281] Cf. Isa. 53:4.

Him,"[282] you have never seen sin. When you stare at Sinlessness and see that He is "made sin," then, for the first time, you are looking at that thing which in your day is as common as dirt. When you see Jesus Christ one raw bleeding wound, His body all but flayed alive; when you gaze on your God and see Him, infinite purity and consummate holiness, utterly naked on a criminal's Cross, His divine blood covering every limb, blurring His eyes as it pours from His thorn-crowned head; when you have heard this consubstantial Son of the Father crying as from the rim of Hell and the brink of despair: "My God, my God, why hast Thou forsaken me?"[283] then and only then will you have some idea of what sin is.

Artists, the most realistic of them, have idealized the Crucified One. It is perfectly justifiable, for there is unsurpassed beauty beneath this culmination of horror and hideousness. Yet, for you who would love your God with all your heart and mind and strength, there is no revolting detail in the whole bleeding monstrosity that is not without intimate meaning.

Ignatius of Loyola would have every retreatant fall passionately in love with Jesus Christ. That is why he has them study sin and self and the Savior in what is almost a brutal fashion. Until you know God, you cannot know sin. Unless your love for Christ becomes a passion, you will not really hate sin. And hate it with all your heart you must if you are ever to stand as straight as God's only Son.

John J. Corbett, S.J., was an aging man when, in 1921, he was sent to Yonkers, New York, to give the annual retreat to the Jesuit novices there. The fifty youngsters who sat before him during that retreat did not average twenty-five years of age. They had come,

---

[282] Isa. 1:6.
[283] Mark 15:34 (Revised Standard Version).

almost one hundred percent, from middle-class, strongly Catholic homes, and you could say that they had led wholesome lives, both at home and in school, and had been wisely protected from the world's unsavory influences. They knew very little of sin. Yet the high point in that retreat, for both the novices and their retreat master, came when this aging Jesuit cried, literally cried, before those youngsters as he prayed, "O God, my God, I want to hate sin! I want to hate sin!"

He was petitioning for himself, of course, and with all sincerity; but as retreat master, he was also praying for each of those retreatants under him. And not one of them, no matter what his experience in later life, can ever forget the sight of that saintly old man at that moment and his desperate cry.

That cry came as colloquy and climax not to the consideration of what sin can do to man, but of the study of what sin has already done to the sinless Son of God. Ignatius' meditations on sin are progressive. But even when you come to their climax and can kneel before your crucified God crying with the sincerity of a Father Corbett, you have not yet reached the point proper for one who is to live ever conscious of the fact that he or she is a member of Christ's Mystical Body.

Yet that is the whole purpose of this stop on the stairs at this particular height. For while it is a good thing to know what sin is, it is a much better thing to know what *your* sin is! For while it is wholesome and healthful to study the effects of Original Sin on man, it can be sanctifying to study the effects of *your* sin on God. If you are to stand as straight as Christ, and stay that way, you must never forget that you, this day, can make Christ as crooked as He was on the Cross!

Going from St. Ignatius to St. Paul, you learn that when *you* sin, you do more than Judas did, more than Pilate did, more than hateful high priests and deluded Jews did, more than rough Roman soldiers did; to the very heart of Christ, you do more than Longinus did with his unerring lance.[284] For you are Christ's member! None of these were. When you, a member of Christ's Mystical Body, sin, you do much more than spit on the face of God, make mockery of Omniscience, and render Omnipotence helpless.

In his letter to the Hebrews, Paul speaks of certain sinners as those who "again crucify the Son of God and expose Him to mockery."[285] No one who has ever followed Christ from the Cenacle to the Garden of Olives, then to the houses of Annas and Caiphas, down to the dirt and dark of the dungeon, on to Pilate's praetorium, across to the hall of mockery ruled by Herod, then to the whipping post and the barrack yard, out to the gallery of the *Ecce Homo*,[286] then stumbled with Him through the tortuous streets of the city and up to Golgotha's top would not quail before the thought of crucifying Him again!

But even that is not the specific horror of sin when committed by a mystical member. To see that, you have to turn to Paul's first letter to the Corinthians and read the indignant lines: "Are you not aware that your bodies are members of Christ's Body?" Then that question which is freighted with horror: "Shall I, then, take the members of Christ and make them the members of a prostitute?"[287]

It is true that Paul was speaking of a specific sin. But you will be wise if you adopt the language and follow the thought of those spiritual writers who liken all sin to adultery; for every sin is a betrayal of love and of your Lover! Now you should be able to understand

[284] Cf. John 19:34.
[285] Heb. 6:6.
[286] "Behold the Man"; John 19:5.
[287] 1 Cor. 6:15.

why Cardinal Newman was so vehement when speaking of sin, even of venial sin. He once said, "The Catholic Church holds it better for the sun and the moon to drop from the heavens, for the earth to fail, and for all the many millions on it to die of starvation in extremest agony, as far as temporal afflictions go, than that one soul, I will not say, should be lost, but should commit one single venial sin."

That is what the Holy Roman Catholic Apostolic Church holds. You now know why. Sin in a mystical member is ever so much more than spitting into the face of God or hammering Him to a tree. Sin in a mystical member is "joining His Body to a prostitute!" And you, a member of His Body, can sin. You will sin if you do not use your liberty aright and obey.

⧸∾

Christ enables you to be sinless

Whoever knows himself or herself to be "bent" and labors to unbend is near the heart of the fire, for he or she realizes that to *be* a Christian is not easy. He or she sees religion in its essence and recognizes it to be what Nero and Diocletian in ages past, what Danton and Robespierre at the time of the French Revolution, what Hitler and Stalin in the recent past have recognized it to be: a challenge, a war cry, an irreconcilable totalitarian force — which they must break if it is not to break them.

A member of Christ cannot be maudlin or mediocre. Chesterton was right when he said, "Christianity has not been tried and found wanting; it has been found difficult and left untried." He was speaking of the masses of men, not of Christ's members. The masses are "bent" and are all but unconscious of their deformity. But the member of Christ, worthy of the name, is straight — as straight as Christ. That straightness means sinlessness.

"But," someone might ask, "how can the sinful be sinless?" That is an old objection. The answer is simple. You are sinful and will be so as long as you live on earth. But realize once and forever that *sinful* does not mean "full of sin." When it is said that every son of Adam and daughter of Eve is sinful, it can never mean that every man and woman is always sinning. You, thank God, are not always sinning — even venially. Like every other human, you are full of faults. You may be guilty of many inclinations to venial sins in the course of a single day. And the inclination to sin will be in you until you see God face-to-face. But between an ever-present inclination to fall and the actual fall into sin yawns a distance that, if not actually infinite, is certainly close to it.

To their dying day, the purest of saints had the inclination to sin; they were sinful. Francis de Sales[288] once humorously said that the inclination to sin will stay with us humans for a full fifteen minutes after we are dead.

But from the opening page of this book you have been asked to stress the positive. Do so now. What is this inclination to evil compared with your innate Godward drive? What is this concupiscence that comes from Original Sin and remains in you even after Baptism compared with that share in Omnipotence that was given you by the pouring of those waters and the flaming Holy Spirit? What is this thing called *concupiscence* but the very thing you have been learning to straighten out in Christ Jesus.

Christ is the ultimate answer to every objection, just as He is the strength for every weakness, and the straightener for every bend. For He is "the power of God and the wisdom of God." How can the sinful be sinless? By the grace of God! By living ever conscious of the fact that you are the member of Him, the sinless Son

[288] St. Francis de Sales (1567-1622), Bishop of Geneva.

of God. The sap that rises from the Vine to the branches is omnipotence. That is why Paul could so daringly say, "I can do all things in him who strengthens me."[289] You can say the same.

The great German theologian Scheeben[290] once exclaimed, "If you only knew your true self, Christian soul, how you would honor yourself." He knew full well that every member of Christ, so long as he or she is on earth, will always have to pray those two great prayers of the Mystical Body: the one to the Father, which says, "Forgive us our trespasses," and the one to the Mother, which says, "Pray for us sinners." He knew the ever-pressing need for humility as deep as God's own humility. Yet he recognized that your ignorance of self, once you are incorporated in Christ, is something of an insult to God.

He then went on to give some of the reasons you should honor yourself. "If you only knew yourself to be holy, beloved of God, His dwelling place, honored and reverenced by the angels! If you only knew you were the fairest paradise in creation, the tabernacle of the Holy Trinity, the nuptial chamber of the great King! If you only knew that you were the Ark of the Covenant, not of the Old, but of the New Testament, the altar of Divine Majesty, the Shrine of the Holy Spirit, the Temple of the Living God! If you only knew that you were the Throne of the Godhead, the Heaven where shine, not the stars, but the three Persons of the Blessed Trinity! If you knew all this, how you would honor yourself, not for what you are by yourself, but for the dignities conferred on you by grace."[291] He could have added what is the most significant truth of all as far

---

[289] Phil. 4:13.

[290] Matthias Joseph Scheeben (1835-1888).

[291] From "Marvels of Divine Grace," quoted by Raoul Plus, S.J., in *Inward Peace* (Westminster, Maryland: Newman Press, 1954), 58.

as you are concerned: "If you only knew that you are Christ's mystical member."

In reality, you have known all these truths almost from the first day you opened the child's catechism, but Scheeben awakes you to the fact that you have been giving only a notional assent to them. Now you ought to realize what "eternal vigilance" means. It means that every hour of the day, there should come from the bottom of your heart the cry "God, make me conscious! Make me conscious of who I am, what I have, and why I live! Make me conscious that I am one who can be as straight as your Christ; that I am one who must be that straight! Straight in thought, in word, in deed; straight in mind and will; straight in body and soul; straight with men, with myself, and, above all, O my God, straight with You. God of liberty, help me to use my liberty right!"

How you, your world, and God Himself need men of rectitude. Basically, the bankruptcy of your present-day world is due to the woeful want of men of rectitude. Straight-thinking, straight-talking, and straight-acting would renew the face of the earth. But before such "straightness" is had, you, and thousands of others like you, will have to use your liberty to cultivate holy habits of thought and will; habits that are shot through and through with Christlikeness; habits that will have you and them ever keenly conscious of who you are, why you are, and what you should actually be doing. Cultivate those habits, and you will be truly free, for you will be truly in love.

Now you can be told that those who define freedom as "an absence of constraint or necessity," and those who put it positively, saying it is "the power to choose according to one's own will from among many possibilities," have said very little about that wondrous reality which is yours. Philosophically they are exact; but life is ever so much more than exact philosophy!

Actually, these men have but scratched the surface of something that is as deep as your soul; for, ultimately, liberty was given to you by God so that, with perfect freedom, you might love no one before God, no one as much as God, no one apart from God. That is sinlessness — or the straightness of Christ — from the positive angle. That is freedom seen in its fullness. That is life lived at its highest. But before you, or any other man, will know that liberty, or live that life, you must become "an uncaught captive in the hands of Love."

Freedom — responsibility — rectitude is your call in Christ Jesus. You answer it by love; only by a generous surrender; only by freely binding yourself in His grasp.

In a unique book, Père François Charmot, S.J., gives a dialogue between Christ Jesus and a human soul, which, of course, might very well be your soul. Christ first says that if He did not love man, He would not ask anything of him. If He loved man only a little, He would ask only a little. But because He loves him so much, He asks much. He concludes by saying, "You can always measure the ardor of my love by the demands of my will." Remember that!

The soul — your soul — remonstrates and draws a parallel between human love that always manifests itself "like beautiful, ripe fruit — full of savor, sweetness, and delight," and the will of Christ, which is so often crucifying. Then that soul — your soul — questions Christ, "Does Thy Heart know how much we love to be free?" He answers:

> My child, what confusions cloud your understanding.
> I myself am the creator of liberty, and I bring it
>   to perfection.
> I love liberty beyond all things.

I will never give you Heaven under compulsion.
The happiness I am preparing for you will be the fruit
  of your liberty.
You will enjoy it only in liberty and through liberty.
But true liberty abides in love. All others are false.
One is free to love or not to love the true life.
No matter what befell me on earth,
My liberty, which was all-powerful, was in my Heart.
All my works, from my birth until my death,
I accomplished freely, because I did them through love.
In the crib, I was wrapped in swaddling clothes; on the
  Cross, I was fastened by nails,
During my whole life, I was fettered to the will of my
  Father, but I always acted freely, because I always
  acted through love.

Men do not see that in following their passions, they
  are slaves of the creatures which seduce them. . . .
They lose the liberty for the best things in life.
My will must be done!
But my will is accomplished only through love; it is
  love that renders man sovereignly free.
Your will united to mine is all-powerful.
Fear, suffering, death do not paralyze it.
The martyrs were free to say no to the tyrants because
  love is stronger than all suffering.
If you wish true liberty, ask it of my pierced Heart.
Because it is the source of love, my Heart will give
  it to you.[292]

[292] François Charmot, *In Retreat with the Sacred Heart* (Westminster, Maryland: Newman Press, 1956), 67-68.

That soul replied, "Ah, Jesus, I understand now: The greatest act of liberty is to do Thy will."

Are you ready to make the same reply, and to act upon it? Do not say you are unworthy. God — and everyone else — knows that. Yet, knowing it, He has made the choice. He has called you to liberty; but it is you who must answer the call, for He "will never give you Heaven under compulsion."

"Those who abide in Christ do not sin." *You* can be sinless. You can stand as straight as the sinless Son of God. God wills it. God is watching and waiting to see if in headlong love, you will plunge into Christ Jesus and live.

Cardinal Newman once wrote, "God beholds thee individually, whoever thou art. He calls thee by name. He sees thee, and understands thee, as He made thee. He knows what is in thee, all thy own peculiar feelings and thoughts, thy dispositions and likings, thy strength and thy weakness. He views thee in thy day of rejoicing and thy day of sorrow. He sympathizes in thy hopes and thy temptations. He interests Himself in all thy anxieties and remembrances, all the risings and failings of thy spirit. He has numbered the very hairs of thy head and the cubits of thy stature. He compasses thee round and bears thee in His arms; He takes thee up and sets thee down. He notes thy very countenance, whether smiling or in tears, whether healthful or sickly. He looks tenderly upon thy hands and thy feet; He hears thy voice, the beating of thy heart, and thy very breathing.

"Thou dost not love thyself better than He loves thee. Thou canst not shrink from pain more than He dislikes thy bearing it; and if He puts it on thee, it is as thou wilt put it on thyself, if thou art wise, for a greater good afterward. Thou art not only His creature (though for the very sparrows He has care, and pitied the 'much cattle' of Nineveh); thou art man, redeemed and sanctified, His adopted son, favored with a portion of that glory and blessedness which flows from Him everlastingly unto the Only-Begotten. Thou art chosen to be His, even above thy fellows, who dwell in the East and the South. Thou wast one of those for whom Christ offered His last prayer and sealed it with His Precious Blood."[293]

Is it not appalling to think that such a one, who lives not only under the eye of God but in His very hands, can sin? Is it not puzzling to think that such a one, a member of Christ's Mystical Body, can keep from falling deeply in love — with God?

"Many things know we," said St. Thomas More,[294] "that we seldom think on: and in the things of the soul, the knowledge without the remembrance little profiteth. What availeth it to know there is a God, which thou not only believest by faith, but knowest by reason? What availeth it that thou knowest Him, if thou think little of Him? The busy minding of thy four last things, and the deep consideration thereof, is the thing that shall keep thee from sin." He was commenting on that verse of Ecclesiasticus which says, "Remember the last things, and thou shalt never sin."[295]

After pausing so long on this height, you are in position to paraphrase that and say, "Lord, let me be ever mindful of my real beginning; of my Baptism, and what You made of me therein, and I will never sin; for, as St. Paul has taught us, 'Christ never knew sin,' yet You 'made Him into sin for us' so that in Him we might be turned into the holiness of God!"[296]

---

[293] John Henry Cardinal Newman, *Plain and Parochial Sermons*, Vol. 3, sermon 9: "A Particular Providence as Revealed in the Gospel."

[294] St. Thomas More (1478-1535), Lord Chancellor of England and martyr.

[295] Ecclus. 7:40 (RSV = Sir. 7:36).

[296] 2 Cor. 5:21.

Chapter Nine

❧

You are one who knows the only answer to the problem of pain

You are now in a position to sum up all history in two words and all time in a single name. Those words are as important to you as your heartbeat. That name is as vital to you as your breath — even a bit more so! From Peter you can get the name; but it will be from Paul that you will take the words.

When Peter was first arrested in Jerusalem and put on trial by the very man who had first tried Jesus — the high priest Annas — he was asked, "By what authority or in what name have you done this?" The Prince of the Apostles answered, "In the name of Jesus Christ. . . . There is no other name under Heaven appointed among men as the necessary means of salvation."[297]

There is the single name that sums up all time for you: *Jesus Christ.* Heretofore you may have thought that He splits all time, since He stands in the middle of history, all of which is dated around Him: B.C., meaning before Christ, and A.D. being after Him. That is a common misconception, and really pagan in content, for it implies that Jesus was not in the Old Testament and is

[297] Acts 4:7, 10, 12.

not existing in present time. Both implications are completely false.

The Old Testament was filled with Him from even before the promise made in the Garden of Eden to after the bestowal of the golden sword on Judas Machabeus.[298] As for the present: who else fills the minds of men, who else captures their hearts, who else is the object of their love and their hate? Your day throbs with Jesus Christ: those "who are not with Him are against Him!"[299] But no one is indifferent to or unconcerned about Him.

With that much as lead, and with the last chapter still in your mind, you might be tempted to think that *sin* and *sinlessness* — or *sin* and *salvation* — are the two words that tell the whole of mankind's history. You would not be far wrong; still you would not be right.

Let St. Paul give you what you need. In the second chapter of his letter to the Philippians, he says that the sinless Son of God "emptied Himself." To state that truth, he used the one word *kenosis*. And in that word is locked up half of history, for as Paul tells you, "Jesus, though He is by nature God, did not consider His equality with God a condition to be clung to, but emptied Himself by taking the nature of a slave, fashioned as He was to the likeness of men and recognized by outward appearance as man."[300] But that was not the ultimate purpose of His *kenosis*; that emptying Himself and taking the nature of a slave was but a necessary condition for the fulfillment of His real purpose, which was to "humble Himself and become obedient to death; yes, to death on a Cross"[301] and

[298] 2 Macc. 15:15.
[299] Cf. Matt. 12:30.
[300] Phil. 2:5-7.
[301] Phil. 2:8.

thus restore to His Father all the glory that had been stolen from Him by sin, and at the same time, and by the same deed, redeem sinning and sinful mankind.

As you know, Jesus did that one work with a thoroughness God alone could achieve. He ended it with a cry only the Son of God could utter: "It is now completed!"[302] That is the triumphant cry that blazoned Golgotha's gloom at history's most hideous hour. The *kenosis* was absolute. He had now emptied Himself even of life.

Yet that cry, although it came from the lips of the Son of God, who once described Himself as "Truth," tells only a half-truth, as far as you are concerned. In a certain sense, it did not tell the full truth even about Jesus Christ. For, while as the *Christ*, or Anointed of God, His work was completed, as *Jesus*, or Savior of men, it had just begun. The *kenosis* — the emptying — called for a *pleroma* — a "filling up"; redemption was absolute, but salvation was conditioned. The first was done by God alone, for only God could do it; He did it through a humanity. The second must be done by man, who can do it only through Christ's divinity.

There is all history for you in two Greek words: *kenosis* and *pleroma*. The first tells of Christ and what He has done for Christians; the second tells of Christians and what they must do for Christ. And history has no other story to tell, nor does it contain any other meaning.

In the last chapter, you learned that you, who were born in sin and who, to the hour of your death, will be sinful, can stand as straight as Christ and thus be sinless. But thrilling as that last truth is, it is only half the truth about the actuality you are living. Learn now what you can do by your freedom from sin and by your lack of the fullness of the third freedom.

[302] John 19:30.

213

A tiny doubt must have entered your mind as you read St. Bernard's analysis of your liberty and learned that your freedom, to be full, must be threefold. For you see clearly enough that you will always be free to choose. You should have been convinced by the last chapter that you are always free to choose aright, and when you are in Christ, "the power of God and the wisdom of God," you have strength enough to carry out that choice and remain sinless. But the question must have occurred at least once to you: "Isn't there something wrong with this analysis, for while I am always free from necessity, and can be free from sin, why is it that I cannot always be free from sin's consequences?"

∽

Your Faith gives you the
answer to the problem of pain

Actually, that is the question that has perplexed the world. For it holds in its depths the problem of evil. In plain fact, you are asking why there is pain, why men suffer, and why the sinless should know misery. The pagan world stood dumb before that query. Most of your modern world — which is pagan enough — is equally perplexed and equally at a loss for a reply. But you have the only answer, for you have seen the face of God and heard His voice.

Deeper grows the mystery of who you are since higher mounts the revelation of what you have already done. You have done what patriarchs, prophets, kings, and judges of the Chosen People, and what the people themselves craved to do, but never did. The desire that burned in every human heart during the time of the Old Testament has already been fulfilled for you, although they died without ever knowing that satisfaction.

That is revelation. Jesus Himself once told His disciples the truth about you. No torturing of the text is necessary; no strain is put on the mind or the imagination for you to see that Christ's words are even more applicable to you this moment than they were to the disciples the day He said, "Happy the eyes that see what you are seeing. Indeed, I tell you, many prophets and kings would have liked to see what you are looking on, but did not see it, and to hear what you are listening to, but did not hear it."[303] What were those disciples looking on that prophet and king would have liked to have seen? What was it that they were listening to that prophet and king would have liked to have heard? Precisely the One you are looking at and listening to — God!

David, "the man after God's own heart,"[304] summed up the heart of mankind perfectly. He put the throbbing desire of the entire Old Testament in a single line: "Thy face, O God, will I seek!"[305]

That cry of David is the voice of the drive modern depth psychologists are just discovering. It is the face of God that every human being is seeking at every hour of the day and night whether he knows it or not; for in the face of God the human soul finds that truth without which its mind will never be at rest and that beauty and goodness without which its will can never know contentment. It is the face of God that makes Heaven Heaven; and Heaven is the proper home of every person on earth. That is why you and every other human being on earth this moment are but an aching nostalgia for the face of God. Every human life has been summed up in that line of the psalm: "Show us thy face, and we shall be saved."[306] You have seen His face!

[303] Luke 10:23-24.
[304] Cf. 1 Sam. 13:14 (Revised Standard Version).
[305] Ps. 26:8 (RSV = Ps. 27:8).
[306] Ps. 79:4 (RSV = Ps. 80:3).

Isaiah saw the throne of God, the skirt of God filling the Temple, and heard the seraphim singing to God, "Holy, holy, holy,"[307] yet he never saw or heard what you have seen and heard. He never knew God as you know Him. Ezekiel sat in exile by the waters of the Chobar when suddenly there swept down on him a whirlwind of fire, and in the midst of it, there amid the wheels, the wings, and the lightning flashes, he saw the Son of Man and he heard "the voice of one who spoke."[308] But he never saw, nor did he ever hear, what you have seen and heard.

Because you were born in a year designated as *anno Domini* (A.D.: "in the year of the Lord"), you have come to know more about the living God, and the very life He lives, than patriarch, prophet, judge, or king, even though these were specially chosen by God and admitted to rarest intimacy. Actually, in the knowledge that is real knowledge, you are wiser than Solomon, that "wisest of men." Because of your hold on actuality and the one Reality's grip on you, you are dearer to the heart of God than was David "that man after God's own heart." Because you live twenty centuries after Christ, you know the answer, the *only* answer, to the problem that perplexed every century before Christ, and is today a complete mystery to all who have not seen what you have seen or heard what you have heard.

Perhaps you have often felt a holy envy stir within you as you read the Old Testament and learned the intimacy that existed between God and His special friends. But now as you see reality, if anything stirs in you, it will be pity for God's Chosen People and His most intimate friends; for you become aware that the God they knew and served, the God they worshiped with all their

---

[307] Isa. 6:3.
[308] Ezek. 1:28.

being, was a God who was almost faceless, while you, who live in Christ Jesus, have not only seen the face of God, but have come to know its every feature. Those are the features that fashion for you the one answer to the problem of pain, the baffling enigma of evil in the world, and the mystery that surrounds human suffering.

Neither Abraham, Isaac, nor Jacob; neither Moses, Aaron, nor Josue; neither Gideon, Samson, nor any one of the judges; neither Saul, David, Solomon, nor any other one of the kings; neither Isaiah, Ezekiel, Daniel, nor Jeremiah, nor any one of the minor prophets ever did once nor could they do once what you have done ten thousand times. Which one of them could ever sign themselves with the Sign of the Cross or bless themselves "in the name of the Father, and of the Son, and of the Holy Spirit"? They worshiped God, and worshiped Him well; but never once could they give Him the worship you give Him when you say, "Glory be to the Father, and to the Son, and to the Holy Spirit." Glory is defined as: "praise that rises from clear knowledge." Hence, compared with yours, their knowledge of God was cloudy, and consequently, their praise was weak when measured by what you can give.

Yahweh — the God of the Chosen People — was a living, personal God. He was the holy, immortal, strong God. Yet, was He not all but faceless? He hugged Israel to His heart and called it "son"; yet what Israelite ever prayed the Our Father as you can pray it? Genesis told of a woman and her crushing heel,[309] Jeremiah of a "woman who would compass a man,"[310] Isaiah of a "virgin who would conceive and bring forth a son,"[311] but who in Old

---

[309] Cf. Gen. 3:15.
[310] Jer. 31:22.
[311] Isa. 7:14.

Testament times could ever say the Hail Mary as you say it? Although the Spirit of God is manifest from the moment of creation, when you find Him "moving above the waters,"[312] and is in evidence in almost every scene up to that last in the Old Testament, when a golden sword, as a gift from God, is given to Judas Machabeus, who in the Old Testament knew God the Holy Spirit? What did they know of the life of this living God? Next to nothing, for they had never seen His face. But you who have looked on it can say, "The Father is God, the Son is God, and the Holy Spirit is God; yet there are not three Gods, but only one God."

You know the very life God lives! You know that the Father, Infinite Intelligence, expressed His knowledge in one Word, a living, substantial Word, who is adequate expression of what the Father is. In uttering that Word, the Father begets a Son, to whom He communicates His whole essence: nature, perfections, and life. "Just as the Father is the source of life, so, too, has He given the Son the power to be a source of life."[313] Divine life has been communicated and received! The Son, being the perfect expression of the Father, is loved by the Father; and the Father, being the source of everything the Son has, is loved by the Son. From this mutual love, as from one principle, proceeds that Spirit of Love — living, substantial, and personal — that Holy Spirit who is the bond of union between the Father and the Son, co-equal and co-eternal with the Son and the Father.

There, very briefly, is the truth about your living God and the life He leads. It is a life of knowledge and love. In that inexpressible, unique, and ever-fruitful life, God finds His essential bliss. He has no need of any other life or any other love. He has no need of

---

[312] Gen. 1:2.
[313] John 5:26.

any creatures. But you know that in His goodness, He willed to create beings to whom He would communicate this life and love, and whom He would have participate in that life which is proper to Himself alone. You also know there is no other life, nor any other, comparable to this. Hence, those who do not share it are not really alive.

You know that God willed to communicate this life and love of His to angels. When they were put to the test, some failed and went to Hell; others passed and entered into eternal bliss. Then God willed to communicate this life and love to men. When put to the test, Adam and Eve both failed. But God willed to restore that life and love and communicate it anew to men through Christ Jesus. That is why there was a *kenosis* — "an emptying." That is why the Second Person of the Blessed Trinity, who, like the First, was a source of life, assumed a human nature in such a way as to make that created humanity the very humanity of the Son of God, and hence, filled to fullness with the divine life. Through this unique humanity, which the Son of God assumed, this same divine life which He received from the Father will be communicated to all men who will receive it.

There is the plan of God as learned from looking on His face and listening to His Word. The people of the Old Testament never knew this plan. Pagans had not the slightest idea of its existence. That is why you find them bewildered by the omnipresence of this thing called pain. They knew not what to do with it, for they knew not why it was. Aristotle, Plato, and Plotinus knew God, but how nebulous was their knowledge of Him! If Yahweh was faceless, what must you call the "immovable Prime Mover" or the "self-thinking Thought" or that "Unity" which was the "dialectical residue of the flight of the mind from multiplicity"? Yet, what else did Aristotle, Plato, or Plotinus have? Such was the knowledge of these much-admired Greek philosophers. The wisdom of Chinese and Hindu sages was no greater. But you have seen the face of God. You know Christ, and "in Him are to be found hidden all the treasures of wisdom and knowledge."[314]

Because the gods of the pagans had no face, these ancients, the best of them, had but two attitudes they could recommend toward pain. One is manifest in the hard, set face of the Stoic. Some people have admired this face. They think they have found something noble in the hard, set features. A closer study would show them fatuous. For Stoicism was, and is, just a foolish flight from reality. Pain is real. Pain is omnipresent. Pain is almost omnipotent. Pain can no more be avoided than can the pressure of atmosphere. Any person who tries to be insensible to it has ceased to be human.

The other face the ancients would turn to this omnipresent thing was that of the hedonist, the pleasure-worshiper, or the Epicurean, whose god was his belly.[315] Again you are faced with the fatuous, for you are faced with flights from reality. Escape is sought from what cannot be fled. The laugh of the roisterer is hollow, when it is not brittle. He who would escape pain by rioting wakes up in greater pain than that which he tried to escape.

∽

Christ has transformed pain

Because the ancients knew so little about history, life, time, and person, what could they possibly make of that which visits every person, is found in every life, fills time, and does much to make history — that thing called pain? But you have seen the face

[314] Col. 2:3.
[315] Phil. 3:19.

of God as He broke into history and time — not to divide time, but to fulfill it; not to disrupt history, but to direct it to triumphant achievement.

Ever since that moment, pain has ceased to be a problem, far less a perplexity. Suffering has been changed from a profound mystery to something pulsing with meaning both personal and divine; and sorrow's face can be lighted with rapture even when drenched with tears. Because of Christ, pain has been all but transubstantiated. It remains pain, and it hurts the human, but it throbs with all the holiness of God for those who, like you, are in Christ Jesus.

Jesus Christ suffered a Passion of pain. Ultimately, it killed Him. But, with it, He redeemed mankind and restored to God all His outraged glory. Christians must do the same even if they have to suffer a "passion" of it — even if it kills them. They are to take it and use it for the salvation of men and for the glory of God, who is still outraged.

Now you are at the heart of the fire, and this truth must burn its way into your being until you are branded with it as ineradicably as you are with the character of Christ.

You have seen the face of God in the features of a Child born in direst poverty — in a cave, bound in swaddling clothes and laid in the trough from which cattle fed. Because you know that that Child's face is the face of God, the pain that will always accompany poverty will be seen by you as something that makes you like unto God. Could anything be more welcome to a human being? It is not only blessed; it is deifying! In it you hear the voice of God speaking the first beatitude.[316]

---

[316] "Blessed are the poor in spirit, for theirs is the kingdom of Heaven"; Matt. 5:3.

You have seen the face of God in the little Jewish exile in Egypt.[317] The pain of your own exile from Heaven, the pain that pierces those deported and displaced, the searing pain of homelessness can be received with greater equanimity, and all the suffering entailed can be used as the little Jewish exile in Egypt used His. He was redeeming men then just as when He was on the Cross, for He was doing the Father's will and making reparation for sin.

You have seen the face of God wet with sweat in the face of the village Carpenter at Nazareth. You know now how to labor and, with your sweat, not only win a living, but fashion a life — a life like that of the Incarnate Son of God. Work, for you, is worship.

You have seen the face of God covered with blood in Gethsemani and on Golgotha. You know now what to do with agony and how to bear a cross.

Pain was in the world before Christ came. It remained in the world after He had gone to Heaven. For He had not come to take away the Cross, but to take it up. Since He took it up and died on it atop that hill outside the Holy City, no man need ever again climb any hill outside any city and die a meaningless crucifixion. Because Christ bore a Passion of it, pain has a divine signification and is endowed with almost infinite power for good. But it must be borne in Christ and for Christ. There is your answer — the *only* answer to the problem of pain: because the Vine climbed the trellis of the Cross, the branches can now spread themselves wide on the same wood and find it is a ladder leading to glory!

That does not mean that pain has lost its power to pierce Christians; or suffering, its ability to sear; or sorrow, that poignancy and weight that can break human hearts. It only means

---

[317] Cf. Matt. 2:13.

that none of these three is evil; that each is the justice, mercy, and love of God to men; that each is to be taken by Christians and used for the *pleroma* ("filling up") of Christ.

∞

You can assist in Christ's plan of salvation

It was Paul who gave you the first word that told you half of history. It is the same Paul who gives you the other that completes the story. He told his Philippians about the *kenosis* of God that wrought redemption. But note well: it did not accomplish salvation. Christ could, and did, redeem alone. But Jesus did not, nor can He, save without assistance. That is where you and all your pains come in. The *kenosis*, the "emptying," of Calvary, accomplished by God, makes possible a *pleroma*, or "filling up," that can be accomplished by men. The first was done in Christ Jesus, for God, as God, cannot suffer. The second must be done the same way — in Christ Jesus — for men, as mere men, cannot save.

So you see how it is that this *pleroma* fills to the brim every split second of earthly existence with significance for eternity. God and men depend on you and what you do with pain. You are to use it as Paul told his Colossians he used it: "to fill up what is wanting to His Passion for His Body, which is the Church."[318]

Once you really know who you are, and what you are to do, time, that commodity which so many recklessly squander, takes on eternal import. And suffering, so universally shunned, is seen as something sacred. The culmination of God's *kenosis*, marked by that "It is finished"[319] of Christ, shows you time's midmost moment, history's center, and the turning point in the drama of mankind.

[318] Col. 1:24.
[319] John 19:30 (Revised Standard Version).

For to that splendid moment, all previous time had anxiously looked forward; and to it, every future moment of time must gratefully look back. For without it, past, present, and future time would be nothing but sand dropping through an hourglass. With it, every flashing moment is alight with the glory of God.

Time is for Christ — all of it. What went before Him was all anticipation; what follows Him should be nothing but fulfillment. Hence, the Epic of Existence — be it that of the individual man or of the human race — is told completely in the two Greek words: *kenosis* and *pleroma*, and each bespeaks both Christ and you!

This fact is the pivot from which swings everything: God's glory, man's happiness, time's meaning, eternity's bliss, Christ's success, and the triumph of Christians. It makes pain look altogether different and gives a new face to all suffering; for with what so many call *misery*, you can help God on to success; for you can "fill up" what is wanting; you can make a *pleroma* of Christ's Passion.

That is the revelation made to you by St. Paul, who, when in chains, and with death bending over him as he wrote, told his Ephesians and Colossians truths that throb with personal meaning for everyone living at this present moment. In the first letter, he "published to the world the plan of God — the mystery hidden from the beginning of time."[320] You have been studying that plan almost from the first page of this book. It tells how "God chose you out in Christ before the foundations of the world . . . to be His adopted child through Jesus Christ."[321]

In his letter to the Colossians, Paul shows you how to implement that plan by telling you what to do with pain. Paul tells you

[320] Eph. 3:9.
[321] Eph. 1:4-5.

that, like him, you can "rejoice in your sufferings," for by them, in them, and through them, you can do what this flame of living love did for God and man: you can "fill up what is lacking to the sufferings of Christ in your flesh, for His body, which is the Church."

"Rejoice in your sufferings?" you ask. "That is beyond human nature."

The unqualified answer comes back: "Of course. But so are you! You are living in Christ Jesus. You are supposed to do things that are beyond human nature, or else you will not be acting in a way that is natural to you! You were 'born again of water and the Spirit' so that you might be the *pleroma Christi*, the 'filling up of Jesus Christ'!"

Awaken to the fact that Christ Himself is crying for that "filling up" this moment; for without it, His Passion and death, yes, His Resurrection and Ascension will have been in vain for many a soul. He is crying to you to "fill up" so that He who has so magnificently been mankind's Redeemer may now become mankind's Savior, and thus live up to His name of *Jesus*.[322] You can help Him do that by offering Him your pain.

The first pain you should offer is the anguish such knowledge as this brings with it. The pain of exile from your true home; the pain of having to earn a living; the pain of possessing a body that can be visited by such ordinary things as head colds, earaches, eyestrain, and countless other minor ailments — you, and every other human in Christ Jesus, can help the almighty Son of God on to real success by cheerfully accepting such things. Such minor but very common irritations such as having to wait for a train, a bus, or a taxicab, the inconvenience involved in getting a wrong number on the phone or having to wait in a doctor's office — these and

[322] The name *Jesus* means "God saves."

every other trifling discomfort, the ordinary pain of human existence, can be taken and made to contribute to the triumph of Christ's Cross. To know this and yet to see the world ignorant of this tremendous fact, or, worse still, indifferent to it, can cause real anguish of soul. It did to St. Paul. It does to the Pope today. It always will to ardent Christians who love their Christ and all their fellowmen who should be in Christ. It pains to know a truth of such splendor and of such personal import for every human who breathes, yet see millions ignorant of it or, worse still, seé them rebelling.

Who is there who loves God and man and would not ache as did St. Paul, then try to do as he did? He strove "to bring consolation to their hearts, and by strengthening their love, to enrich them with the fullness of understanding and to bring them to the deep knowledge of the divine mystery, Christ. In him are to be found all the treasures of wisdom and knowledge."[323]

The tragedy of your day is not that there is so much pain in the world, but that so much of that pain is not turned to profit for man and for God by making it contribute to the filling up of Christ's Passion.

The fundamental fact that must never be lost sight of is the intimate connection between suffering and sin. John Henry Cardinal Newman and Gilbert Keith Chesterton each found the world so filled with suffering that they fashioned an argument along the same lines as the famous "cosmological argument" of St. Thomas Aquinas, but came to what looked like the opposite conclusion!

Newman, with his usual minuteness of detail, enumerated every kind of suffering, and then ended with the words: "All this is a vision to dizzy and appall; and inflicts upon the mind the sense of

[323] Col. 2:2-3.

a profound mystery, which is absolutely beyond human solution. What shall be said of this heart-piercing, reason-bewildering fact? I can only answer that either there is no Creator, or this living society of men is in a true sense discarded from His presence."

Chesterton was briefer and more devastating. He concluded, "Either there is no God; or, if there is One, He is evil!" Such is the universality of suffering and pain; such is its seeming uselessness. Hence the imperious demand for the only answer — the one you have!

Newman and Chesterton, being believers, had, as the ultimate purpose of their clever reasoning, the heightening of the force of revelation — especially the revelation about Original Sin. Reason alone is completely baffled by this problem of pain. It can be solved only by those who have seen the face of God and heard His voice.

Newman in his *Apologia pro Vita Sua* closed his argument with the words: "Since there is a God, it is obvious that the human race is implicated in some terrible aboriginal calamity. It is out of joint with the purpose of its Creator. This is a fact, a fact as true as the fact of existence; and thus the doctrine of what is theologically called Original Sin becomes as certain as that the world exists, and as the existence of God." Chesterton's conclusion was identical.

∞

Sufferings can be a blessing

Pain had no place in the original plan of God. It is manmade. If Adam had not sinned, you would never have shed a single tear or experienced the tiniest dull ache. Pain is a punishment. Both Christ and Christianity affirm that solidly — not only with words but with the testimony of blood. Yet, since Christ died, pain is no longer *only* a punishment. It can be a privilege. It can be taken as a most precious gift from God, a testimony of His trust in the individual visited by it. It can ever be seized as an opportunity to help His Son on to success by transforming it into that which is needed for salvation.

Since Christ suffered a Passion of pain, one of the purposes of human suffering now is to show men the face of God and let them hear His voice, as Christ Himself once taught His disciples through a miracle. "One day he saw, in passing, a man blind from birth. So his disciples asked him, 'Rabbi, who has sinned, this man or his parents, to account for his having been born blind?' "[324]

There you have the Old Testament mind regarding the source of suffering and its purpose. There also you have the mind of many an uninformed modern. As far as it goes, that mind is sound. Had there been no sin, there never would have been any pain. That is why the Jews in the Old Testament looked on every affliction as a punishment from Heaven on account of sin. But in the New Testament, and very explicitly in this particular passage, Jesus shows you that neither the Old Testament mind nor the uninformed modern mind goes far enough. Pain can have another purpose. " 'Neither this man has sinned,' replied Jesus, 'nor his parents. No. God simply wants to make use of him to reveal His ways.' "[325]

There is revelation for you! On the testimony of Incarnate Truth, affliction can come from God and, far from being a punishment for sin, can be meant merely to open men's eyes to the face of God and their ears to His voice.

Read the rest of that episode for yourself in the ninth chapter of St. John. Never did he or any other Evangelist write a more human story, nor one more palpably divine. You will see why every

[324] John 9:1-2.
[325] John 9:3.

reader must conclude that this man's blindness was meant by God to be a brightness as intense as that of the Star of Bethlehem, and had exactly the same purpose. How can anyone escape that conclusion when the story itself closes with the man expelled from the synagogue kneeling at the feet of Jesus and listening to His voice asking, " 'Do you believe in the Son of God?' 'Well, who is He, Sir' the man answered; 'I want to believe in Him.' 'You are now looking in His face,' replied Jesus; 'yes, it is He who is now speaking to you!' "[326]

As you look out on your world today, you are looking into the face of Christ, and it is He who is speaking to you. You find a face of one in agony, for Christ will be on the Cross until the end of time. There will be a *Parousia* — "a final coming of Christ" — only when there has been a *pleroma* — a "filling up of Christ."

That is why the voice you hear today is saying the same as He said on Calvary. He is crying, "I thirst!"[327] That cry was misunderstood. The soldiers reached Him a sponge filled with vinegar. Though His lips were cracked, His tongue cleaving to the roof of His mouth, His very veins dried and shriveled, He did not drink. For neither wine nor water, nor any other material liquid was what He wanted. The early Fathers of the Church were much more correct when they interpreted that cry as indicative of a spiritual thirst — a thirst for souls. But as you hear it today, you will be most right when you interpret it as a cry for mystical members who will "fill up what is wanting to His sufferings." It is a cry for the *pleroma* — a cry that pain be used rightly.

Christ is in agony, and you can help Him. Today you can do more than Veronica did with her veil; you can do more than the

---

[326] John 9:35-37.
[327] John 19:28.

Cyrenean did with his back; you can do more than the angel of consolation did when he ministered to Him in the Garden of Gethsemani. Today, in a certain sense, you can do more for Him even than His Mother did when she stood beneath His Cross; for while she was Co-Redemptrix, you can be co-savior.

Does the climbing grow more steep? Do you think you are reading just pious rhetoric? Then turn to a man who taught with all the authority of God. Read his sober statements of this identical truth. "Dying on the Cross," says Pius XII in his encyclical *Mystici Corporis*, "Christ left His Church the immense treasury of the Redemption. Toward this she contributed nothing. But when those graces come to be distributed, not only does He share this task of sanctification, but He wants it to be due, in a way, to her action. . . ."

Is that not saying what you have already learned: redemption was accomplished by Christ alone in His physical body; salvation is the work of Christ and His mystical members? "Deep mystery this," continues the Pope, "subject of inexhaustible meditation: that the salvation of many depends on the prayers and the voluntary penances which the members of the Mystical Body of Jesus offer for this intention, and on the assistance of the pastors of souls and of the faithful, especially fathers and mothers of families, which they must offer to our Divine Savior as if they were His associates."

Associates with the Son of God! Associates in the work of salvation! Always practical, the Pope tells you precisely how: "Although our Savior's cruel Passion and death merited for His Church an infinite treasury of graces, God's inscrutable Providence has decreed that these abundant graces should not be granted us all at once; and the amount of grace to be given depends in no small part on our good deeds. They draw to the souls of men this ready flow of heavenly gifts granted by God. These heavenly gifts will surely flow more abundantly if we not only pray fervently to God, especially by participating devoutly every day if possible in the Eucharistic Sacrifice, if we not only try to relieve the distress of the needy by works of Christian charity, but if we also set our hearts on eternal treasure rather than on the passing things of this world; restrain this mortal body by voluntary mortification, denying it what is forbidden, forcing it to do what is hard and distasteful; and, finally, humbly accept as from God's hands, the burdens and sorrows of the present life. Thus, according to the Apostles, we shall fill up those things that are wanting of the sufferings of Christ, in our flesh, for his Body, which is the Church.' "

How simple! Yet how we mortals miss our golden opportunities! If the angels could envy, they would envy you. They have everything in Heaven, yet they lack the glorious burdens of earth! Yes, those burdens, while never ceasing to be burdens, are glorious when they are borne as they should be: as part of the *pleroma*. Because you can suffer the ordinary burdens of everyday life, you are capable of more than the seraphim and cherubim, more than the entire nine choirs of angels. They can, and do, adore Christ. They can, and do, sing His praise. But they cannot, and hence, they do not, help Him in the one work His Father gave Him to do. They cannot, and, hence, do not, help Him save mankind. They are pure spirit. Not so you; you also have flesh. Therefore you can do what no angel will ever be able to do: you can "fill up what is wanting."

There is the highest potentiality of your human nature: the power to be a coadjutor to Christ, an associate with the Son of God, a collaborator in the work of the world's salvation — and all that very particularly by suffering.

∽

You are called to embrace the Cross

To say you are going to suffer is to state the obvious. *Human existence* and *pain* are not synonymous; but they most certainly are correlatives. No one can live without suffering something. Modern medicine can relieve you of much pain, but it cannot kill it entirely. Present-day psychiatry and psychotherapy can do marvels for your mind, but they cannot do away with all anxiety, nor bring perfect and lasting peace. Science can, and has, prolonged life, but science will never banish death. So you are going to suffer. The only question facing you is: How are you going to do it?

You can do it like an animal, for you are part animal. You can howl and flee. You can do it like a mere man, for, in part, you are mere man. You can grit your teeth and bear it. You can set your face like a steely Stoic. Or you can suffer gladly and thus be what God made you to be: a member of Him who once said of Himself, "To throw a firebrand upon the earth — that is my mission! And oh, how I wish it were already in a blaze! But then, I have yet to undergo a baptism, and oh, in what an agony I am until it is accomplished!"[328]

That baptism was a baptism of blood — His own blood. But that shows you what attitude of mind and heart the member of Christ should have toward suffering. It is not something to which you should be simply *resigned*; nor yet something that you more or less willingly *accept*. Suffering is something you should gratefully and gladly *embrace*; something you should *be in an agony* to endure!

Heroic, of course. But no one who has been baptized into Christ Jesus can be anything less.

[328] Luke 12:49-50.

Burn these truths into your being. The cross, as you dramatically, yet truthfully enough, call your afflictions, is still "to the Jews certainly a stumbling block and to the Gentiles an absurdity, but to those who are called, to the Jews and Greeks alike, Christ, the power of God and the wisdom of God."[329]

You have been called. Hence, like Paul, you are to find more wisdom in the "absurdity" of God than in all the wisdom of men and more might in the "weakness" of God than in all the might of men.[330]

Those are texts a lifetime of meditation will not exhaust. But right now they ought to tell you clearly that suffering, when rightly borne, is one of the supreme goods on earth. In a private revelation to one of the greatest mystics of the fourteenth century, the Blessed Henry Suso,[331] God said, "Affliction is a reproach in the eyes of the world, but in my sight, an immense dignity. . . . By suffering, all the virtues are strengthened, a man's soul is made beautiful, his neighbor is edified, and God is glorified. To keep patience in time of adversity is more admirable than to raise the dead or work any other miracles. The world, indeed, calls men who suffer miserable; but I declare them happy, because I have chosen them for myself."

Chosen by God are those who suffer rightly, and chosen for Himself! But weigh that adverb well. Suffering of itself does not sanctify nor save. It must be borne *rightly*. For as St. Augustine observed, "The world is a furnace; sufferings are the fires that burn therein. God is the Artificer who fans those flames. The good are there like gold, the wicked like straw; and the same fire that

---

[329] 1 Cor. 1:23-24.

[330] Cf. 1 Cor. 1:25.

[331] Blessed Henry Suso (c. 1295-1366), German mystic.

purifies the gold consumes the straw. One is reduced to ashes; the other is cleansed of its dross." Suffering must be borne *rightly*.

For you, a member of Christ, who have the privilege of "filling up what is wanting," simple resignation, even if meriting the high title of "Christian resignation," is too negative a manner in which to meet pain. It is good as far as it goes. It is meritorious. But it is nothing compared with what it can be in those who are apprecia-tive of the honor that is theirs: of associating with God in man's salvation.

Acceptance is better than mere resignation. It shows more faith. But it does not yet show enough *fire*. It still leaves you too passive. Christhood calls for passion and a constant consciousness that you are to be the *pleroma* of Christ's Passion. Once you have acquired that consciousness, you will grow in gratitude for every pain, be it of the body or of the mind. You must never forget that Jesus suf-fered a mental agony as well as a physical Passion. He needs mem-bers who will do the same.

There is your answer for those who cannot understand why there is so much mental sickness in your day. Alan Keenan, O.F.M., struck it off beautifully when he named every hospital for the men-tally afflicted "Gethsemani." In them, Christ again suffers what He suffered in the garden. A modern poet put it in telling verse shortly after she had been subjected to shock treatment, during which the attendants had been gentle neither in word nor in work:

> Lord, for the pain I cursed You for last night
> I do most gladly offer thanks today. . . .
> For not in pride, but in deep humility,
> In me, and by me, and through me, I find You!
> In my stripped loneliness, Your own imprisonment —
> My bruises mark Your scourging; and the same

Rude jests ring in my ears that rang in Yours —
And round my aching head I seem to feel
Even today, the racking crown of thorns. . . .
I, too, was bound and though I never died,
I was like You, Jesus — my spirit crucified.[332]

There you have something more than resignation or mere passive acceptance. There you have gratitude! You can have the same if you will take what Cardinal Newman said about himself and make it part of the very substance of your soul. He said, and you can say:

God has committed some work to me
which He has not committed to another.
I have my mission. I may never know it in this life,
but I shall be told it in the next. I shall do good.
I shall do His work, if I but keep His Commandments
and serve Him in my calling.

Therefore, I will trust Him.
Whatever, wherever I am, I can never be thrown away.
If I am in sickness, my sickness may serve Him;
if I am in sorrow, my sorrow may serve Him.
My sickness, or perplexity, or sorrow may be necessary
causes of some great end, which is quite beyond us.
He does nothing in vain. He may prolong my life;
He may shorten it. He knows what He is about.
He may take away my friends; He may throw me among
strangers; He may make me feel desolate, make my spirits sink,
hide the future from me — still He knows what He is about.

[332] Eithne Tabor, *The Cliff's Edge* (New York: Sheed and Ward, 1950).

O my God, I will put myself without reserve into Thy hands.
Wealth or woe, joy or sorrow, friends or bereavement,
honor or humiliation, good report or ill report,
comfort or discomfort, Thy presence or the hiding of
Thy countenance — all is good if it comes from Thee.

There is your answer to what is called the enigma of evil or the problem of pain. It lies in the one word *God*. For if you believe that God exists, you must believe that He is good. If you believe that He is good, you must believe that pain is a privilege, suffering a gift, and sorrow something sent for your glory. It takes faith to see that; but never forget you are a being who breathes faith, for you are a breath of God in a vessel of clay.[333]

Realize, then, that when you have something difficult to bear, God is showing you exceptional mercy and being tenderly kind, for, as Paul said, "If we suffer with Him, we shall be glorified with Him."[334] And there is your final solution to this perplexing problem: you are to suffer *with Him*.

You have seen two ways of handling pain. The first is Christian resignation. It is good; even very good. The second, however, is much better. It is glad and even grateful acceptance. It is saying *yes* to God, who asks you to suffer, and saying it with a smile.

But there is yet "a more excellent way,"[335] and this is truly the Christian way. It is that of joyful oblation or consecration! That is the way Christ did it; that is the way true Christians should do it. "Christ proved His love," says Pius XII in his *Mystici Corporis*, ". . . not only by His tireless labors and constant prayers, but by His sorrows and His sufferings, gladly, lovingly endured. . . . Let us,

[333] Cf. 2 Cor. 4:7.
[334] Rom. 8:17.
[335] 1 Cor. 12:31.

then, not be unwilling to follow in the bloodstained footsteps of our King. The security of our salvation demands it: 'For if we have been planted together in the likeness of His death, we shall also be in the likeness of His Resurrection,' and 'if we be dead with Him, we shall also live with Him.' "

How sacred a thing, then, is suffering. Squander not so much as the smallest crumb of pain. It is priceless. That is why Pius XII pleaded, "From a father's heart, We appeal to all who, from whatever cause, are plunged into grief, to lift their eyes in confidence to Heaven and to offer their sorrows to Him who will one day reward them abundantly. Let them remember that their sufferings are not in vain, but will be to their great gain and that of the Church, if for this purpose they but take courage and bear them with patience. To make this intention more efficacious, the daily use of the offering made by the members of the Apostleship of Prayer[336] will contribute very, very much. . . ."

⁂

Only suffering that is offered to God can save

Note well what the Pope is saying: Suffering of itself does not save. Pain of itself will never purify nor contribute to Christ's *pleroma*. Sorrow of itself will never sanctify. All must be offered to God "for this purpose," the Pontiff says. All must be "consecrated." Because you are a child of Adam, you are going to suffer. But because Baptism made you a member of the Mystical Body of Christ, you can sublimate suffering into something sacred; you can

---

[336] "O Jesus, through the Immaculate Heart of Mary, I offer Thee my prayers, works, and sufferings of this day in union with the Holy Sacrifice of the Mass throughout the world, in reparation for my sins, and for the intention recommended by the Holy Father."

take pain and make of it a *pleroma Christi*, and thus save souls; you can "consecrate" sorrow to the glory of God. This is what you will do if you are true to your real self.

"There never was a time, Venerable Brothers," says Pope Pius XII, "when the salvation of souls did not impose on all the duty of associating their sufferings with the torments of our Divine Redeemer. But today that duty is clearer than ever when a gigantic conflict has set almost the whole world on fire. . . ." Now, note in what your salvific sufferings can consist. As was stressed before, no gory martyrdom is necessary. See what Pius XII prescribes: "Today imposes on everyone, with particular stress, the duty to flee the vices and blandishments of the world, and to renounce the unrestrained pleasures of the body and that worldly frivolity and vanity which contribute nothing to the Christian formation of the soul, nothing toward gaining Heaven. Rather let those words of Our Immortal Predecessor, Leo the Great, be deeply engraven in your minds, that Baptism has made us flesh of the Crucified One. . . . We cannot but plead with all to love Holy Mother Church with a devoted and active love. Let us pray every day to the Eternal Father for her safety and for her happy and large increase. For this intention let us offer to Him our works and our sufferings, if the salvation of the whole human family, bought by divine blood, is really dear to our hearts."

It is very probable that one day you may be gripped by a sickness that will not only throw you prone upon a hospital bed, but will absorb your full consciousness by its burning pain. What are you going to do? You can answer that question fully and infallibly today. For never are habit patterns made more manifest; never is Belloc's statement, "A man is his mind," more clearly borne out, nor can you find more complete proof that we are what our thoughts are than when great suffering grips a person. If one has habitually allowed the animal in his or her make-up to dominate, the animal will come out in the pain. If his or her habitual thoughts have been those of a mere human, an earth dweller merely, then the not-very-inspiring human side will be shown. But if one has drilled into himself the truth that he or she is a member of Christ, then Christ is seen saving mankind; for habit will have taken over, and the sufferer, looking up, will see what the man born blind saw when Jesus asked him, "Do you believe in the Son of God?"

Turn to Chapter 15 of St. John again. "I am the real vine," says Christ, "and my Father is the vinedresser. He prunes away any branch of mine that bears no fruit, and cleans any branch that does bear fruit, that it may bear yet more abundant fruit. . . . I am the vine, you are the branches."[337] Pain is God the Father cleaning one of the Son's branches so that it may bend lower with richer, fuller grapes. Suffering exists so that Jesus, the Vine, may have more fruit. There is sorrow so that the Father may be more highly glorified by branches "bearing more abundantly."

The voice that spoke those truths in the Cenacle was heard in more recent times from the Vatican. The accent is unmistakable. On Valentine's Day of the Marian Year — February 14, 1954 — Christ's Vicar spoke on the radio to the shut-ins and the sick. Just as Jesus relies on His suffering members to make His Redemption a success, so did Pius XII rely on the shut-ins and the sick ones to make the Marian Year a success. He told them so, as he named them "the precious jewels of the Church of God." He then went on to assure them that they had a mission from God in their very sickness and called them "the Church of God's powerful source of spiritual energy."

[337] John 15:1-2, 5.

Pius XII knows the only answer to the problem of pain. That is why he said so lovingly, "Certainly We wish We had the omnipresence of God; We wish We could draw near to each one of you . . . languishing in hospitals large and small, in sanatoriums, clinics, rest-homes, prisons, barracks, under desolate roofs of the poorest, or in rooms set apart in your own homes. Little children with faces pale as flowers which grew without the warmth of the sun; young people whose rare smile expresses strength of soul rather than the fresh bloom of youth; middle-aged people cruelly torn from their usually active lives; the aged, to whose natural weariness sickness has added discomfort and suffering."

Then from the depths of his heart, he exclaimed, "We have always begged Jesus to make Our heart in some way like His: a good heart, a meek heart, a heart open to all sufferings, to all pains. But how greatly We wish We had some reflection of His Omnipotence. How We long to pass in the midst of you, drying tears, bringing comfort, healing wounds, giving back again strength and health."

His Holiness would work miracles if he could. He longs for omnipresence and omnipotence so that he might stand beside each sufferer and do what Jesus did when lepers called out to Him, the blind besought Him, the paralytics lay before Him, or He was brought to the dead. But knowing the overall plan of God for the glory that is to come from creation; knowing how Christ's *kenosis* cries for a *pleroma*; knowing the value of suffering, Pius XII used the radio to give him a species of omnipresence and used the truth of God about sickness to give him some semblance of omnipotence as he worked the miracle of changing men's minds regarding afflictions.

He went first to those who rebel. He found them with contorted features, anger in their hearts, curses on their lips. He bent over them lovingly and whispered, "Soul in anguish, why do you rebel? Let the rays of light, which come from the Cross of Jesus, fall on this dark mystery of suffering. What evil had He done? Look over your bed in the hospital ward; perhaps there is a picture of the Madonna. What evil did she do?"

That is the first point the Pontiff scored: Christ, the Head, and that loveliest, loftiest member, who is also Mother, of the Mystical Body, suffered as no other members will ever suffer, but certainly not because of any evil they had done. Suffering, then, is not always a punishment for personal sins. The Pope calls it "God's mercy, not His revenge."

Yet he does point out that sin merits punishment; mortal sin, eternal damnation. "Think back," says the Pontiff. "Perhaps you have offended God many times, in many ways . . . yet, you are still alive, under the merciful gaze of God, and in the loving arms of Mary. If, then, the Lord is now punishing some sin of yours, you should not on that account curse and debase yourself. You are not a slave being punished by a cruel master, but a child of God, your Father, who wishes not to take revenge, but to correct you. He wants you to say to Him, 'I have sinned,' so He can pardon you and restore you to the life of the soul."

That is a consoling truth for sinners. For the sinless who are suffering and rebelling, the Pope had this startling parallel: "Even the misfortunes of the innocent are a mysterious manifestation of divine glory," he says. Then he points to the Pietà. "Look at the Holy and Immaculate Mother: she holds in her lap the lifeless body of her divine Son. Could you possibly imagine that the sorrowful Mother would curse God — that she would ask the reasons for such sufferings?"

The Pope then gives those reasons and shows how precious is this thing called pain. "We would not have been redeemed if that

Mother had not seen her Son die in torment, and there would not have been for us any possibility of salvation." The Pope is saying Redemption was not salvation. But just as the first was wrought by suffering borne by the Mystical Body's Head and its Mother; so will the second be achieved by suffering borne by its members.

"Perhaps," the Pope continues, "you have desired martyrdom. You have dreamed that the chance might be offered you to suffer for Jesus. Give glory to God! Your bodily affliction is like shedding blood; it is a real form of martyrdom."

But even with that, the Pope is not finished. To be like the martyrs is great, but it is not all. "Do you want to be like Jesus?" asks the Pontiff. "Do you want to transform yourself into Him? Do you want to be a channel of life for Him? In sickness you will find the Cross. Be nailed to it, and thus die to yourself so that He may live in you and make use of you. . . . Would you like to help Jesus save souls? Then offer Him your sufferings. . . . Your sacrifice, united to the Sacrifice of Jesus, will bring many sinners back to the Father; many without faith will find the true faith; many weak Christians will receive strength to live fully the teaching and the law of Christ. And on the day on which the mystery of Providence in the economy of salvation will be revealed in Heaven, you will see at last to what extent the world of the healthy is your debtor."

You will have "filled up what is wanting" and brought success to the woman who sorrowed over the dead One who is the Source of life.

Chapter Ten

ɔ๑๑

You are one who can pay God back
in his own coin — superabundantly

God gave hearts as well as minds to men. When those hearts find
gift after gift given them by God, they cry out instinctively, "What
return can I make to this lavishly giving God?"[338]

The answer to that question will never be given until you know
yourself as you really are. When first posed, this question finds you
feeling bankrupt; for you believe that were you to barter your all
and give it to God, you would still be deep in debt. But you have
enough, and more than enough, to pay God back. You can do it
"superabundantly."

ɔ๑๑

God Himself fashioned you

Look into your eyes, and ask yourself who chose their color.
Most certainly you did not. Nor did your parents. No one had a
word to say about their color but your God. There is the first revelation, and it should arouse a surge of holy respect for self, a respect
that is tinged with reverence; for the Infinite, the omniscient God

---

[338] Cf. Ps. 115:12 (RSV = Ps. 116:12).

was the one who chose the color of your eyes, and He did it, as He does everything, from eternity! How near is God! Who but He could have made possible for you the marvel of sight?

Who was it that kindled the light of life in those eyes of yours? Who keeps it burning? You know the answer: He alone who is Life could kindle such flames. He alone can keep them glowing. Think of all the pleasure you have had by means of those two eyes: the silent wonder of His night sky, the restless green and blue of His seas, the hushed glory of this morning's dawn, and the flaming beauty He so often uses to mark the day's end. And what of the love light you have seen in other eyes — the warm affection you have watched suffuse some other human face? Had you no light, you would never have seen anything. And never forget that God is the Light of the World! How near is your God!

Think of the brain that is lodged behind those eyes. You know that there are over two billion cells there, all interconnected by fleshy wires, thinner than any thread, yet truer to their specific tasks than the compass needle in pointing to the north. It was God who arranged every last "wire." It is He who keeps them functioning so flawlessly. Thanks to His management of such an intricate "exchange," you can enjoy anything and everything from the light kiss of a summer's breeze to the eloquent pressure from the palm of a friend's hand; anything and everything from the peculiarly soothing scent and sound of rain to the touch of the sun and the silent symphony of the summer night. As you look at your eyes and think, the one word *God* is about all you can gasp, but the subtle question forms itself: "What return shall I make?"

From time to time, you must have marveled at the ingenuity of man that, by means of the radio, can take the thin, clear note of a violin, fling it across a modern city's harsh din, then bring it into your room with all the delicate loveliness it had when the artist brought it to birth by his bow. You have reason to marvel at such ingenuity. To think that you can sit in your room and, by a twist of a tiny dial, have the metallic fingers of your radio reach out into space and pluck from it a melody that is being played two, five, maybe ten thousand miles away.

But have you ever given any thought or study to the delicate organs that catch, condense, concentrate, sharpen, or soften sound so that you can hear? God tuned many thousands of harp strings, then strung them within the shelter of your shell-like ear. They are sensitive enough to catch the lullaby of the leaves, yet strong enough to report the crashing of a world. Who but God could have fashioned so wondrous an instrument? Those thousands upon thousands of strings do not stretch or shrink in extremes of temperature; they are not worn by weather, nor rendered untrue by constant use. Who but God could give you such a marvel?

Who but God could give you the sense organ by which you distinguish the fragrance of a rose from the still more delicate scent of a violet? When you think of the equally delicate and complex senses of taste and touch, your heart makes you ask, "How can I requite the Lord?"

If this heart question tends to become urgent from scanning the surface of your senses, what will it be when you stare at the light in your eyes and realize it is evidence of the presence of an immortal soul within you? That flickering light in your eyes tells of eternity! Twenty, thirty, fifty, surely one hundred short years ago, you were nothing. Now you are living, and will go on living forever! A brief moment of time back, you were not even a name — no, not even dust. Today you are splendor in some way kin to the seraphim — and can be such forever! Unknown to any human just a few decades back, hence, utterly unloved by man or woman, you have always been, and always will be, a name to the everlasting

God and can be an object of love to Him forever! Before time was, you were with Him who always was and ever will be. Your eternity has already begun and because you, as you, have always been known and loved by the only Eternal One, you have always been eternal.

∞

God has given you countless blessings

He who is timeless chose the exact moment of time you were to be changed from a possible being into an actual one. He selected your parents, and like all His choices, it was an infinitely wise one. He endowed your soul with memory, intellect, and will. He made your will free with His own freedom and thus fashioned you into His very image and likeness. With that mind of yours, you can come to know not only an almost infinite number of truths, but actually to know Him who is infinite truth. With that will of yours, you can love not only everything that is good, but Him who gave that goodness to all things, simply because He *is*, by His very essence, good. With that memory of yours, you can recall all that is beautiful and, as you have already learned, know an aching nostalgia for Him who *is* beauty. This kind of thinking has you breathlessly asking, "How can I ever pay?"

But what will you do if you use your memory to go back over all your years, recalling every joy that has been yours — joys that came through your faculties and senses, joys that came from parents, family, relatives, friends, and mere acquaintances? Can you count those joys? Each came from God ultimately! What of the limitless love He has allowed you from the day you first recognized the face of her who gave you birth, down to the latest friend who has shown you real love? Every morsel of it came from God and, ultimately, simply because He loves you!

God has been prodigal in His giving to you. Each new day is like a new birth, and it is a day loaded with "birthday presents" from God! But think now of the wonder of your rebirth by Baptism.

God could have blessed you with brains and beauty; given you power and popularity; granted you every success in the social, economic, academic, and political spheres; and favored you above all your fellows, yet these "and all the world besides" would be nothing compared with that one gift which enables you to lift your eyes and say from your heart, "I believe in God, the Father Almighty . . . and in Jesus Christ, His only Son, our Lord. . . ."[339] For in granting you that gift, God really struck all scales from your eyes and allowed you to see reality, and view it in the light that never fades. Faith is the gift of gifts. God gave it to you!

You have already reviewed the fact that some smart, but not very wise, scientists would have you looking on the earth as little more than a grain of sand lost in immeasurable space, and on man as those mites that move across the surface of that sand. They like to impress people with the fact that those mites move for only the merest flash of time. From such "cosmic views" you cannot view fellowmen or yourself as other than infinitesimal.

But as you, in the quiet of your room, look into your eyes and realize that you were known and loved by the omniscient and omnipotent God before time was or space began to be; that He so loved you as to give His only-begotten Son; that this Son loved you enough to "empty Himself" not only of divine glory but even of human life; then you can only pity these "learned" scientists, for you, and every other "mite" on this grain of sand called the earth, are of more import and concern to the infinite God than the Milky Way with all its galaxies or even the entire universe.

[339] Apostles' Creed.

You also know that the "flash" of time which is your earthly existence means more to God than all the eons of time it has taken for the solar system to evolve. One beat of your heart, properly directed, the slightest movement of your free will, can mean more to the triune God than all the gyrations of sun, moon, stars, and sea from time's first moment until time's final end. In order that you might say, "I believe in God . . ." the heavens were one time moved as "darkness fell upon the whole land, the earth shook, the rocks were rent, tombs were opened and many of the dead rose to life."[340] In order that you might say, "I believe in Jesus Christ . . ." God not only became a beggar on earth, but a corpse on a criminal's Cross. The price paid for your act of faith was infinite! What return can you make?

∞

You are a member of God's family

Realize now that, thanks to Baptism, you have been taken into the family of God! With perfect right and truth you can call the Trinity's First Person "Father," the Second Person "Brother," and the Third Person your "Spouse." Since you are a member of God's own household, you have angels — nine choirs of them — as friends, all the saints as intimates, and the Mother of God as your own Mother.

Thanks to this gift of faith, while still in exile and far from home, you can hold converse with God and with all in Heaven any hour of the day or night; for you can pray. Think of the gift God gave you in the Church with her Seven Sacraments. When your eyes were closed to the sight of God, He opened them by the miracle of Baptism. When they were still youthful eyes, He

[340] Matt. 28:45, 51-52.

cleared them of fear by Confirmation. When they were guilty eyes, He gently cleansed them by His miracle of Penance. When they were lonely eyes, He came to them in Holy Communion. If they glow with human love, He will sanctify that glow by Matrimony. If they should burn with holy ardor, He will chrism them with Holy Orders. If they become sick, dim, and hold the glint of death, He hurries to them with the Sacrament of the Sick. What return can you make?

How near is your God? If you are looking in the right manner, you can see God everywhere and in everything. The good poets, who are seers, have expressed this truth well. Joseph Mary Plunkett saw ". . . His Blood upon the rose, and in the stars the glory of His eyes." Joyce Kilmer, looking at the loveliness of a tree, sang, "Only God could make a tree." Of a wildflower Francis Thompson exclaimed, "His finger pushed it through the sod; that flower is redolent of God!" He closed his *Orient Ode* with those magnificent lines:

> When men shall say to you: "Lo, Christ is here!"
> When men shall say to you: "Lo, Christ is there!"
>   Believe them!
>   And know that thou art seer
>   When all thy crying clear
> Is but: "Lo, here! Lo, there! Ah me, lo, everywhere!"

"Blessed are the pure of heart," said Christ in His first sermon, "for they shall see God."[341] You can be pure of heart. You can see God everywhere, but nowhere so wonderfully as under the snowy garb of a consecrated wafer of wheat or in a golden cup that holds what looks like wine, but is the Blood of Christ Jesus. How near is

[341] Matt. 5:8.

God — near enough to take Him into your mouth — Body and Blood, Soul and Divinity! God — your food and drink! How can you make a return?

So many go to the grave before ever reaching boyhood or girl-hood. God has kept you alive. He has to have an infinitely wise purpose. Part of that purpose is that you pay Him back in some sort of just measure for the countless gifts He has given you. Never forget the Gospel story of the lepers, and the anguished query of the Christ: "Were not the ten made clean? Where are the other nine? Oh, to find that not one has returned to give glory to God except this foreigner!"[342] God loves gratitude.

Faced with the same problem, Ignatius of Loyola finally made reply by saying, "Take, O Lord, and receive my liberty. Take my will, my mind, my memory; take and receive whatever I hold or possess: my body with all its senses and every organ; my talents, my toils, my time — take all!" Then he adds, "Thou didst give them all to me; I now restore them all to Thee." Magnificent oblation. A lover's tribute. Nothing is held back. Complete, all-out surrender. Such is the only fitting reply to give to a God who has dowered man with all man holds. But Ignatius asked one thing. It is a lover's request — legitimate, and even necessary if he was to go on loving: "Give me Thy love and Thy grace. With these I am rich enough and ask for nothing more."

That famed prayer "Take and Receive" of St. Ignatius is a magnificent reply to "How can I make a return?" Yet, when you make it, although you have given your all, you know you have not given enough. So the question perdures and becomes even more pressing. It can be answered — answered by you and answered more than adequately. You can pay God back in His own coin and even

[342] Luke 17:17-18.

in His own measure! You have something to offer God that is worthy of Him and commensurate with His donations to you, for you can tender Infinity to the Infinite.

∞

You are a priest of God

Now you are at a point where you wonder if your earthy words have lost their meaning. Yet, when you know yourself, you know that the words just written about you and your power to repay are literally true. But do you know yourself? Do you know yourself as priest of the Most High God? That word *priest* is used in its literal sense and with its ordinary meaning. You are a priest according to the order of Melchisedech — and you are a priest forever.[343]

Stamped on your soul is a character that the fires of Hell cannot burn away. It is the character of the priesthood of Jesus Christ, the New Law's only High Priest. It was stamped there by Baptism, and it can never be effaced. When you were reborn of "water and the Spirit," you were sealed with the seal of God. Nothing, absolutely nothing, can remove that seal. When you were confirmed with chrism and the Holy Spirit, deeper into your being was burned the character of Christ — the character of high priest. You may not have received Holy Orders; you may even be one who could not receive holy orders; yet, the fact remains that so long as you have been baptized and confirmed, you have already been "ordained" — and "ordained" a priest of God! Being a priest, you can offer God sacrifice that is *acceptable!* You can pay God back in His own coin — and even in His own measure, which is "pressed down, shaken together, running over."[344] Lift up your heart! Rejoice with

[343] Cf. Ps. 109:4 (RSV = Ps.110:4).
[344] Luke 6:38.

great joy! For you can make requital that is superabundant, for you are one who can offer Mass!

Never again may you say that you will "go" to Mass, or that you will "attend" Mass, or that you will "hear" Mass. You go to a show; you attend a meeting; you hear an opera. In each case, you are passive; you are receiving something. But the Mass is action itself. It is the action of the New Law and of the Mystical Body. And you, because you are a priest, must be highly active in it!

You "assist" at Mass. That is to say, you actively cooperate in the great action. It was St. Pius X[345] who told you to "pray" the Mass. By that he meant that you were to say the same prayers the priest at the altar says. When you follow that directive, you cooperate; you assist; very truly you "say" Mass. So the best and truest formula for you to use in the future is that you are going to "offer Mass." That is not only the liturgically correct but the theologically exact formula. And it is to be used by man, woman, and child who has reached the age of reason.

It was the first Pope, Christ's own apostle and appointee, who originally told this wondrous truth to mankind; and he told it in the first letter he ever wrote. Because it speaks of all you have been learning about yourself — your rebirth, salvation, oneness with Christ, and your manner of requiting God — it has special force and fittingness here. "You have been born anew," says St. Peter, not of perishable seed, but of imperishable, through the living and abiding word of God."[346] "As newborn babes, long for the unadulterated spiritual milk, so that you may grow up to salvation in the Lord. You have already tasted how sweet He is. Draw near to Him, the living Stone, rejected indeed by men, but chosen and honored

---

[345] St. Pius X (1835-1914), Pope from 1903.
[346] 1 Pet. 1:23 (Revised Standard Version).

by God. You also, as living stones, are being built into a spiritual edifice."[347]

That is Peter's paraphrase of the "Vine and branches" mentioned by Christ, and of the "Head and members" so dear to St. Paul. It is the first Pope's presentation of the Mystical Body; his insistence on your oneness with Christ Jesus. The Prince of the Apostles goes on to say, "You are being built . . . so as to be a holy priesthood to offer up spiritual sacrifices which will be acceptable to God through Jesus Christ." Then Christ's first Vicar concludes with these resounding truths: "You, however, are a chosen race, a royal priesthood, a holy nation, a people that is God's possession, that you may proclaim the excellence of Him who called you out of darkness into His marvelous light."[348]

Pius XI, in that moving encyclical of his on Reparation to the Sacred Heart,[349] proclaimed the priesthood of the laity plainly when he said, "For not only are they partakers in the mysteries of this priesthood and in the duty of offering sacrifices and satisfaction to God, who have been appointed by Jesus Christ the High Priest as ministers of such sacrifices . . . but also those Christians called, and rightly so, by the Prince of the Apostles, 'a chosen generation, a kingly priesthood,' who are to offer 'sacrifices for sin,' not only for themselves but for all mankind, and this in much the same way as every priest and 'high priest taken from among men is ordained for men in the things that appertain to God.' "

Pius XII, in his encyclical on the Mystical Body, taught the same truth and with even more appositeness for the lesson you are learning about paying God back superabundantly; for the Pope

---

[347] 1 Pet. 2:2-5.

[348] 1 Pet. 2:9.

[349] *Miserentissimus Redemptor*, May 8, 1928.

says, "Through the Eucharistic Sacrifice, Our Lord wished to give special evidence to the faithful of our union among ourselves and with our Divine Head, marvelous as it is and beyond all praise. For here the sacred ministers act in the person not only of the Savior, but of the whole Mystical Body and of every one of the faithful. In this act of sacrifice through the hands of the priest, whose word alone had brought the Immaculate Lamb to be present on the altar, the faithful themselves, with one desire and one prayer offer it to the Eternal Father — the most acceptable Victim of praise and propitiation for the Church's universal needs."

That you are a priest is a truth that has always been held by the Church, but not always insisted upon with equal force and clarity in every age. The early Fathers of the Church, both Latin and Greek, taught it clearly enough. Irenaeus said, "All the just have the priestly order."[350] St. Jerome, in his dialogue against the Luciferians, spoke of "the priesthood of the laity, that is, Baptism."[351] Augustine, in his *City of God*, wrote, "We say that all Christians are priests, seeing that they are the members of the one Priest."[352] Chrysostom, with his wonted eloquence, says, "Thou wert made a priest in Baptism."[353]

Just how this sacrament bestowed the priesthood of Christ on the layman remained somewhat obscure for centuries. In a dim way, it was recognized that there was some connection between the character it imposed and this ordination. But it waited for Aquinas, who was really intrigued by this matter of sacramental

---

[350] St. Irenaeus (c. 130-c. 200; Bishop of Lyons), *Adversus Haereses*, 4, 8, 3.

[351] St. Jerome (c. 342-420; biblical scholar), *Dialogue against the Luciferians*, ch. 4.

[352] St. Augustine, *City of God*, Bk. 20, ch. 10.

[353] St. John Chrysostom, Homily 3 on II Corinthians.

character, to elucidate the point. In a passage that has become classical, St. Thomas wrote: "The whole rite of the Christian religion is derived from Christ's Priesthood. Consequently it is clear that the sacramental character is specially the character of Christ, to whose character the faithful are likened by reason of the sacramental characters, which are nothing else than certain participations of Christ's Priesthood, flowing from Christ Himself."[354]

So there can be no question about it: you are a priest. You have been twice stamped with that character which is a sharing in the only priesthood of the New Law — Christ's own!

What a person you are: summoned by God out of nothingness to share in His life; summoned again by the same God out of your grave of sin and given a share in His own holiness, His divine life, for grace made you a "partaker in the divine nature."[355] It rendered you like unto God. But Baptism and Confirmation did more than give you grace; they branded you with the character of Christ and made you a sharer in His priesthood.

Strange as it may seem, that is as far as St. Thomas went. He did not draw out the natural and inescapable conclusions from his marvelous discovery. He did not show the world the connection between the character received in Baptism and Confirmation and the offering of the Holy Sacrifice of the Mass. True, he distinguished clearly between "consecrating priests" and those who may only "offer." But he went no further.

Undoubtedly it was because God wished you to thrill to the full truth about your priesthood, just as it is obvious that He wanted you to know the breathtaking joy that comes from the complete truth of your membership in Christ's Mystical Body. That is why

[354] *Summa Theologica*, III, Q. 63, art. 3.
[355] 2 Pet. 1:4.

He exercised His Providence in such a way that, while He had His Council of Trent condemn Luther, Wycliff, the Lollards, the Waldensians, and all others who would in any way distort this magnificent truth about the priesthood of the laity, and try to make every baptized person equally a priest with those who have received Holy Orders — and condemn with anathemas that leave no loophole — yet He did not have that Council do anything more positive in this matter than to define the *existence* of these three characters as the result of reception of these three sacraments.

God then had a humble Jesuit, a mere commentator on Sacred Scripture, start the curtain rising on the magnificence of you and your life as priest of the Most High. Cornelius a Lapide, S.J.,[356] commenting on the words of St. Peter you have seen so often already, after clearly setting forth the fact that *priesthood* may be taken in a twofold sense, added these thought-provoking words: "The faithful layman is therefore called, and is, a priest; but a mystic one. First, because he is a member of a Church which has true priests, and of Christ, who is sovereign High Priest. Secondly, because by assisting the true priests, by serving them, supporting them, cooperating with them, he offers a true sacrifice at Mass."

It was not too explicit a statement of the relation between the character of Baptism and the Sacrifice of the Mass, but it was something. It started theologians weighing the words of St. Augustine, found in his 351st Sermon: "The Priest alone [Jesus Christ] . . . yet, clearly, the whole Priest, will stand there . . . that is, with the Body added of which He is the Head. . . . It is to Him that the apostle Peter said, 'Chosen race, royal Priesthood.' "

The weighing of these words brought results, as is evidenced by Matthias Joseph Scheeben, who has been called "the greatest

---

[356] Cornelius a Lapide (1567-1637), Flemish Jesuit and exegete.

genius among nineteenth-century theologians." He states very directly how you are to offer Mass. "With regard to the worship that is to be offered to God," he writes, "the designation or consecration which the character confers on us is obviously of far greater and more universal import. For all the characters empower and oblige us to participate, in greater or lesser degree, in Christ's acts of worship. Above all, the character conferred by the sacrament of Holy Orders so conforms the priest to offer the sacrifice of Christ. . . . But the baptismal character enables all others, if not to re-enact, at any rate, to offer this Sacrifice to God as their own, as a Sacrifice truly belonging to them in the strength of their membership in the Body of Christ."[357]

∞

You can repay God by offering Him the Mass

The Mass, then, is *yours!* You *are* a priest! You can offer the Mass to Almighty God. But the Mass is the only Son of God, co-infinite, co-eternal, co-equal to the Father in all things, consubstantial with Him. Therefore, *you* can pay God back — in *His own* coin — and pay Him back *superabundantly.* For "where sin abounded, grace did more abound."[358] You, a finite creature, can offer your infinite Creator, Him who is Infinite.

Now your eyes ought to tell you whatever the last chapter failed to tell. If those eyes of yours fill with pain, you have wheat for tomorrow's Sacrifice. If those eyes cloud with sorrow, you have wine that can be offered to the Father "in Christ, through Christ, with Christ." But never forget that if those eyes light with joy, you

---

[357] Quoted by Gerald Ellard in *The Mass of the Future* (Milwaukee: The Bruce Publishing Company, 1948), 181.
[358] Rom. 5:20.

again have something that can be "transubstantiated." Is life, at last, becoming life for you? Do you begin to see how real religion is! Are you commencing to know yourself truly?

Pius XI tells you how to live and be your real self in these words: "Though the ample Redemption of Christ more than abundantly satisfied for all offenses, nevertheless, by reason of the marvelous disposition of Divine Wisdom by which we may 'fill up those things that are wanting to the sufferings of Christ in our flesh, for His Body, which is the Church,' we are able, in fact we should add to the acts of praise and satisfaction which 'Christ in the name of sinners has presented to God,' our own acts of praise and satisfaction. . . . For this reason we must bring together, in the august Sacrifice of the Blessed Eucharist, the act of immolation made by the priest with that of the faithful, so that they, too, may offer themselves up as 'living sacrifice, holy, well-pleasing unto God.' . . .

"The Apostle admonished us that 'bearing about in our body the mortifications of Jesus' and 'buried together with Him by Baptism unto death,' not only should we 'crucify our flesh with the vices and concupiscences,' 'flying the corruption of that concupiscence which is in the world,' but also that 'the life of Jesus be made manifest in our bodies,' and, having become partakers in His holy and eternal priesthood, we should offer up 'gifts and sacrifices for sin.' "

That passage, in unmistakable language, tells you who you are, and what you are to do. It comes much more from God the Holy Spirit, through the apostles Peter and Paul, than it does from Pope Pius XI. Nevertheless there have been those who claim that even here it is not said that laymen actually offer the Sacrifice of the Mass. So turn to Pius XII. In words that are most direct, he tells you, "In this act of Sacrifice through the hands of the priest, whose word alone has brought the Immaculate Lamb to be present on the altar, the faithful themselves with one desire and one prayer offer it to the Eternal Father."

That clear statement is found in the encyclical on the Mystical Body. But some enthusiasts exaggerated this truth and, perhaps all unwittingly, revived the error of Luther, Wycliff, and the rest, which would have all the faithful on the same level of priesthood as those men who have received Holy Orders. This, of course, could not be countenanced.

That is why you read in *Mediator Dei*,[359] "There are today, Venerable Brethren, those who, approximating to errors long since condemned, teach that, in the New Testament, by the word *priesthood* is meant only that priesthood which applies to all who have been baptized. . . . It is superfluous to explain how captious errors of this sort completely contradict the truths we have just stated above, when treating of the place of the priest in the Mystical Body of Jesus Christ. But we must not forget that the priest acts for the people only because he represents Jesus Christ, who is Head of all the members and offers Himself in their stead. Hence he goes to the altar as the minister of Christ, inferior to Christ, but superior to the people. The people, on the other hand, since they in no sense represent the divine Redeemer and are not a mediator between themselves and God, can in no way possess the sacerdotal power, that is, the power to consecrate. All this has the certitude of faith. However, it must be added that the faithful do offer the divine Victim, though in a different sense."

He immediately goes on to stress the truth, saying, "This has already been stated in the dearest terms by some of our predecessors and some doctors of the Church. 'Not only,' says Innocent III of immortal memory, 'do the priests offer the Sacrifice, but also all

[359] On the Sacred Liturgy, November 20, 1947.

the faithful: for what the priest does personally by virtue of his ministry, the faithful do collectively by virtue of their intention.' We are happy to recall one of St. Robert Bellarmine's[360] statements on this subject. 'The Sacrifice,' he says, 'is principally offered in the person of Christ. Thus the oblation that follows the Consecration is a sort of attestation that the whole Church consents in the oblation made by Christ, and offers it along with Him.' "

But to bring this truth home more realistically, the Pope turns to the very prayers of the Mass and says they "signify and show no less clearly that the oblation of the Victim is made by the priests in company with the people. For not only does the sacred minister, after the oblation of the bread and wine, when he turns to the people, say the significant prayer, 'Pray, brethren, that our sacrifice may be acceptable to God the Father Almighty'; but also the prayers by which the divine Victim is offered to God are generally expressed in the plural number; and in those it is indicated more than once that the people also participate in this august Sacrifice inasmuch as they offer the same."

There is only one other place in the Mass where the purpose of your offering is brought out with like clarity. That is at the end of the Canon proper, where you, through the lips of the priest, say, "Through Him, with Him, in Him, in the unity of the Holy Spirit, all glory and honor is Yours, Almighty Father, forever and ever." That prayer tells you explicitly that you go to Church to *give* something to God. You give God to God "a pure Victim, a holy Victim, a spotless Victim" and "through Him, with Him, and in Him" you give God "all glory and honor."

Pius XII quoted that prayer and then pointed out that you ratify it by your *amen*. Then he added, "Nor should Christians forget

---

[360] St. Robert Bellarmine (1542-1621), cardinal and theologian.

to offer themselves, their sorrows, their distresses, and their necessities in union with their divine Savior upon the Cross."

You will want also to offer to God in Christ Jesus and through Christ Jesus all your joys! But the climax, as far as you are concerned right now, comes when Pius XII says: "Nor is it to be wondered at, that the faithful should be raised to this dignity. By the waters of Baptism, as by common right, Christians are made members of the Mystical Body of Christ the Priest, and by the 'character' which is imprinted on their souls, they are appointed to give worship to God; thus they participate, according to their condition, in the priesthood of Christ."

Pius XII concludes this passage on your priesthood with the words: "Now, the Sacrifice of the New Law signifies that supreme worship by which the principal offerer Himself, who is Christ, and in union with Him, and through Him, all the members of the Mystical Body, pay God the honor and reverence that are due Him."

There you have an official and authoritative confirmation of the fact that you can pay God back, pay Him in His own coin, and pay Him back superabundantly. Nothing but the Mass really matters for you or for any other member of Christ's Mystical Body, be that membership actual or only potential.

But you, and they, must know just what the Mass is. St. Augustine called the Mass the "Sacrifice of the Mystical Body" and spoke, as you have already seen, of the "whole Priest." By that very expression he intimates that there are differences in your representation of the Sacrifice of Calvary from the Sacrifice Christ Himself offered liturgically in the Cenacle and consummated sacrificially on the Cross.

Emile Mersch, S.J., who has given the world two classics in *The Whole Christ* and *The Theology of the Mystical Body*, tells you definitely in the latter book that there *is* a new element in the Mass.

After insisting that the Mass is "the perpetual pouring out of Christ's life," that it is the "visible coming of the Sacrifice of the Cross to the whole Christian life," he concludes, "The Mass adds nothing to the Cross. God is no more glorified than He was before, and no graces are merited beyond what had already been merited. The fruits which the Mass distributes are those of the Sacrifice of the Cross. But the Mass does distribute them." That is important for you and your work in the Mystical Body. His next few lines are even more important. He says, "What it [the Mass] adds to the Cross, by the power of the Cross, is the universal expansion of the Cross. The Sacrifice of Calvary becomes the Sacrifice of mankind, and the glory it gives to God ascends from mankind. . . . This is the new element contributed by the Mass: The Mass enables mankind to offer to God the supreme worship offered by Christ."

∞

You must make your life a "Mass"

Now you have your answer to that persistent question: "What return shall I make to God for all that He has given me?" Give Him the only Gift that will enable you to pay your debt with anything like proper measure. Give Him Himself in His Son.

But never forget that God also wants *you* in His Christ. "My child, give me thy heart"[361] was His command in the Old Law. It has not changed in the New; but your heart has changed, and the way you are to give it to Him is really new. With a directness quite characteristic, and an eloquence all his own, St. Augustine, pointing to the bread and the wine that was to be offered in the Mass, said, "It is you who lie here on the altar table; it is you who are in the chalice; and we ourselves are there with you." You are one

---

[361] Prov. 23:26.

with Christ. But never forget that in the Cenacle and on the Cross, Christ was not only Priest, he was also Victim. And you, since you have been "Christed," are not only priest; you are victim as well.

Victim is not a welcome word in your century. But its repulsiveness is subjective rather than objective. It is due to the myopia developed by materialism. But you must never forget who you are. You are a person who has been reborn in Christ Jesus. He was born to say Mass. He said it in the Cenacle and on Calvary. You were reborn for no other purpose. That is your life's work, and your only real work in life. You must make the Mass of Christ your life — for there is where you get the "Bread of Life," there you find the "Fountain of Life," and there, from the Headwaters, you drink the "waters of life." And you must make your life a Mass for Christ. It must be exactly what His life was — a Sacrifice!

There is another word that is not welcome in your day. The attitude toward the word *sacrifice* is due largely to ignorance of its root and real meaning.

Sacrifice comes from *sacrum* and *facere*. It means "to make sacred." When a thing is set apart for God's use, for God's glory, for God's good pleasure, it is said to be *sacred*. When God takes a thing to be His own, then, in all truth, the thing is sacred. The Greeks had a beautiful word for it: *theothotos*. It seems to show you man placing the thing before God, and God taking it. That is sacrifice. And nothing else is. Sacrifice is the action of a lover who cannot find words for his love; it is the silent eloquence of a heart speaking through symbols, signs, and deeds.

You have been asking a lover's question: "What return shall I make?" You have received a Lover's reply: "Give me thy heart." Could you do anything less after seeing all that God has given you? Would you do anything less after learning who you really are?

Could you possibly think of doing anything less after staring at a crucifix and seeing what it is?

You must see that in making your life a Mass, in being what God made you to be — priest and victim — you not only give God what is His due, and give it in proper measure, but you gain incredibly for yourself! Making your life a Mass will be costly, but also to your immense profit. It may even be somewhat grievous at times, but that will only be to bring you greater blessings. In a certain sense, it will be literally death-dealing — how could there be sacrifice worthy of the name without a death? — but it will be death-dealing only to be life-giving. Realize what the Mass is, and what it means to make your life a Mass, and you will be like a newly ordained priest who cannot wait for the dawn so that he may go unto the altar of God and begin that action which is the greatest action in all the world: Sacrifice. Never let the thought that you are but a finite, frail creature hold you back; for Christ, who is the Mass, is not only *before* you as a Model; He is *within* you as a Force — a vital Force for a truly Christian life.

∞

In the Mass, Christ offers Himself with His members

If you have been shocked by the statement that there are differences between the Sacrifice of Calvary and the Sacrifice of the Mass, it may be good to stop a moment and study those differences. On Golgotha, Christ was the sole Priest and the lone Victim. That is not true in the Mass. The entire Church — the ordained priest who will consecrate, you, and every other actual member of the Mystical Body who will offer — will be with Christ; and with Him in the dual role of priest and victim. In the words of Augustine: "The Mass is the Sacrifice of the Mystical Body." You know that Calvary was the Sacrifice of Christ in His physical body. On the Cross Jesus offered Himself to the Father as vicarious Victim for all men. In the Mass, He offers Himself along with His members: those "who have been baptized and profess the true Faith, and who have not unhappily withdrawn from Body-unity or for grave faults been excluded by legitimate authority." There is the official definition of a member of Christ, as given by Pope Pius XII in his *Mystici Corporis*.

Abbé Anger gives you this whole matter with rare precision. He writes, "Christ is ever the principal, the sovereign priest. But as principal He has given us of His sacerdotal power. He raises those who have received the baptismal character to the dignity of in-struments of His Priesthood. He gives this power unequally. All the faithful offer; only [ordained] priests consecrate. We have al-ready stated that in the Mass Christ is not the sole Victim, as He was upon the Cross. The Church, who offers through Him and with Him, offers herself also with Him. She does not do this on the same plane and by the same title as does Christ. The natural body of Christ constitutes above all else the offering, that is, the thing offered. But, as every external sacrifice is sign and symbol of an in-terior sacrifice, the Mystical Body offers the natural body of Christ as seal, pledge, and testimony of the offering of itself, of its own consecration. 'By the Sacrifice of her Chief,' writes St. Augustine, 'the Church learns to sacrifice herself.' "[362]

You were present on Calvary only potentially, for Christ had not yet died so that the Mystical Body might be born. But in the Mass, you are present actually, so that through Christ, with Christ, and in Christ, you may offer to God the tribute of praise, thanksgiv-ing, adoration, and reparation that is His due.

[362] Joseph Anger, *The Doctrine of the Mystical Body*, trans. John J. Burke (New York: Benziger Brothers, 1932), 198.

This offering is not only a right; it is an obligation. "From the fact that the faithful are associated in the priesthood of Christ," Abbé Anger writes, "arises their obligation of sharing in the Sacrifice . . . priests as they are with Jesus Christ, the faithful are also victims, everyone in himself a sacrifice, a sacrifice with Jesus Christ. This is one of those truths that command the whole sweep of the Christian life."[363] That came as climax to the teaching that "the heart of the Catholic Worship is the Mass, the full, efficacious repetition and application of the one Sacrifice of Calvary. The active participation of the faithful in the mysteries of the Eucharist is pre-eminently the carrying out of the mandate, and of those rights which they received in Baptism."[364]

So you have title, right, and obligation to offer yourself as victim. St. Augustine sounds almost angry as he speaks to his faithful in his eighty-second sermon and tells them, "God wants you rather than your gifts." St. Gregory the Great[365] was equally emphatic, though somewhat softer in his tone. "We must offer ourselves," he says in his Dialogues, "for the Mass will be sacrifice for us when we have made an offering of us." Even more authoritative is the voice of Pius XI in his *Miserentissimus Redemptor*: "In the very august Eucharistic Sacrifice the priest and the rest of the faithful must join their immolation in such a way that they offer themselves as living hosts, holy and agreeable to God."

Here is an experience you may have had; if not, you can make it an experience right now. In front of you is a priest offering Mass. As he lifts the white host and offers the chalice of wine, ask yourself what you are giving to God in this Mass. You have given no

[363] Ibid., 154.

[364] Ibid., 153.

[365] St. Gregory the Great (c. 540-604), Pope from 590.

stipend for it. You have perhaps not even contributed to the Offertory collection. The young priest offers the bread and wine and says, "Pray brethren that our sacrifice may be acceptable to God the Father Almighty." But what have you given to God? The wheat is not yours. The wine is not yours, nor is the water. Where are you in this offering? How is this your Mass?

Although you are at what St. Pius X called "the very center of our Faith, the final goal of all our devotions, the fulfillment of all the Sacraments, the very summary of all the divine mysteries," you stand with empty hands and watch a priest making offerings. Must you confess as did one honest layman that you are "still vague about why God wants us to offer Sacrifice to Him, why it should please Him, how it honors Him"? Must you admit, as did he, that "although they sacrifice to idols, benighted savages understand what they do better than do I"?

If you have to echo that honest fellow, it is a good thing that you have just studied yourself. For if that study did not tell you why God wants Sacrifice, it most certainly alerted you to the fact that you want to offer the same to Him, and even showed you why. It is a demand of your nature. You must make return for all He has given you. Sacrifice and the need for it go deeper than that, but that will suffice for the moment.

At the beginning of man's history, Abel offered God a lamb. Later in that history, a strange king, Melchisedech by name, who was also priest of the Most High God, offered bread and wine. Later still, there came that strangest of all offerings, the one made by Abraham, the man who was ready to sacrifice his only son. In the center of the Canon of your Mass, those three men and their three sacrifices are mentioned. With deepest insight, Holy Mother Church has chosen three examples that let the dullest see and understand what sacrifice is and how it pleases God. God accepted

Abel's offering because it was the offering of a grateful lover. Melchisedech tendered God bread and wine, symbols that spoke to God, saying that the giver was ready to offer his very life to God out of love. By binding his son, placing him on the sacrificial pile of wood, and even raising the death-dealing knife, Abraham told God by action that he was ready to give to the Almighty what was dearer to him than life. Sacrifice is the language of love.

∞

You must offer yourself in the Mass

Yet these three, eloquent as they are, were but mere figures and types, shadows only, of what God's only-begotten Son would do. Mass is always celebrated before a crucifix. It is to remind us that Christ is at the altar to do in an unbloody manner exactly what He did years ago on Calvary in that terribly bloody manner. Yet the sign of the Crucified should tell people and priest that while the Mass is Calvary, there are differences. There He was alone; here He is not. You, the priest, and every member of the Mystical Body are present, and each present as a victim. That should enable you to understand Paul as he exhorts his Romans "to offer your bodies as a sacrifice, living, holy, pleasing to God — such is the worship reason requires of you."[366]

St. Augustine, addressing neophytes and explaining the Mass to them, said, "If you will understand what the Body of Christ is, hear what the apostle says to the faithful: 'You are Christ's Body and individually its members.' Since, then, you are the Body of Christ and His members, it is your mystery that is placed on the Lord's Table; it is your mystery that you receive. . . . But why is this mystery accomplished with bread? Let us offer no reason of our

---

[366] Rom. 12:1.

own invention, but listen to the apostle as he speaks of this sacrament: 'Because the bread is one, we, the many who partake of that one bread, form one Body.' Understand this and rejoice. Unity, truth, piety, charity. 'One bread.' What is this one bread? It is one Body formed of many. Remember that bread is not made of one grain, but of many. . . . Baptism water was poured over you, as flour is mingled with water; and the Holy Spirit entered you like the fire that bakes the bread. Be what you see, and receive what you are. This is what the apostle teaches concerning the bread. Although he does not say what we are to understand of the chalice, his meaning is easily seen. . . . Recall, my brothers, how wine is made. Many grapes hang from the vine, but the juice of all the grapes is fused into unity. Thus did the Lord Christ manifest us in Himself. He willed that we should belong to Him, and He has consecrated on His altar the mystery of our peace and unity."[367]

The Mass will be but a ceremony, a mere external bit of action, which, as far as you are concerned, is meaningless, unless, as Augustine says, "the visible sacrifice, outwardly offered to God, is a sign of the invisible sacrifice by which one offers to God himself and all his possessions." That statement will enable you to grasp the full import of St. Cyprian's profound remark: "The Sacrifice of our Savior is not celebrated with the requisite sanctity if our offering of our self, and our sacrifice of our self correspond not to His Passion."

On the paten and into the chalice you must put *yourself* — all that you have, all that you are. Read again what Pius XI said in his *Miserentissimus Redemptor*: "The more our oblation and sacrifice of self resemble the Sacrifice of Christ, in other words, the more perfect the immolation of self-love and the passions, and the more

[367] Sermon 272.

the crucifixion of our flesh approaches the mystical crucifixion of which the apostle speaks, the more abundant are the fruits of propitiation and expiation we receive for ourselves and others."

Now remind yourself of who you are! You are priest of the Most High God — and victim with Jesus Christ. The priest, as he offers wheat and wine and water, is holding *you* out on that paten; he has *you* in that water and wine! At this moment, be it morning, noon, or night, you are being held up to God in Jesus Christ by many an unknown priest; you are thus held up between three and four hundred thousand times a day. You are mystically one with over four hundred million other members of Christ's Body and, with them, are now offering sacrifice acceptable to God in Christ Jesus — and being offered with them. That stranger priest is no stranger mystically; through him, you, all that you have, and all that you are, are being offered to God.

Have you ever known that water is necessary for the Mass — just a tiny drop of it? Without it, no priest can licitly offer the Holy Sacrifice. St. Cyprian tells you, "The water represents the people, and the wine represents the Blood of Christ." In a letter to Caecilius, the saint explained the symbolism in this striking fashion: "When water is mingled with wine in the chalice, the people are united to Christ. . . . So perfectly are the water and wine united in the cup of the Lord that they cannot be separated. In like manner, the Church, that is, the multitude of the faithful united in the Church and persevering in the Faith, can never be separated from Christ. She will ever adhere to Him with an undivided love. For this reason, it is not lawful to offer either water alone or wine alone in the cup of the Sacrifice. For if wine alone is offered, Christ's Blood would be present without us; if only water, then the people are without Christ. . . ." There is proof that even in the Holy Sacrifice of the Mass, you "fill out Christ." See how He needs you to complete His Passion, to make available for you, for His Church, and all mankind, the graces He won on Calvary.

Sacrifice, offered by man, is symbolic. You employ external signs to speak for your internal disposition. You offer water, wine, and bread — those things which sustain life — as symbols that you are not only ready to die for God, but to live for Him! That is what the priest is saying to God on your behalf — and what every priest who lifts the paten and prays over the cup does in your stead. Those signs are never to be empty signs. Those symbols must represent reality. Your life, and all your living, must be a Mass, or else you lie by your Baptism and render the very blood of God valueless in your regard.

God speaks through David, the "man after God's own heart," the man who would not offer God holocausts that cost him nothing. Yet it is not so much David who speaks as God the Holy Spirit, and truly His words are words of fire:

> Our God comes; He does not keep silence,
> before Him is a devouring fire,
> round about Him a mighty tempest.
>
> He calls to the heavens above
> and to the earth, that He may judge His people:
> "Gather to me my faithful ones,
> who made a covenant with me by sacrifice!"
> The heavens declare His righteousness,
>   for God Himself is judge!
>
> "Hear, O my people, and I will speak,
> O Israel, I will testify against you.
> I am God, your God.
> I do not reprove you for your sacrifices;

your burnt offerings are continually before me.
I will accept no bull from your house,
    nor he-goat from your folds.

If I were hungry, I would not tell you;
for the world and all that is in it is mine.
Do I eat the flesh of bulls,
    or drink the blood of goats?
Offer to God a sacrifice of thanksgiving,
    and pay your vows to the Most High;
    and call upon me in the day of trouble;
I will deliver you, and you shall glorify me."[368]

In those lines, God is telling you with infinite severity that your signs must signify and your symbols truly symbolize. He is saying that He does not want mere words or inanimate wheat from your fields, wine from your vats, or water from your wells. He wants *you* — your heart, and all that is meant by that term. Do not have God saying again today what He had to say before Christ was born: "This people honors me with its lips, but its heart is far from me."[369]

Read the rest of the psalm above and learn how direct God can be in His speech — especially with the insincere, those whose lives are not a Mass, not acceptable water, wheat, and wine. But take His last lines as addressed to you, and read them as promise and prophecy: "He who brings thanksgiving as his sacrifice honors me; to him who orders his way aright, I will show the salvation of God!"

"Him who orders his way aright": that is to be the fitting description of you. For with Ignatius of Antioch, you can bravely say,

[368] Ps. 50:3-9, 12-15 (Revised Standard Version).
[369] Isa. 29:13.

"I am the wheat of God." You are His member! That dignity lays on you the challenging and thrilling obligation to be wheat, wine, and water!

∞

The acceptability of the Mass depends on you

The fact that you act in the Host with Christ and in the sacred cup should clarify for you some Mass prayers that have often puzzled the less informed. Frequently the priest begs God the Father to accept the Sacrifice. Since these people know that Christ is being offered, and that the Mass is the Sacrifice of Calvary, which God has already accepted — as is shown by Christ's Resurrection from the dead — these prayers are puzzling. But you, who know that the Mass is not exactly the same as Calvary, that Christ is not the sole offerer, that Jesus is not alone as Victim, can explain to them that there is water in the wine which will be changed into Christ's Blood; it is water of the world. You can tell them that while you are the "wheat of God," you are not the same wholesome wheat that Christ was and is; hence the host offered is not utterly unspotted.

Father de la Taille, S.J., the man who did so much to focus the attention of theology and theologians on the essence of the Mass, points out that while every Mass will be acceptable, and accepted, by reason of the merits of Jesus Christ, there will always be another reason for their being both acceptable and accepted, and that is the holiness which is a mark of Christ's Church and which will never be wanting to His Mystical Body. But he immediately adds that this holiness will vary, for it is subject to increase and decrease. And that is the fact that will bring this study of yourself to perfect focus, for implicitly it tells you that the acceptability of all Masses depends on *you*.

While every Mass is acceptable, the holier the priest is who offers the Sacrifice, the more acceptable is the Mass to God and the more efficacious for mankind. But since you are priest and victim, you are, in a way, concelebrant with every priest who vests for the Sacrifice, since with him you are going to co-offer and be offered! The conclusion is inescapable: the acceptability and the efficacy of every Mass depends, in definite measure, on you and the life you lead!

How urgent it is, then, that you become holier and holier! Listen to Father de la Taille: "Devout people, men and women, should be urged by every means to higher sanctity, so that through them the value of our Masses may be increased, and the tireless voice of the Blood of Christ crying from the earth may ring with greater clearness and insistency in the ears of God. His Blood cries on the altars of the Church, but since it cries through us, since our lips and hearts are its organs of expression, it follows that the warmer the heart, and the purer the lips, the more clearly will its cry be heard at the throne of God."

What a chivalry toward God that makes your life! What a romance with men that fashions out of all your living! The truer you are, the more human-divine you show yourself every hour of the day and night, the more will Almighty God be honored and the more sinful man will be saved.

It is the same learned Jesuit who furnishes you with food for thought about your times, and gives you reason to push on to higher sanctity. He points to the first Pentecost and the years immediately after, and asks how was it that the Gospel was so marvelously propagated in those days. Peter converted three thousand with a single short sermon![370] How was it that those early Christians were

---

[370] Acts 2:41.

so saintly — filled to overflowing with all spiritual gifts? How was it that there was such purity of mind, heart, and morals; so much genuine charity and perfect unity?

His answer is unexpected, somewhat startling, yet perfectly satisfying: "Because the Mother of God was still on earth, giving her precious aid in all the Masses celebrated by the Church." Think of the blinding sanctity in her who, as St. Thomas wrote, "borders on the Infinite." How the Masses celebrated while she was still on earth, and in which she, the Co-Redemptrix, would be co-offerer and co-victim, must have cried to God!

You are a child of Mary. You must prove it by giving each priest who lifts a paten a whiter host, and pour ever richer wine and purer water into his golden cup. You can do that by your every joy and every sorrow, by every disappointment and every triumph, by every thought, deed, and desire of your day — every day!

Life, and everything in life, becomes more serious when you know who you are. But it also becomes more stimulating. To know that *you* — with all you have and all you are and all you do — are held up to God in Christ Jesus every moment, each hour of the day and night, kills any idea that there can be such a thing as a meaningless movement or an idle moment in all your earthly existence. You and your life are flung against a background that burns with holiness — the holiness of God's own Son.

You will not be unwise if you tell yourself a hundred times a day that "you are the wheat of God, and wine for a thirsting world." It will be the height of discretion to remind yourself hourly of the words of Pius XII: "In the Mystical [Body], no good can be done, no virtue practiced by an individual, without it contributing something to the salvation of all." Recall this same Pontiff's words in *Mystici Corporis* to the effect that "just as on the Cross, the Divine Redeemer offered Himself as Head of the whole human race to the

Eternal Father, so now in this pure Oblation, He offers not only Himself as Head of the Church to the heavenly Father, but in Himself His Mystical members as well."

With that in mind, you can realize that every hour of your day and night, you sit down with Christ to His Last Supper; with Him you climb Calvary, stretch yourself out on the Cross, and even let Longinus pierce your heart. For you are held out on every paten in the world, you are lifted up in every cup that is blessed, and over you are spoken sacred words — the most important words in all the world! In effect, and in fact, with every breath, you are saying, "This is my Body. This is my Blood. Take them, O God, in Christ Jesus, Your Son, our Lord, and transubstantiate me!"

Eugene Masure, once director of the Grand Seminary at Lille, France, claims he has advanced the theory of de la Taille one step further by laying heavy stress on this idea of transubstantiation. He shows how the prayers of the Mass become meaningful when we fully realize that while Christ is always acceptable, we, who offer our all in Christ, will be acceptable only if we are changed into Him. Unquestionably, the Church shows anxiety about the acceptability and the acceptance of her offering. You can feel it not only before the Consecration, but even after the Communion, and on to the very end.

Yet the Church never fears that her offering will not be accepted; for she knows she is following that command: "Do this . . ." She well knows what that command means. It means changing bread into a Body that was offered and wine into Blood that was shed.

But what the Church does not know — and this causes her some concern — is how much grace will be poured out on men by her Sacrifice. There is where you can help her; for you are not only one who can pay God back in His own coin — and pay Him superabundantly; but you are one who can aid every human being who breathes the air of earth and those who are not yet in Heaven, yet will not be condemned to Hell. You are not only someone, but you are one who can do something!

Chapter Eleven

∽

You are one who truly is someone and who can do something

You are building your soul by thinking these thoughts, which, in ultimate analysis, are God's thoughts. The night before He died, knowing how short man's memory was, Jesus Christ said, "Do this in remembrance of me."[371] With those words, He ordained the first priests of the New Law and empowered them to offer the New Law's only Sacrifice. That Sacrifice is very rightly named the "memorial of His Passion," for, thanks to it, men may never again forget that God died — and died for them! But that Sacrifice is a "living memorial"; for in it is the living Christ, and from Him alone can men receive true life.

As He sat in the Cenacle, surrounded by His Apostles, Christ was thinking of you in this century. His command to those Apostles was an invitation to you and all other men of this century to sit in with Him at His Last Supper every day of your life, and every hour of your day — so that you might have your fill!

The Mass, as all Christ's actions, is for the glory of the Father. But that glory is obtained by the salvation of men. That is why

---

[371] Luke 22:19 (Douay version).

you can call the Mass *your* Mass. It is very definitely yours. For you cannot enrich God. He is infinite. But God can almost infinitely enrich you. St. Augustine observed that "God does not grow rich on our payments, but makes them who pay Him grow rich in Him."

Hence, the Mass takes on an ever more personal meaning, for the greatest riches you can ever receive are more Christhood, more godliness, and more grace. Nowhere can you receive them more surely than from the Mass.

As you read this line, some priest is somewhere praying those marvelous prayers of the Liturgy. By them he is slowly but very surely drawing you into the sacrificial center of the Mass, where Christ Himself will seize you and plunge you deep into His obedience. That was the core of Calvary. That is the core of the Mass: obedience. And when God says, "Son, give me thy heart," that is exactly what He is asking: obedience. For your heart is your free will. God wants that, not to enrich Himself, but to bless you in time so that He can bless you for eternity. You give Him that heart and that obedience in Christ Jesus — especially in the Mass.

This is the very pinnacle of Christianity, for it is the summit of Christ's mysteries. Here, and here alone, you can live; for just as a spark cannot live outside the fire, neither can a Christian live outside of Christ. And where, if not in the Mass, when you are plunged into His world-redeeming obedience, can you be closer to this Life-giver and His life-giving?

"All wise though He be," says St. Augustine, "God knows nothing better. All-powerful though He be, God can do nothing more excellent. Infinitely rich though He be, God can give nothing more precious than the Most Holy Eucharist."

Grasp this truth so that you can never let it go, and you will live! Never will you know a dull moment. Never will you see what

men call lowly, mean, and menial tasks as other than they are —
glowing with the splendor of God — for there is nothing that you
cannot have "transubstantiated."

∞

You can offer God every aspect of your day

Each morning as the priest ascends the altar of God, he has
need of a new host, fresh water, and more wine, for what he offered
yesterday gave of its substance so that God might live beneath its
appearances. Your new day, with it new trials and triumphs, its new,
even though recurrent, annoyances, defeats, and disappointments,
its new pleasures and joys, will furnish you with the fresh wheat,
the clean water, and the rich wine you need to make new offering
and again "do this" as His memorial. Offer to God your every
thought, word, action, and operation; offer Him every single happening of your new day; with them, offer yourself afresh for "transubstantiation." Let Him take their substance, so that you, while
retaining your own appearances, may in them and through them
be changed ever more and more into Jesus, and thus be enabled to
radiate Christ to your not-too-Christian world.

You may feel small. Undoubtedly the greatest human being is
small. But never forget what happens to that drop of water which
is mingled with the wine. Repeat again and again that prayer the
priest must say as he mingles that water with the wine: "By the
mystery of this water and wine, may we come to share in the divinity of Christ, who humbled Himself to share in our humanity." Do
all that as His memorial, and every hour of your day, you will grow
in godliness.

What keeps you from becoming more and more like Christ
every minute of your earthly existence? Not God. His desire for
your divinization — your deification — is eloquently expressed

by Bethlehem's crib, Calvary's Cross, and the white Host in the ciborium. One thing, and one thing only, prevents you from making your every moment sacramental — grace-laden and God-filled — and that is your failure to pronounce the words that will bring about transubstantiation.

The Mass is God's infinite gift to man. Yet, for that gift to be of any value to Giver or receiver, puny man must use what costs him least: his breath. Unless the consecrated and consecrating priest says, "This is my Body" over wheat and "This is my Blood" over the water mingled with wine, there will be no transubstantiation; and without transubstantiation there is no Mass.

In like manner, unless you take today's headaches and heart-aches, today's trials, troubles, and thrills, today's encouraging successes and whatever depressing defeats it holds, and offer them to God in Christ Jesus, they may well remain sterile happenings in a meaningless flight of hours. Then your day, no matter what manifestations of what you call *life* be in it, is actually dead. God made you a priest, but you must actualize that priestliness. God gives you the morning, but it is you, and only you, who can make it a "morning offering" — one that will consecrate your every moment to God who can then "transubstantiate" your every breath and heartbeat into a Sacrifice "holy and acceptable." That is something God desires with all the warmth of His infinitely warm heart. And you?

You already know that your heart is an ever-present ache to *be someone* and a persistently gnawing hunger to *do something*. That gnawing and ache was in the heart of Adam. He sought to appease them and fell. That same gnawing and ache is in the tiny heart of the latest child born of woman. He will seek to appease them, too; and fall he must unless he comes to learn some of the truths you have been learning; fall he will unless he is thoroughly taught who

he is. In you, and in every human who breathes, there is an inerad-
icable impulse to *be* godlike and to *do* godly deeds. Destruction —
and even eternal damnation — can follow on it unless you and
they realize that there is only one way to follow that urge, appease
that ache, and satisfy that hunger. That way is Jesus Christ.

∞

Your sacrifices will improve the world

Apart from Him, who are *you?* A syllable outside its word is
meaningless. A branch outside its vine is deadwood. A Christian
outside Jesus Christ is an insult to Heaven and a drag on the human race.

You can find one very complete and convincing answer to the
question "What is wrong with the world?" by looking at yourself. If
you were holier, the world — the entire universe: earth, Heaven,
and what lies between — would be better! Were you holier, the
bridge that spans the infinite gulf between God and man would be
more solid and much safer for traffic, for you are a priest, and every
priest is a *pontifex,* or bridge builder. Were you holier, the conduits
through which the life-giving and life-sustaining waters of grace
come to man would be clearer. Were you holier, the arteries
through which the lifeblood of the heart of the world must flow
would be ever so much more functional.

If you find the world something of a mess, look to your Mass! If
you find few saints in your civilization, check on your own surrender to God. If you find civil and even domestic society swaying,
look to your own stability in Christ Jesus. If modern man seems on
the verge of bankruptcy, it may well be because you have not offered the holocaust that costs!

Christ's own ancestor, David, one day looked around his world
and, like you, was grieved. A pestilence lay upon the land. People

were dying by the thousands. And David knew that he was somehow responsible for their deaths. He prayed to God earnestly. But his prayer was not enough. Then Gad, the prophet of God, "came before the king and said, 'Go up and build an altar in the threshing floor of Areuna, the Jebusite.' And David went up according to the word of Gad which the Lord had commanded him.

"And Areuna looked, and saw the king and his servants coming toward him . . . and said, 'Wherefore is my lord, the king, come to his servant?' And David said to him, 'To buy the threshing floor of thee, and build an altar to the Lord, that the plague which rageth among the people may cease.'

"And Areuna said to David, 'Let my lord the king take, and offer, as it seemeth good to him: thou hast here oxen for a holocaust, and the wain, and the yokes of the oxen for wood.'

"And the king answered, and said, 'Nay, but I will buy it of thee at a price, and I will not offer to the Lord my God holocausts free of cost.' So David bought the floor and the oxen for fifty sicles of silver. And David built there an altar to the Lord and offered holocausts and peace offerings; and the Lord became merciful to the land, and the plague was stayed from Israel."[372]

Do you pay for your holocausts? Are they truly costly? If not, how are you a Christian? How are you like Christ? He could have redeemed the world with a sigh; repaired the outraged majesty of God with a gesture. But what did He do? He emptied Himself! He would not offer God holocausts that did not cost. He took an agony in the garden, a scourging at the pillar, a crowning with thorns, a staggering, stumbling Way of the Cross, all as mere prelude to those three endless hours when He prayed the slow Rosary of Redemption on the costly crimson beads of His own blood.

[372] 2 Kings 24:18-22, 24-25 (RSV = 2 Sam. 24:18-22, 24-25).

Thus did He actualize His priesthood and victimhood. You have been stamped with that same priesthood and victimhood as never was Christ's ancestor David.

Now you are face-to-face with the fundamental reason your world is not better. You, and thousands of others like you, do not really believe what you profess to believe. You do not really believe in your predestined role in the one work of this world, which is to give glory to God in and through Christ Jesus. You do not believe with anything like a fervid belief that your Baptism and Confirmation made you Christ, that God has chosen you out to complete the work of Jesus; that you are "to fill up" — to be the *pleroma Christi*. You do not believe with anything like a dynamic, vibrant, vital belief that it is the Mass that matters, that costly sacrifices save. The basic belief that will rebuild your life and your world is the belief that you are *one* with God and *one* with all men.

∞

You have solidarity with Christ

Christianity is a religion of solidarity. It recognizes a solidarity in sin, a solidarity in redemption, and a solidarity in salvation. It is this triple recognition that allows our religion to give the only valid and satisfying explanation of the blood-drenched history of man and to account for so much that seems utterly unaccountable in the life history of any one individual. Until you come to a vivid realization of these three solidarities, you will never know yourself fully and never know what has been going on in your own century or what life on earth is all about.

St. Paul explained these solidarities as no man before him or after him. In writing to the Romans, proclaiming to them the Good News made known by God, he says, "This Good News concerns His Son, who, as regards the flesh, was born of the line of David, but according to the spirit of holiness was constituted the mighty Son of God by His Resurrection from the dead, Jesus Christ, our Lord. Through Him we have received grace and the apostolic office, whose purpose is to bring men of all nations to honor His name by the submission of faith."[373]

The axis of man's world is *faith!* That faith is "faith in Jesus Christ," a faith that brings "sanctification," a sanctification that is wrought by "grace," grace that is won through the "shedding of His blood."[374]

Paul concludes, "Having, therefore, been sanctified by faith, let us have peace with God through our Lord Jesus Christ, through whom also we have found entrance into this state of grace in which we now abide, and exult in the hope of participating in God's glory."[375]

The motion of man's world is *hope!* That hope Paul specified in proclaiming the Good News. That Good News has been proclaimed to you. You live by faith, spurred on by the hope of "participating in God's glory." But all that marvel is thanks to Jesus Christ, as Paul specifically points out, saying, "While we were still helpless, Christ, at the appointed hour, died for us wicked people. Why, it is only with difficulty that a person will die to save a good man. Yes, it is only for a worthy person that a man may, perhaps, have the courage to face death. But God proves His love for us, because, when we were still sinners, Christ died for us."[376]

There is the substance of man's world: *love!* And "God's love is poured forth in our hearts by the Holy Spirit who has been given

[373] Rom. 1:3-5.
[374] Cf. Rom. 3:22, 24-25.
[375] Rom. 5:1-2.
[376] Rom. 5:6-9.

us."[377] Your hope will not be disappointed, for the God who proved His love for you by dying for you when you were a sinner will save you as Paul says: "Much more now that we are sanctified by His blood shall we be saved through Him from God's avenging justice. Surely, if when we were enemies, we were reconciled to God by the death of His Son, much more, once we are reconciled, shall we be saved by His life."[378]

You know that Christ lives. But do you realize that He lives to give you life and, through you, pour out life on many dead men? In the letter to the Hebrews, this is made plain. Paul tells how Christ is "able at all times to save those that come to God through Him, living always, as He does, to make intercession on their behalf."[379]

Paul's words give you a flawlessly clear picture of actuality. He says Christ is living. He is living in that body which rose all glorious from the borrowed tomb. But that was the body that had been spiked to Calvary's tree. So it is still scarred from His encounter with sin, Satan, and death. Those sacred stigmata are the mouths through which He "makes intercession." It can safely be said, then, that those "mouths" are opened by the men and women who follow His command: "Do this in remembrance of me."

Get that picture not only in your mind but also in your imagination. Christ with His glorious stigmata stands before the throne of God. Men and women who pay the price, men and women who offer no holocaust to God that does not cost, men and women who make the Mass their lives, and their lives a Mass, set those wounds glowing, and grace is poured out! That is actuality, for the sanctification, salvation, and grace that was won on Calvary pours out

[377] Rom. 5:5.
[378] Cf. Rom. 5:9-10.
[379] Heb. 7:25.

through the Mass. It is from Christ that life comes to men — and the Mass is Christ.

"Through one man," says St. Paul, "sin entered into the world, and through sin death. . . . But the gift is not like the offense. For if by the offense of one, many died, much more has the grace of God, and the gift which consists in the grace of the one man, Jesus Christ, overflowed unto many. . . . For if by reason of the one man's offense, death reigned through the one man, much more will they who have received the abundance of the grace and of the gift of holiness reign in life through the one Jesus Christ. Therefore as from the offense of the one man, the result was condemnation to all men, so from the one's fulfillment of a mandate, the result is the sanctification, which gives life to all men. In other words, just as by the disobedience of the one man, many were constituted sinners, so also by the obedience of the one, many will be constituted holy."[380]

Now, that is the Good News, and Paul certainly stresses your double solidarity. But do not miss the real import of this celebrated passage. Father Mersch, in his *Theology of the Mystical Body*, points out that most theologians confine their comments and focus attention on the common Fall in Adam. But that was not Paul's prime purpose at all! Just the opposite. He wanted men to recognize their common restoration in Christ!

Christianity is positive. Christianity is optimistic. Christianity is filled with bright hope and warm love. Christianity lifts the human heart and sets it pounding with joy as it insists that while the original clay fell and broke, Christ came along, gathered the scattered fragments, and fashioned them into better form. Paul's passage begins with sin, it is true, but that is only a point of departure.

[380] Cf. Rom. 5:12, 15, 17-19.

He moves on resolutely, rapidly, and with almost breathless ascent. The first Adam with his sin appears only to introduce the glorious second Adam with His generous life-giving grace. "Where sin abounded, grace did more abound."[381]

Paul was a man of one idea. That idea became his obsession. The most rapid and superficial reading of his letters leaves no doubt that here was a man who "knew only Jesus Christ," and was determined that all men should "come to the same knowledge."[382]

St. Augustine, ever the most lucid commentator on St. Paul, is not only the Doctor of Grace, but the Doctor of Original Sin as well; for the two are but the separate sides of the one coin — man. In his thirtieth sermon, Augustine briefly draws the complete picture, saying, "Such is our faith; such is truth; this is the foundation of Christian Faith: one man and one man. Through the former comes ruin, through the latter restoration. He who did not remain standing fell; He who did not fall raises up. The former fell because he abandoned Him who remained standing; the latter, still standing, stooped down to him who was lying prostrate."

As with Paul, so with Augustine, solidarity in good is given stronger accent than the solidarity in evil. So must it be with you. You were born of the sinner Adam, it is true; but the greater truth is that you were reborn of the ever-sinless second Adam, and He is God.

But the truth that will drive you to constant action and become your very life and love is that, while all men are born members of the mystical body of Adam, and hence in sin, it is only through the free choice of men that any can ever be reborn into the Mystical Body of Christ and, hence, be given life that is true life.

[381] Rom. 5:20.
[382] 1 Cor. 2:2; cf. Eph. 4:13.

Why should that truth drive you? Because it tells you that in the mysterious Providence of God, life for the lifeless, veritable resurrection from the dead, Christhood for the Christless, depends on *you*. If the Son of God is actually to take the shattered clay of individual mortals and remold it, shaping it to His own likeness, you must pick up the pieces and put them in His all-holy hands. You *are* your brother's keeper. You are Good Samaritan and Good Shepherd. You must seek out the lost. You must save your fellow-man. You do so by simply being your real self in Christ Jesus. For if there was solidarity in sin (all being in Adam) and solidarity in redemption (all being in Christ), there must be solidarity in salvation — and there will be, if you allow Christ to reach out through your hands to take into unity those men who, although potentially, are not actually His members!

Think of it: you can save men for God! Frightening responsibility? Yes. But so brimmed with wonder and love that it casts out fear.

⚭

Your least action affects the entire Church

The ache in your heart to *be* someone was soothed, even taken away, by Baptism; it made you Christ! The hunger in your heart to *do* something can now be fully appeased; you can build up the Body of the God-Man by helping Him save your fellowmen. You do that by becoming an ever-holier member yourself, for health in the Mystical Body means holiness.

When one has a broken arm, the other arm does double service while the broken member rests and recuperates. Every organ, every cell, in the body is affected by that break; every organ and every cell in the body will contribute something toward the mending of that break, for the human body is a unit.

Christ's Mystical Body is just as tight a unity. You are His member. Are you a healthy, wholesome member that can help parts that are not well? You hardly need to be told that there is a difference between the perfect physical body Christ took from the sinless womb of His immaculate Mother and the Mystical Body He has taken from the womb of ever-sinful mankind. The first was flawless; the second, alas, because made up of members with free will, is far from flawless. Not only the sinful, but sinners are members of this Body. It is hideously scarred. More than one member suffers from worse than broken bones. You can aid each and every one of them!

But perhaps you deem yourself too small to do double duty for any organ that is diseased or any limb that is broken. Every man, as man, is small. But once incorporated in Christ, no smallest cell is without some semblance of omnipotence. Let your own estimate of yourself stand; you are small — too small to do a big work. You are but a tiny, inconspicuous, all-but-invisible member of the mighty, world-embracing Catholic Church. Agreed.

Now, ask yourself if you have ever seen a phagocyte — one of those leukocytes in your bloodstream. The chances are about a thousand to one that you have never even heard of a phagocyte, let alone seen one. You would almost need an electronic microscope to bring such a corpuscle into anything like satisfying focus. Yet, when you suffer an infection anywhere in that body of yours, watch those phagocytes!

Suppose you cut the tip of your little finger, and it becomes infected. Immediately, from every part of your body, those healthy, vigorous, life-giving phagocytes will rush to the area of infection. From the tip of your toes to the tip of your ear they will come and, at the tip of your little finger, do battle to the death with the bacteria that are there causing the infection, because your body is a unit, and every member of it is concerned with the well-being of the whole.

The Mystical Body of Christ is just as tight a unit. On your own estimation, you are small, as small as a phagocyte. Then be a healthy, holy, vigorous, life-giving "phagocyte" and rush to the parts of Christ's Mystical Body that are infected.

On the wakefulness and watchfulness of a single sentinel, the welfare of an entire army can depend. On that army, the fate of an entire country can depend. On that country, the immediate future of the civilized world can rest. And, as you well know, the fortune or the fate of untold unborn generations are in the pregnant womb of the present. Is a lone individual important?

Leon Bloy once hazarded the statement that the surprising and fate-filled victory won by Foch at the Battle of the Marne in World War I could have been due to the innocent prayers of a little girl to be born some twenty centuries from now. With God there is no time; and with Him the prayers of the innocent are powerful. Scientists tell you the slightest shake of a baby's tiny rattle affects not only the sun and the moon, not only Betelgeuse, Venus, Saturn, and Mars, but even the unknown and most distant star, whose radiance may be billions of light-years away from us. The universe is a unit; the smallest action of the lowest and least affects all.

You are distinct from all other men, but you are not separated from any one of them, least of all from those who are incorporated in Christ. Hence, what scientists tell you of the universe and your own body, Pius XII has told you about that unit which is Christ's Mystical Body. "In that Body," says that Pontiff, "thanks to the Communion of Saints, no good can be done, no virtue practiced by individual members, without its contributing something to the salvation of all."

Will you dare now ask, "What can I do?" Not if you have once read *Mystici Corporis*. For almost as soon as he had opened that encyclical, the Pope was telling you, "As in our mortal composite being, when one member suffers, all the members share its pain, and the healthy members come to the assistance of those that are ailing; so in the Church, the individual members do not live for themselves alone, but also help their fellows, and all work in mutual collaboration for their common comfort and for the more perfect building up of the whole Body."

A page earlier, he told you that this was God's own plan. "As He hung on the Cross, Christ Jesus not only avenged the justice of the Eternal Father that had been flouted, but He also won for us, His brothers, an unending flow of graces. It was possible for Him personally, immediately to impart these graces to men; but He wished to do so only through a visible Church that would be formed by the union of men, and thus, through that Church, every man would perform a work of collaboration with Him in dispensing the graces of Redemption.

The Holy Father said, "The salvation of many depends on the prayers and voluntary penances which the members of the Mystical Body of Jesus Christ offer for this intention, and on the assistance of pastors of souls and of the faithful, especially of fathers and mothers, which they must offer to our Divine Savior as though they were His associates."

Associate of God! What an answer you now have for that original question: "Who are you?" and to that other one: "What can you do?" Associated with Almighty God — wonderful as that is, it does not tell the whole story at all.

Pope Pius XII knew this. That is why later he labored to show you just how closely you are united to God, not only associated with Him. His Holiness quoted St. Augustine, who named this union "something sublime, mysterious, and divine," and then went on: "It is at once evident that this union is very close. In Sacred Scripture it is likened to the pure union of man and wife, and is compared to the vital union of branch and vine, and with the cohesion found in our body. Even more, it is represented as being so close that the apostle says, '[Christ] is Head of the Body of the Church,' and the unbroken tradition of the Fathers, from earliest times, teaches that the Divine Redeemer and the society which is His Body form but one mystical person, that is to say, to quote Augustine, 'the whole Christ.' Our Savior Himself, in His high-priestly prayer, has gone so far as to liken this union with that marvelous oneness by which the Son is in the Father and the Father in the Son."

Pure union, as between husband and wife; *vital* union between Vine and branch; *substantial* union between parts of body; *personal* union between Head and members; *that ineffable oneness* between divine Father and divine Son. Small wonder His Holiness gives vent to the exclamation: "Nothing more glorious, nothing nobler, nothing surely more ennobling can be imagined than to belong to the Holy, Catholic, Apostolic, and Roman Church."

∞

You must love others as Christ did

Indeed you *are* someone: you are Jesus Christ and one with the Father! And, therefore, it is up to you to *do* something; for Christ and His Cross is the mystery of *generosity*. Hence, no one dares call himself or herself a Christian unless he or she is willing to love the entire human race as Christ did — "to death, even to death on a Cross."[383] In the Mystical Body of Jesus Christ, there is no room for mediocrity, no room for shriveled hearts or small souls.

[383] Phil. 2:8.

"Let us imitate the breadth of His love," says Pius XII. "One only is the Spouse of Christ, the Church; but the love of the Divine Spouse is so vast that it embraces in His Spouse the whole human race without exception. Men may be separated by nationality and race, but our Savior poured out His blood to reconcile all men to God through the Cross, and to bid them all unite in one Body."

That being the case, you can do something that will have worldwide influence and affect, not only every man living, but even the generations yet unborn. If that seems absurdly exaggerated, just think a moment! Is there a single organ in your body — your heart, your lungs, your kidneys — that has not benefited by the food you ate today? Is there a single cell in your whole being that was left unaffected? No. You are a living unit. Each part in you works for the whole.

Christ's Mystical Body is just as much a unit; and in it, every cell lives and labors for the good of the whole. If you took Food — *the* Food, Holy Communion — into your mouth today, there is not a cell in Christ's worldwide Body, from the Pope down through the College of Cardinals, on to every archbishop, bishop, prelate, and priest, on to every religious male and female, every layman from the most well-known down to the all-but-utterly unknown nonviable fetus who was baptized just before he died, who has not benefited by your action. If you have prayed once in Christ Jesus today, you have bettered the entire world of men!

Your sympathy, both natural and supernatural, went out to Cardinal Mindszenty when he was arrested, imprisoned, tortured, drugged, then pilloried by that farce of a public trial. Your sympathy, both natural and supernatural, has gone out to every bishop, prelate, and priest, to every nun who has been first placed under house arrest, then led to solitary confinement, where they have been brainwashed, abused physically and psychologically, then readied for what Christ Himself experienced just before Calvary: the presentation to a frenzied mob, duped, and driven by a few satanically clever men who are past masters at intimidation and mob psychology. Your sympathy, natural and supernatural, goes out today to those millions of the faithful, clerical and lay, who suffer diabolical tortures behind those curtains which would shut out God. But have you done anything more than feel sympathy? Have you stood ringing your hands in impotence, or let your arms hang limp in helplessness, when all the while you could have been lifting those arms in aid and pouring out assistance from those hands by so simple a thing as prayer?

There is no one, no matter what his or her condition of incarceration, whom you cannot help this moment by a reverent, prayer-filled, fruitful pronunciation of the holy name of *Jesus!* Those who are being starved, you can feed; those who have stripped naked, you can clothe; wounds made in body and mind you can bind up; and to those who have almost been robbed of heart and courage, you can give heart, hope, and heroic courage, by being a bit more holy, more filled with grace, and more mindful of who you are. The Mystical Body of Christ is so compact a unit that, to it, space means nothing, distance proves no barrier, and physical limitations are without meaning. Your influence can be worldwide. Make it so!

To your generation, this can never sound like theory. It will read rather like a truism. For what generation before yours ever saw this truth about the importance of the individual in a unit ever more completely or as convincingly demonstrated?

It is a fact that before World War II, there were certain centers of civilization where the individual, as an individual, had been stripped of all dignity and reduced to a mere number. In Russia a human being was but a pair of hands to produce what would help the progress of the Red Revolution. In Germany he was but a pair of feet that were to goose-step that little caricature of a man, Hitler, to world domination. In Italy he was as individualistic as a grain of sand that was to be poured into the concrete that Mussolini would use to raise up his Fascist State.

But then came World War II, and country after country, your own included, was shaken into the realization that, fundamentally, a nation is only a collection of individuals; that unity means a totality of related parts; that effectiveness depends on the coordination of various units. In short, the world was alerted to the importance of the individual as an individual and the contribution he could make to the whole; each citizen was recognized as a "cell" in the "body" of the nation. During the war, your own nation saw that the munition worker in Bayonne was as important as the bomber over Berlin, the garment-maker in Brooklyn or the Bronx as much a part of "Uncle Sam" as the boy in Guadalcanal or on New Guinea, the steelworker in Pittsburgh as necessary for V-day as the GI at the front. It was a providential lesson; it prepared the world for a keener appreciation of what the individual Christian means to Christ. World War II was the hand of God readying the world for the acceptance of the doctrine of the Mystical Body. The epoch-making encyclical *Mystici Corporis* was released on June 29, 1943.

On that date, the world was writhing in agony. Nation after nation in western Europe had been blitzkrieged almost out of existence. The civilization, built up through countless centuries was being reduced to rubble. Mankind was almost paralyzed by the multitudinous and often mountainous problems that faced it in every realm from economics and politics to morality. To that world, frantic and warfrenzied, Christ's Vicar gave an encyclical describing the Mystical Body of Christ.

That would be scandal were it not revelation. The history of papal encyclicals — especially during this past hundred years — is such that no well-informed person would ever dream of any one of Christ's vicars handing mankind a stone when it was calling for bread.

What Pius XII offered a blasted world is anything but the stuff dreams are made of. No intelligent person will pick up this encyclical without reverence, nor read it without that same intentness revelation deserves.

To you, and to all men of the twentieth century, this has the same kind of meaning as had the Sermon on the Mount, in which the Son of God proclaimed to the multitude the beauty of the Beatitudes. How Christ thrilled men that day! Never before had the poor, the meek, or the mourning been called *blessed*. Never had those who thirsted after justice been promised their fill, nor the merciful told that they would receive mercy. Those people — so representative of the vast majority of humans, since life pressed heavily on them — were told by authority that their human lives, far from being barren, were actually *blessed!*

This encyclical tells you truths that are even more personal and wonderful; it gives you facts that satisfy the hunger of your heart. It shows you how you can do something great, not only for the dead and the living, but even for the generations unborn. You have the wealth of God in your hands. You have the blood of Christ at your disposal.

Because there are some three hundred thousand Masses offered every day, by an intention of your free will you can hold up a chalice to God four times every second and say, "We offer Thee, O God, this chalice of salvation, begging Thy mercy that it may come into the presence of Thy Majesty for our salvation and for that of the entire world."

Do that, and God the Father will hear the Son crying again as He cried on Calvary: "I thirst!"[384] He will understand the source of that thirst and know the only thing that will quench it: *souls!* He will answer it, and you, in Christ Jesus, and through Christ Jesus, and with Christ Jesus, will have been saved.

Pius XII pinpoints your lifework once again in *Mediator Dei*. The teaching is the same as in *Mystici Corporis*, but there is more anguish in the voice as His Holiness says, "See how we were bought: Christ hangs upon the Cross; see at what a price He makes His purchase. . . . He buys with Blood; He buys with the Blood of the spotless Lamb; He buys with the Blood of God's only Son. He who buys is Christ; the price is His Blood; the possession bought is the world." That, as you see, was Redemption: Christ bought back with Blood. You had nothing to do with that except, possibly, to make the price higher by your personal sins.

But with what that Pope says next you have much to do. "This purchase," says Pius, "does not immediately have its full effect; since Christ, after redeeming the world at the lavish cost of His own Blood, must yet come into the complete possession of the souls of men. Wherefore, that the redemption and salvation of each person of the future generations unto the end of time may be effectively accomplished, and be acceptable to God, it is necessary that men, individually, should come into vital contact with the Sacrifice of the Cross, so that the merits which flow from it should be imparted to them. In a certain sense, it can be said that on Calvary Christ built a font of purification and salvation which He filled with the Blood He shed; but if men do not bathe in it, and there wash away the stains of their iniquities, they can never be purified and saved."

[384] John 19:28.

Then the Holy Father says something very personal and pertinent to you: "The cooperation of the faithful is required so that sinners may be individually purified in the Blood of the Lamb." Pius XII is ever bringing you and all members of Christ's Body back to the Mass, for there you find the heart of His Mystical Body, the font of life, and the center of your world. "To participate in the Eucharistic Sacrifice is their chief duty and supreme dignity," says Pius, and immediately tells you how to participate: not in any "inert, negligent fashion, giving way to distraction and daydreaming, but with such earnestness and concentration that they may be united as closely as possible with the High Priest, according to the apostle: 'Let this mind be in you which was also in Christ Jesus.' And together with Him and through Him let them make their oblation, and in union with Him let them offer up themselves."

With his accustomed practicality, Pius XII tells what it means to have "the mind of Christ." He says you should possess "as far as it is humanly possible, the same dispositions as those which the Divine Redeemer had when He offered Himself in Sacrifice: that is to say . . . in a humble attitude of mind pay adoration, honor, praise, and thanksgiving to the Supreme Majesty of God. Moreover, it means that they should assume to some extent the character of victim, that they deny themselves as the Gospel demands, that freely and of their own accord they do penance, and that each detests and satisfies for his sins. In a word, it means that we must all undergo with Christ a mystical death."

You know what mystical death means — not that you are to be without life, but rather that you be filled and overflowing with real life, the life of grace. It means death to sin and to that self which would sin.

Chapter Twelve

∞

You are one who can serve
Christ in your work

By this time, you know there are only two classes of people in the world: those who "fill up" by making their lives a "Mass," and those who "empty" by letting God's blood sink into sand instead of into their souls. Yet there is only one way for *you* to see men — all of them! And that is the way Caryll Houselander once saw them.

She tells you that she was riding in the subway "on a crowded train in which all sorts of people jostled together, sitting and strap-hanging workers of every description going home at the end of the day. Quite suddenly I saw with my mind, but as vividly as a wonderful picture, Christ in them all." That "vision" was, of course, a very special gift of God to that one girl. She left the train and came out on the street. For a long time, she walked amid the crowds. The marvelous experience continued: "on every side, in every passerby, everywhere — *Christ.*" For several days, with this same intensity, the "vision" lasted. Then she makes the remark that should help clear your vision. "After a few days . . . people looked the same again. . . . Christ was hidden. . . . Through the years to come . . . I would find Him in others — only through a deliberate and blind act of faith. But if the 'vision' had faded, *the knowledge had not.*"[385]

You possess that knowledge without ever having had the "vision." Thanks to it, you can always make a "deliberate and blind act of faith" that will never fail to open your eyes to reality and will enable you to see men — especially workingmen — for what they are!

Those who lack this knowledge too often look at workingmen and see only functioning machines, mere instruments of production and nothing more. It might well be that even you, at times, have looked at workingmen in this way and, because of your education and environment, have viewed work simply as a function. To countless persons among your contemporaries, it is that and nothing more. What a fallacy! What a heresy! Yet, how easily accounted for.

The Industrial Revolution of the past century changed men into "hands," made labor a commodity that is purchased the same way that medicine or pork and beans, coffee or beef are purchased. That concept of man and his labor potential explains all. Capital became interested in men's work, not in man. Efficiency, achievement, and output were what concerned the employer; the personality of the employee, not at all. Man became a machine, valuable so long as he was in running order; to be cast aside if he broke down or ceased to function with highest efficiency.

Leo XIII was Christ's Vicar when the Industrial Revolution came into being. With that wisdom and clarity which is so characteristic of the Watchman in the Vatican, he saw a wind was being sown that was sure to reap a whirlwind if someone did not stop

---

[385] Caryll Houselander, *A Rocking-Horse Catholic* (New York: Sheed and Ward, 1955), 139 ff.

that seeding. So he wrote what has become the *Magna Carta* for the world of labor, his encyclical *Rerum novarum*.[386] In it the Pope championed the cause of the workingman as it had never been championed before. With a fearless, strong hand he attacked and overthrew the idols of Liberalism, so openly worshiped by the rich. At the same time, he prevented Socialism from erecting any temple for its gods, by showing the workingmen how to form their own labor unions.

∞

There is dignity in work

Laying down the fundamental principles that were to govern the relative rights and mutual duties of Capital and Labor, then specifying the part to be taken by the Church, the state, and the individual concerned, His Holiness gave the world a new social philosophy. In time, that philosophy gave birth to a Christian social science. As this science grew, it gave the human race as its common possession the Catholic principles of sociology; and workmen ceased to be "hands," for they were made very conscious of their God-given dignity. These men were reminded that they were men, created by God to His own image and likeness; hence, they had certain inalienable rights and definite duties. They were convinced that they could develop and choose their own leaders.

In no time, these Catholic principles brought a whole new branch of jurisprudence into being, as laws concerning the welfare of the workers were passed, thus compelling the entire economic universe to recognize the person of the worker and respect it. Those laws had to do with such personal things as health, housing, working conditions, and the like. Then more stringent and reverential

[386] On capital and labor, May 15, 1891.

laws regarding women and children as workers were enacted. Thus the Social Revolution, sired by the Pope, checked the Industrial Revolution from growing that whirlwind it surely was sowing.

But, you may ask what right the Pope has to speak out on such matters. In practically every economic question, morality is involved. Economics has its own laws and its own end, it is true. But that end is only one of the many means to be employed by man to attain his ultimate goal, which, you well know, is God. Dollars and cents, production and distribution, work and wages, supply and demand, all ultimately lead to God — whenever they are used humanly.

"No man may with impunity outrage that human dignity which God Himself treats with *reverence*," wrote Leo XIII in his *Rerum novarum*. He told the wealthy owner that he "must respect the dignity and the worth [of the worker] as a man and as a Christian." He told him that he could not regard workers as "so much muscle and physical power," mere "chattels to make money by." His Holiness did not use the words, but he most certainly taught the truth that when these men hired and fired Christians, they were really hiring and firing Christ. When he came to address the workers, however, he did employ that text which is of such paramount importance in the doctrine of the Mystical Body; the one that tells everyone who is abused that "if we suffer with Him, we shall also reign with Him."[387] He also cheered them by showing them that Christ Himself had been a workingman, a hired laborer, and thus had dignified toil and shed divine luster about every man who labors.

After admitting that there always was and always will be two classes, the rich and the poor, he pointed out that God seemed to

[387] 2 Tim. 2:12.

favor the poor because He had chosen to be one of them. He had called the poor *blessed* — something He never called the rich. And He had invited all who "labor and are burdened" to come to Him.[388]

Yet that Pope would never be inadequate, so he commands both rich and poor, the employer and the employee, to have respect and even reverence for every member of each class. The reason is God. His Holiness set it down briefly: "Each and all are redeemed and made sons of God by Jesus Christ." That is the ultimate and only solid basis on which society can build. That is the only bond that will ever bind men successfully and bring them to true peace and happy living.

Leo XIII used the undeniable facts of history and showed that when the Gospel of Jesus Christ broke upon the world, there was a veritable resurrection from the dead. Civil society was renovated in its every part. On the strength of that renewal, the human race was lifted up, "brought back from death to life," says Leo, "and to so excellent a life that nothing more perfect had been known before, nor will come to be known in the ages that are yet to be. Of this beneficent transformation, Jesus Christ was at once the First Cause and the final end, as from Him all came, and to Him all was brought back."

Although this encyclical was written before you or your century were born, the truths it tells are as fresh as this morning, and are as pertinent and personal to you as this new day's atmosphere; not only because of the economic milieu in which you move, but for the far more basic and ontological fact that Job expressed so aptly the day he said, "Man is born to labor as birds to fly."[389] It is the all-holy will of God that you and every other human work.

[388] Matt. 11:28.
[389] Job 5:7.

∞

Work can bring you joy

All too many people look upon all work as burdensome and boring. God never meant it to be that. Originally He planned work as a means of pleasure that was ultimately to lead you to happiness. Sin changed that plan somewhat. It brought in sweat and weariness.

But it did not essentially change work. Work can still be a source of joy as God made it to be. Thanks to Jesus Christ, even toil and labor can be sacramental; they can be taken as penance and thus transformed from a curse into a means of acquiring merit. In other words, if you work as a Christian — that is, in the spirit of Christ — you not only make a living, but you acquire more real life: grace!

But the attitude of so many of your contemporaries toward work is actually childish. Very young and unformed children look on school as the serious side of life, and after-school hours and long vacations as the only time they really live; for it is the only time they can enjoy themselves. In school all is discipline; the child feels fettered. Classroom work is not only serious work; it is dry, burdensome. But once school is out, the child can play!

Do you or your fellow adults view your work in any other light? Is not life, for you, divided into work and play — work being the serious side of living, the time when you have to hold yourself in check, do what you are told, show discipline, and manifest obedience? It is the time of day when you are not really yourself, but only some sort of a puppet who must answer to the pull of the strings in the hands of the boss; or that time when you are little more than an inanimate machine that must function in a way that will produce. Once work is over, then you can be yourself; you can live, for you can play!

That attitude of mind can rightly be called pathological; for it is a sickness that actually stops human growth.

Sunday — the Lord's day — is supposed to be a day of rest, a day of peace and recollection, a day for family reunion, true piety, and some real prayer. Sunday is supposed to be the *Antiphon* for the week — the day that blessed the six days on which man works. But in your time, what has Sunday become? It has been replaced by the *weekend*.

Again your generation gives evidence of that childishness which is a pathological state, since it divides all life into work and play. What is more, you have allowed the dichotomy to become so deep and divisive that man's primary vocation is lost sight of; both work and play have lost their real identities; and earth has been changed from what God made it into a workshop that has a playground attached. The pathology is deadly, for when it obscures man's primary vocation, inevitably the One who issued that call fades from view. Then, in all truth, the weekend completely supplants Sunday with the inevitable result: God dies!

Those who traveled behind the Iron Curtain were aghast at the fact that, actually, on God's earth, there was a land without God. A land without a Sunday is just that. You see, then, that if the weekend has supplanted Sunday in your land, a childish error, which became a philosophical perversion of truth, ends by being dogmatic heresy — an affront to the infinitely good God.

∞

You are called to holiness, not to efficiency

But has man's God-given vocation been entirely lost sight of? Look around you. You live in a world that has lost faith. Religion has been replaced by work and achievement. In such a world, men take work very seriously. They want nothing less than perfection

307

in it. Hence, their goal and their norm of judgment is efficiency. Consequently men are judged not by what they *are*, but by what they can *do*. No wonder your economic world wobbles. It has lost its center of gravity.

Your primary vocation, like that of every other human, is to *be*, not to *do*. Your life's aim is holiness, not efficiency. God and godliness, not production, is your goal, for you have an immortal soul; you are not a machine. Every work and every profession, even the highest, is but a means for man to express his inner wholeness and to acquire more holiness; none of them is ever to become any man's idol or total absorption.

You are now grappling with truths that have been horribly distorted in your day. Twist them back into shape so that you will be able to live twenty-four hours a day as a human, a child of God, and not spend a great part of your life on earth as a robot that keeps going through the motions so that it can make a living, but which is really only waiting for the whistle that will allow it to go out and play.

Realize first that while all men are *created* equal, all men are not *born* equal. Far from it! Some are born with silver spoons in their mouths; others with a pick and shovel by their side. In his encyclical on labor, Leo XIII showed that society always was and always will be stratified. God so wills it, as is evident from the fact that "among mankind, differences of the most important kind exist: people differ in capacity, skill, health, strength. Unequal fortune is the result of unequal condition."

But note well that for attaining their last end, for getting back to God whole and holy, each human has been liberally endowed by His Maker. No man has grounds for complaint. You may not be gifted enough to conquer the world, but you have more than enough to conquer your sinful self — and that is, of course, the only conquest that counts. In eternity, you will not be judged on productivity, but only on Christlikeness. Hence it is essential that you learn how you can grow in Christlikeness while at work, for work you must. It is the God-given law of life.

Work is part of God's plan for humans. But God is your Father, and God is all-good. Therefore, the work potentials He gave you must be for your happiness.

∞

Work is holy

The second step is easy. If work is God's will, it must be sanctifying; for, in ultimate analysis, sanctity is only doing the will of God. Therefore, work is a sacred thing; it is a "sacramental" — an outward sign that can give grace. Hence, you can go to work for the same reason you go to church to worship God! Work is a religious thing. It is holy.

That view, of course, is the antithesis of the way many modern men conceive work. They exalt it, but only by a complete reversal of values and truths. The person who helps produce impersonal goods is placed far below the goods he helps to produce and is thus completely dehumanized. Pius XI exposed this situation in his *Quadragesimo Anno*,[390] saying, "Conditions of social and economic life are such that vast multitudes of men can only with great difficulty pay attention to the one thing necessary; namely, their eternal salvation." But you can combat those conditions and overcome that very real difficulty. All you need to do is to think with the mind of Christ and will with the will of God; then you will go to work for the same purpose you go to church.

[390] Commemorating the fortieth anniversary of Leo XIII's *Rerum novarum*: on reconstruction of the social order, May 15, 1931.

Is that possible? Well, you are what your thoughts are. A man is his mind. What are your thoughts and motives for going to church? The same can be had for going to work, for first it is God's will. Therefore, you can make it an act of obedience to your Father. Faith, hope, and charity are already exercised in that one act and attitude of mind. Further, since you know it was the first penance laid on a sinner, you can make it reparation for your own sins and the sins of the world. You can make it plead with God for mercy on all who toil and thus fulfill those two commandments of love of God and love of neighbor which Christ said was all that is required of man.

Have you ever realized that, in making you a worker, God has given you a share in that universal Providence by which He governs the human race and in His act of conservation by which He keeps the world in being? If you are a farmer, you well know you work hand in hand with God in the production of food for man's body and, hence, indirectly for his soul. The multiplications of bread and fishes, twice told about in the New Testament,[391] were truly marvelous happenings. Yet St. Augustine is right to laugh at those who marvel, as he points to the relatively few seeds that are sown in the earth and the millions that are fed from their harvests. He reminds you that this annual miracle is due to God just as much as those multiplications you read of in the Gospels.

But God's Providence does not end in the fields. He rules the entire process from the sowing of the seeds to the growth, the harvest, then the threshing, milling, and marketing. He has a hand, too, in the baking of the bread and putting it on your table. So, in all truth, every human who helps in the process is actually working hand in hand with God.

[391] Matt. 14:15-21, 15:32-38.

This truth brings Heaven very near. Prunes may grow in California, potatoes in Idaho, peaches in Georgia, wheat in Kansas, and corn in Kentucky; beef may be raised in Texas, and hogs butchered in Chicago. But none of these commodities will ever be served at any table miles and miles away unless all sorts of men and women cooperate with God in producing, processing, preserving, shipping, selling, and preparing them. So everyone from the grower to the boy who pastes on the labels to the housewife or the hired chef are God's helpers — so that you may have a meal.

Viewed in that perspective, how can work be anything other than worship? Since Adam fell, work should be a sacred thing! For it can be offered to God in thanksgiving for the pardon He extended to the sinner, as expiation for the sin committed, in petition that there be no more falls, but rather an ever-increasing adoration of God's will and His Providence. But those four ends are the four ends of the Mass. Hence, your work can be, and should be, eucharistic: sacrifice and sacrament.

Only out-and-out pagans can consider work servile. In the Roman Empire, before Christ and Christianity, slaves did all the work. The so-called cultured class deemed it beneath their dignity to toil. But since the Son of God became the village Carpenter, no truly cultured person can look upon work — hard, manual labor — as anything less than ennobling, even deifying.

The Council of Trent has taught that the Passion and death of Christ were the principal means He used to redeem mankind. That explicit bit of dogma teaches you implicitly that it was not on Calvary alone that Christ redeemed. In other words, when Jesus was down in Nazareth working on wood, He was redeeming mankind just as truly as when He was on Calvary nailed to wood. It tells you that when Jesus' hands held a plane or a saw, He was doing His Father's will and thus making salvation possible for you, just as truly as when these same hands held spikes and were held by them! The Son of God was redeeming men at the carpenter's bench in the obscurity of Nazareth just as surely as when He was followed by crowds that would take Him and make Him king[392] — just as surely as when He was followed by that other crowd that had taken Him, mocked Him, and crucified Him for being King!

∝

Obedience redeems

The public life and the Passion of Christ have often drawn attention away from the longer, but no less important, part of His life on earth: those eighteen, and even thirty, years of obscurity. You sometimes forget that Christ was anointed Priest in the womb of Mary; that from the moment she said *fiat* and conceived by the Holy Spirit, the Mass or the drama of the redeeming was underway. From that moment on, Jesus was offering Himself to the Father in reparation for sin and winning the grace that is to be your means to salvation. "Then said I, 'Behold I come.' In the head of the book it is written of me that I should do Thy will."[393]

There is the central fact of God's life on earth: obedience. And it should be the central fact of your life on earth. Redemption was not achieved by passion so much as by action. It was not Christ's sufferings so much as His submission that pleased God and redeemed man. Mary's obedience, expressed in her *fiat* began the drama of the redeeming. Christ's obedience, expressed in His *fiat* in the garden, brought that drama to its perfection, for it was oblation rather than immolation that redeemed. It will be your *fiat* that will save. Pound that truth into your being: *it is simple to save!*

[392] Cf. John 6:15.
[393] Ps. 39:8-9 (RSV = Ps. 40:7-8).

Strictly speaking, neither the sweat of blood, the spittle, the thorns, the biting scourge, the burning nails, the lance, no, not even the Cross itself was necessary that you be bought back from Satan, sin, and death. Obedience was! Golgotha and its blood-filled gloom was but the climax of that obedience which was the beginning, the continuation, and the consummation of your redemption. What redeemed in the first century will save in this century. The manner of offering alone will be different: then it was Christ by Himself, now it will be Christ in, by, and through you!

You should feel holy, then, as you punch the time clock, open the store, or enter your office. You should feel that you are worshiping God and saving men as you answer the alarm that wakens you for work.

As you set out for your work, you can be exercising the infused theological virtues of faith, hope, and charity and give free, full play to the four infused moral virtues as you labor through the day. It takes a stout heart to work day in and day out, year after year. There is where *fortitude* has place. Since you know that work is not only penance but part of God's original plan and present Providence, *justice* will prompt you to obey, and thus, while earning a living, *prudence* and *temperance* will tell you how to glorify God and gain eternal life for self and others.

But now for the deeper lesson that lies in labor.

∝∞

You must serve Christ in others

The whole twenty-fifth chapter of the Gospel according to St. Matthew merits prayerful meditation, but the last third demands the most careful consideration, for it is there that Christ tells you why people go to Heaven — or to Hell. Since life is a wind and eternity tomorrow, you will be in one of those two classes

313

"tomorrow"! You will have gone to Heaven — or to Hell — for what you did or what you left undone — to Jesus Christ.

With that truth before you, life becomes serious, it is true, but also both sacred and simple. Not only is its complexity resolved, but its very mystery melts away; for in startling simplicity and wondrous unity it stands before you: not something, but Someone. Life is Jesus Christ.

Him you can see as clearly as did the Magi who followed a star until they found the Child;[394] as clearly as did the Baptist when he heard the Father's voice and saw the Spirit descend and rest upon the Man he had just baptized;[395] as clearly as did the two on the road to Emmaus when they saw the Stranger breaking bread.[396] You can be the "other wise man," for you can find Christ in all your workers and minister unto Him through all your works.

In *The Other Wise Man*, Henry Van Dyke told of a fourth member of the group of Magi, the one who missed meeting the three whom the Gospel tells about because he stopped to help one who reminds you of the man who fell among robbers as he went from Jerusalem to Jericho.[397] But this fourth wise man, whom Van Dyke names Artaban, is determined to follow that star and give the newborn King the three precious stones he has purchased by the sale of all his possessions: a sapphire "as blue as a fragment of the night sky," a ruby "redder than a ray of sunrise," and a pearl "as pure as the peak of a snow mountain at twilight." But now that he has missed the caravan of the three with whom he was to make the search, he must part with that sapphire as payment for the camels

---

[394] Matt. 2:10-11.
[395] Cf. Matt. 3:16-17; John 1:32-34.
[396] Luke 24:30-31.
[397] Cf. Luke 10:30.

he needs to cross the desert. When he arrives in Bethlehem, not only have his friends departed, but the Mother and the Child have fled to Egypt. Before he can set out in quest of them, he meets Herod's soldiers as they are slaughtering the innocents. To purchase life for one young male whose mother had given him shelter, Artaban parts with the second of the precious stones he wanted to give the newborn King. The ruby that glistened like a drop of blood goes to the captain of the soldiers so that he will pass this house without a search.

Thirty years later, Artaban is back in Judea. One Friday afternoon, he finds himself in Jerusalem, and the city is all astir because two thieves were being crucified with Jesus of Nazareth. When Artaban learns that this Jesus is being crucified "because He made Himself out to be the Son of God,"[398] he turns toward Golgotha with breathless haste, thinking that at last his quest is at an end. He will offer his pearl as ransom for the "King of the Jews" before He is nailed to the Cross. But as he hastens toward Calvary, he meets a band of Macedonian soldiers dragging a young girl, whose dress is torn and hair disheveled, off to slavery. The pearl that was as pure as a snow peak buys her freedom. Just then, the darkness that had been over the land is shattered and the earth shakes. A tile falls from a roof and strikes Artaban. He falls and dies. But the girl whose freedom he had just purchased, as she kneels there holding his bleeding head on her lap, hears God welcoming the fourth wise man. She hears the surprised Artaban asking, "When saw I Thee hungering and fed Thee, or thirsty, and gave Thee drink? . . . Three and thirty years have I looked for Thee, but I have never seen Thy face, or ministered to Thee, my King." Then comes the reply of replies: "Verily I say unto thee, inasmuch as

[398] John 19:7.

315

thou hast done it unto the least of these, my brethren, thou hast done it unto me." The other wise man had found the King.

The Gospel and that story are for you! You will be judged on what you do or fail to do to Christ Jesus *in His brethren* — the members of His Mystical Body. You will be the other wise man if you give *God* your gifts as you give your well-earned wages to your parents, wife, children, brothers, sisters, relatives, friends, and dependents. You have your "sapphire, ruby, and pearl" in your pay envelope. You give them to Christ as you tender your earnings to His members.

Religion is real, as palpable as a pay envelope. Work can be worship. If you are a father with a family to support or a wife and mother with a home to keep and children to rear, how holy your labors can be! Your children are Christ, whom you must feed, clothe, house, and educate. Whatsoever you do to them or for them, you do to Him, for they are His members. Make that truth a habitual thought, and all your labors will be light because they will be love; further, all your work will be real worship, for no longer will you be working for your children alone, but for Him, the omnipotent God, who became a Child for you.

God was very small at Bethlehem, in Egypt, and for years at Nazareth. He is no bigger today as He again becomes incarnate in the children of young married couples. If these same couples miss Christ, it will have been because He was too near! It takes faith to see Almighty God in a helpless, crying baby. But what more did the wise men find in that house over which the star stopped? If Leonidus, the father of Origen, could tiptoe in to his newborn, sleeping son, press an adoring kiss on the child's breast "because God was there," why cannot you go to work every day in order to worship your God by obedience, and do service to Christ as you win sustenance and support for your family?

∞

You can make your work an act of worship

It is simple to make work worship, but it is not easy to keep it such. The atmosphere for most workers is anything but church-like, so you must have techniques that will enable you to make it what God means it to be.

First, get into the habit of blessing yourself before you begin to labor. It will remind you of who you are and what you are doing. Then, as you work, keep united to God — not by dividing your attention between your work and your worship, but rather by focusing all your attention on your work so that it will be worthy to offer as worship. But you know that as you work, God is living in the depths of your soul, and to those depths you drop down every now and then by so simple a device as thinking the name *Jesus* or the one word *God*. Do that, and your work will be a prayer of praise, a petition for grace, a veritable Mass; for you will be offering all your labor to God in Christ Jesus, who will transubstantiate it for you, since you are His and always in communion with Him.

Remember that you, the person, are the one who is the responsible agent for all the acts of your members, just as it is you, the person, who is the recipient of all the suffering experienced through your members. Your *eyes* did not read that sentence; *you* read it through your eyes. When you have what you call a headache, it is not your *head* that aches, but *you* who ache in your head. Rewards and punishments are given to human individuals not to their separate members. You do not execute the gunman's trigger finger; you execute the gunman. You do not pay the stenographer's eyes or hands; you pay the stenographer.

Now, if you apply this to the teaching of St. Thomas Aquinas that says, "The Head and the members of Christ are as one mystical person," you learn what your works are worth.

Cardinal Cajetan,[399] the great Dominican theologian, followed St. Thomas's lead and taught that "Christ and ourselves, His members, make up one mystical person. Therefore, my satisfactions (that is, my meritorious works, offered as satisfaction) when joined to the satisfaction of Christ, and considered as the satisfaction of the one mystical person, become strictly equal to the offense, and at times even superabundant."

In commenting on St. Paul's words to the Galatians: "It is now no longer I who live, but Christ in me,"[400] this cardinal teaches things that are even more directly pertinent to your labors of every day and shows you how the infinitesimal can be lifted into the sphere of the infinite. "Note," says the cardinal, "how the apostle explains the words he had just written: 'that I may live for God.' He does so by correcting the use of the first person. 'No,' he continues, 'it is not I who live, but it is Christ who lives in me. Hence, all my vital acts, such as to know and to think, to love, to rejoice or be sad, to desire, to labor are mine no longer; they no longer come from me, but from Christ within me.' "

∞

Christ works in you

Actions and sufferings belong to the person, not the members. You have learned how your sufferings, the *pleroma Christi*, are the filling up of Christ's Passion. What now of your actions?

Let Cardinal Cajetan answer: "We must suppose, as the apostle does when he writes to the Romans, to the Ephesians, and to the Colossians that men in the state of grace are living members of Christ. We must also suppose . . . that the Head and the members

---

[399] Thomas de Vio Cajetan (1469-1534), Dominican theologian.
[400] Gal. 2:20.

form one body, as in a natural body. . . . Again we must suppose, as the Scripture teaches, that the sufferings and actions of Christ's living members are the sufferings and actions of Christ, their Head. On the subject of their sufferings, we have Christ's own words: 'Saul, Saul, why persecutest thou me?' Yet Paul was persecuting only His members. And Paul reminds the Galatians that Christ was crucified in them, by which he clearly means, in the sufferings they have endured for Christ. On the subject of their actions, St. Paul writes to the Corinthians, 'Seek ye a proof of Christ who speaketh in me.' Finally, speaking in general, he tells the Galatians, 'I live, now not I, but Christ liveth in me.' From all this, I conclude that it is perfectly true for me to say, 'I merit; no, it is not I who merit, but Christ who merits in me. I fast; now not I, for it is Christ that fasts within me,' and so of all the free actions that the living members of Christ perform for God."[401]

Bishop after bishop who addressed the fourteenth session of the Council of Trent expressed the same ideas in almost the identical words. About a year after that fourteenth session, Cardinal Hosius, who had been Papal Legate to the Council, created a sensation by bringing out this doctrine in a *Confession of Catholic Faith*. In one place, he wrote, "If Christ lives in us, He cannot do so without acting in us. . . . What we do in this manner must necessarily be worthy of eternal life, not because of the merit of the works themselves, but because of the merit of Him who lives and acts within us."

To some, that may sound deep and difficult, so let Francis de Sales put this doctrine into language that will speak to your heart

---

[401] Quoted in Emile Mersch, trans. John R. Kelly, S.J., *The Whole Christ* (Milwaukee: The Bruce Publishing Company, 1938), 516.

as well as to your head. Treating of the love of God, the saint writes, "Scarlet and purple or deep crimson is a most precious and princely material, not because of the wool, but because of the color. The works of good Christians possess so great a value that, in return for them, we obtain Heaven; yet, Theotimus, it is not because they proceed from us, and are the wool of our hearts, but because they are reddened with the blood of the Son of God, or in other words, because the Lord sanctifies our works by the merits of His blood. The branch, united and joined to the vine, bears fruit, not by its own power, but by the power of the vine. Now, we are united through charity to our Redeemer, as the members are united with the head; hence it is that our fruits and good works draw their virtue from Him, and so merit eternal life."[402]

There are theologians, even today, who insist that you are only a finite being and can never be anything else. Then they show that your actions, the greatest of them, will be only finite. They seem to have you stopped. For they will argue that "no effect can be greater than its cause." Stones cannot run or even walk. Dogs cannot argue in syllogistic form or any other form. Neither can you, or any other human, bring forth an action that is in any way, shape, or manner infinite. They will go so far as to point out that grace itself is but a creature of God and therefore finite. Hence, it cannot take away your essential limitation as a finite being. They readily admit that by incorporating you into His Christ, God bestowed an immense dignity on you. But they smile and tell you that you cannot get a quart of milk, or a quart of anything else, into a pint bottle; neither can you squeeze the infinite into the finite. Your capacity for receiving is limited; hence, this very gift of God can be received by you only according to your capacity — which is finite.

[402] St. Francis de Sales, *Treatise on the Love of God*, Bk. 11, ch. 6.

They argue well, these men, and seem to receive confirmation for their argumentation in Pius XII's encyclical on the Mystical Body. When he writes about certain errors that have cropped up in this doctrine, the first he cites and condemns is that false mysticism which would have the Head and members forming "one *physical* person." That Pope shows just how erroneous these people are by saying, "While they bestow divine attributes on man, they make Christ our Lord subject to error and to human inclination to evil."

But you must note that Cardinal Cajetan followed St. Thomas Aquinas and insisted that Christ and His members form one *mystical* person, not one physical person. Note also that neither he nor any of his followers ever attributed infinity to the members, but only and always to the Head. What they teach is that the Christ, who lives and works in you, takes your actions, and (while leaving them yours) makes them His own. Hence, you can agree with these men who say that man, as man, can produce only what is human and finite. But then you can quietly insist that that is the precise point: when you work, you do not work as man; you work as Christ's member. And that makes all the difference in the world, for you can be bold enough to parallel St. Paul and say, "I work; no, it is no longer I who work, but Christ works in me."

If these men should say they fear that you are close to error, you can turn to Emile Mersch, S.J., who admits that those theologians knew they were walking on the edge of the abyss when they taught such a doctrine, but says, "They also knew that truth extends as far as error exclusively . . . and to place any further restriction on truth, even under the pretext of more surely avoiding error, is simply to fall into another error."[403]

---

[403] Mersch, *The Whole Christ,* 521.

Or you can quote the Council of Trent itself: "All our glory is in Christ, in whom we live, in whom we move, in whom we make satisfaction, bringing forth worthy fruits of penance which have their virtue from Him, which by Him are offered to the Father, and which because of Him are accepted by the Father."

You could argue, too, from St. Augustine. But you need only limit yourself to Christ's own words. At the Last Supper, did He not speak of the Vine and the branches and the fruit thereof? He said that the fruit came from the branch joined to the Vine or from the Vine that has branches — in other words, from both, but principally from the Vine! About your oneness with Jesus no one can testify more clearly than did He Himself when He cried out in His mystical Passion as He had never cried out in His physical Passion, "Saul, Saul, why persecutest thou me?"

Finally, it was Christ Himself who told you how to be the "other wise man," by saying, "Whatsoever you do [or leave undone] to the least of these . . . you do to me." Since it is your works that build your eternal mansion and win for you everlasting bliss with God and His Christ, are you exaggerating when you say their value is really infinite? Go to your work, then, as a Christian — not merely as a man. Look into yourself and your fellow workers and find Christ. Realize that no matter what the nature of your work, you are collaborating with Omnipotence and helping Him with His Divine Providence. You are God's coadjutor!

When talking to some Italian pottery workers Pius XII spoke a parable applicable to every worker in the world: "Jesus loved to teach through parables," said that Pope. "He compared our souls to the earth where He sows the seeds of nature and grace, which we must make fruitful. We have no right to let these talents sleep, useless to ourselves and to others; for He will demand an accounting. He works this earth Himself and teaches us to work it with Him."

∞

God perfects you through your work

That could be the last word in this chapter. But, despite all you have learned about work, it may still prove a burden. So you can profit from the rest of the parable Pius spoke. It is reminiscent of the prophecy of Malachy wherein your God is likened to a silver-smith who sits by His fires cleansing and refining His silver[404] — which is your soul. Pius builds his parable from the way the potters work. Speaking still of your soul as earth, the Pontiff says, "God kneads it into the daily vicissitudes of life, and submits it to the fire of trials to make His greatest masterpiece out of the lowliest soul, the one most pitiable in the eyes of men. If in your pottery works, the earth could speak, do you think it would lament the vigor of the hands that fashion it, or that it would complain of the burning caress of the fire which gives it hardness, beauty, and splendor?"

Draw the inescapable conclusion: when your work is hard, when you find it trying to your very spirit and a wearying burning in the very marrow of your bones, you can rejoice. For God is then fashioning His masterpiece! And you — if you are working as a member of Christ Jesus — are not only honoring God but helping all men as you win bread for your wife and family or whosoever de-pends on you. Be the other wise man, and find the incarnate God in your work and in your fellow workers.

[404] Mal. 3:3.

Chapter Thirteen

∞

You are one to whom God has surrendered His future[405]

Your ship now enters the deepest part of the sea.

Although you have seen that, as an individual, you are one sent by God and one whom Almighty God actually needs; although you have learned what that need is and how you can fulfill it; although, as a worker, you have just been told how you are God's own coadjutor, helping Him with His Divine Providence and being of real assistance to Him in the preservation of the world He made, you have not yet mounted the highest step. Rise now to one more height, and learn how God the Father, God the Son, and God the Holy Spirit have surrendered Themselves and Their very future on earth and even in Heaven to you.

Dietrich von Hildebrand in his *New Tower of Babel* tells how God speaks to every man as He once spoke to Adam, calling each by name, and asking, "Where art thou?"[406] Although that reads

---

[405] Although this chapter speaks primarily to married people, readers who are not married may profit from it as well.

[406] Dietrich von Hildebrand, *New Tower of Babel* (Manchester, New Hampshire: Sophia Institute Press, 1994), 22; Gen. 3:9.

like fancy, it is actual fact. As you stand on this latest step, hear that friendly call, and although you be as sin-sodden as was Adam when he first heard it, respond! What does God want of you this moment? Exactly what He has wanted since before time was, when He "chose you out in Christ Jesus before the foundations of the world."[407] He wants to entrust Himself, His Son, Their Spirit, and Their future to *you*.

At that grace-filled moment which was your Baptism, the Trinity surrendered Themselves to you. Omnipotence put aside power; the one Eternal became a mendicant in time, begging for a continuance of existence in your life. Father, Son, and Holy Spirit took up their abode in your soul; but there They dwell defenseless, dependent, completely at the mercy of your will. At any moment, for some trifle, you can expel the Trinity from the temple. They fashioned in your sin-freed soul. For some foolish fancy, you can make God an exile, banish Him from your world, and see Him wandering, as the Russian legend has it, limp and lame, begging His way, pleading for a refuge in the world He made.

But that is only one aspect of this surrender of God. His existence on earth in your soul is dependent on your free will. But the more startling truth is that the triune God has entrusted a part of His everlasting glory — the future happiness, as it were, of the Father, Son, and Holy Spirit — to you. Whether the Son will have the joy of presenting you to the Father as one who has been sanctified by His Spirit, and whether these three Persons are to enjoy your presence and your praise for all eternity, depends again on your free will.

What a challenge to generosity, to chivalry, to unassailable loyalty is the fact that the majesty of God, the eternal happiness and

---

[407] Eph. 1:4.

You are one to whom God has surrendered His future

glory of God, is without a single defense in your life, save your love!

∞

Married couples are vital to the Mystical Body

True as that is for each human being, it is doubly true, hence, twice as challenging, for married couples. Christ cannot live in this world of yours eucharistically unless there are men who love Him enough to give Him their lives and become His priests. Christ cannot continue to live in this world of yours mystically unless there are men and women who love Him enough to give their lives to one another in His great sacrament so that mystical members may be born. There is the fact that is stranger than any fiction: the future of God — Father, Son, and Holy Spirit — in this world and in the next, has been entrusted, surrendered even, to men and women who become husbands and wives.

With that truth before you, you can understand why it was that Pius XII, although addressing his encyclical on the Mystical Body to the "Patriarchs, Primates, Archbishops, Bishops, and other Ordinaries in peace and communion with the Apostolic See," should break off four times to address himself to "mothers and fathers of families." In the very first section of the encyclical, the Pope announced two tremendously important truths for married people: first, in the Mystical Body, they hold an honorable place, hence, the building up of that Body is not the concern of priests and religious alone, but of all who live in the world, and especially of fathers and mothers; second, holiness is their goal, even the highest height of holiness — "the peak."

Many have always thought that the summit of sanctity was reserved for priests and religious; that the convent and the cloister had something of a monopoly on holiness. Now they learn that those in the world and those who are married are called to the heights. Let them be assured, here and now, that if they or anyone else fail to arrive at the summit, the fault will not have been God's. He gives everyone sufficient grace to make the grade.

A little further along in his encyclical, Pius XII tells married people that personal holiness is not their only goal as members of Christ's Mystical Body, but that they have another duty; His Holiness goes so far as to say that "without it, the Mystical Body would be in grave danger." If modern psychologists are right in saying that one must feel important if one is to be happy, what happiness that Pope has provided for married people! Could anyone feel more important than those without whom the Mystical Body of the only Son of God would be in danger?

The sentence to which that clause is climax holds four wondrous truths for parents. The first is that "through Matrimony . . . the contracting parties are ministers of grace to one another. . . ." How Godlike that makes each! Grace is supernatural life, the very life of God; yet a man and a woman really "give" grace to one another as they become channels for the very blood of Christ, animated "sacraments," as it were.

The Pope goes on: "Through Matrimony . . . provision is made for the external and properly regulated increase of Christian society. . . ." Normally, conjugal society is not to remain static. Its primary aim is not your happiness and holiness, but the "increase of Christian society," as the Pope puts it. You are to multiply cells for Christ's Mystical Body. You are to help God grow! What a divine romance that makes of life!

"But, what is of greater importance," the Pope continues, "provision is made for the correct religious education of the offspring. . . ." In this great sacrament, God constitutes you the teacher of His and your children. That is your inalienable right, and your inescapable duty; but will any man or woman see it now in any other light than that of an exalted and exalting dignity? What Mary and Joseph did in Nazareth you married people are to do in your own home: teach the Christ Child; for once your child has been baptized, he or she is Christ.

Pius XII ends this last sentence with: ". . . without which this Mystical Body would be in grave danger." How important modern parents are to Almighty God, His only Son, and Their bond of love, the Holy Spirit!

As he neared the end of his letter, the Pope pleaded with "all who claim the Church as their Mother," begging them to realize that "not only the sacred ministers and those who have consecrated themselves to God in the religious life, but the other members as well have the obligation of working hard and constantly for the upbuilding and increase of this Body." Then came the characteristic pause and the subsequent emphasis. "In this connection, We cannot pass over in silence the fathers and mothers of families, to whom our Savior has entrusted the most delicate members of His Mystical Body. We plead with them for the love of Christ and the Church to give the greatest possible care to the children confided to them, and to look to protecting them from the multiplicity of snares into which they can fall so easily today."

As an individual, you can be Christ's complement; as a worker, you can be God's coadjutor; but it is only as parent that you step into that bewildering, intimate association with Omnipotence and become *procreator*. No human being could ask for more. Beyond here stands God — and God alone!

Angels, ministers of God though they be, assistants in the governing of the world, never had opportunities equal to yours. "Our human nature [in itself]," said Pius XII, "is inferior to angelic nature; yet, be it observed, through God's goodness it has risen above angelic nature . . ." for "in respect to similarity of nature, Christ is not Head of the Angels, because He did not take hold of the angels — to quote the apostle — but of the seed of Abraham."

Your guardian angel is a marvelous being, pure spirit, close associate of God. But he never became, nor can he become, what you are: Christ's own member. Never once has he received as food and drink the Body and Blood, Soul and Divinity of God's only Son. Never once has he, or any other angel in the entire angelic host, been allowed to do what you can do continually: offer to God the Body of His only Son. And, of course, no angel can ever have the opportunity of sharing with Omnipotence the begetting of children who are to become Christ's members, and whom you are to raise up as "fellow citizens of the saints, and members of God's household."[408]

∞

Love necessitates giving

The Holy Eucharist is called the "Sacrament of Love" because in it God gives Himself completely. If you read the encyclical on Christian marriage, *Casti connubii*,[409] in which Pius XI confesses he is confirming and making his own what Leo XIII had said in his *Arcanum Divinae Sapientiae*,[410] you will see why you can very justly name Matrimony the "Sacrament of Love," too. For once again, it is a sacrament of total giving.

If you wish to learn how to love, go to the school of God, for God is love. St. Paul wrote for the Ephesians what can be taken as a perfect prayer for every parent: "I bow my knees to the Father of

---

[408] Eph. 2:19.

[409] On Christian Marriage, December 31, 1930.

[410] On Christian Marriage, February 10, 1880.

our Lord Jesus Christ, of whom all paternity in Heaven and earth is named, that He would grant you, according to the riches of His glory, to be strengthened by His Spirit with might unto the inward man, that Christ may dwell by faith in your hearts . . . rooted and founded in charity." In the same letter, Paul would have you "rooted and founded in charity," not only for the strengthening of your inward self, but for a higher, more glorious reason: so that "you may be able to comprehend, with all the saints, what is the breadth, and length, and height, and depth [of this mystery]; and to know also the charity of Christ, which surpasseth all knowledge, that you may be filled unto all the fullness of God."[411]

"The fullness of God" — marriage, too, is for that *pleroma Christi*, although in a sense different from the one you learned when studying suffering. Now you learn you are to "fill out" God the Father's plan for His Son; you are to carry on the Incarnation by giving.

God and the God-Man teach you that the art of living is the art of loving and that the perfection of the art of loving lies in the consummate art of giving. No one ever loves until he or she has given himself or herself away — totally and entirely — to the beloved. If the child would be worthy of the Father and the member of the Head, you must give yourself as God has given Himself.

Marriage is the sacrament of giving. That it is very dear to God and His Christ is evident from the Gospels. There is deep significance in the fact that Christ worked His first miracle at a wedding feast, that He spoke so many parables about wedding guests and wedding garments, and that He makes so many references to brides and bridegrooms. Knowing what you do of the intimacy of marriage, can you conceive any greater intimacy for a human with

[411] Eph. 3:14-19.

God than to be a member of that Church which is Christ's own Bride and entering a union to which mystics give the name "nuptials"?

The terms are inescapable, for marriage speaks of life, union, and fecundity; and Jesus Christ is life, who wedded humanity so that humans might "have life and have it in abundance."[412] But although He is God and omnipotent, Christ cannot give that abundant life to other humans unless some husbands and wives give themselves to one another. Human life will not go on unless humans love. Divine-human, or supernatural, life will not go on unless humans love as God wills.

"Christian spouses, even if sanctified themselves, cannot transmit sanctification to their progeny," says Pius XI, ". . . nevertheless, they share to some extent in the blessings of that primeval marriage of Paradise, since it is theirs to offer their offspring to the Church in order that by this fruitful Mother of the children of God they may be regenerated . . . and finally be made living members of Christ."

That shows you how dependent God, His Christ, and that Christ's Church are on you. Christ's own Church will never become Mother of your child unless you offer your child to her. God's Christ will never have your child as His member unless you present your child to Him. God the Creator cannot become Father to your child unless you freely will it. So you see how profoundly true it is to say that God has surrendered Himself and His future to you.

Pius XI could have had that in mind when he immediately added, "Both husband and wife, receiving these children with joy from the hand of God, will regard them as a talent committed to their charge by God, not only to be employed for their own

---

[412] John 10:10.

advantage or for that of an earthly commonwealth, but to be restored to God with interest on the day of reckoning." See how intimately bound up with you and your children is God's eternal happiness. They are God's children even more than yours; for you gave them only flesh and blood: it is God who gave them life — and life eternal.

God lends you for a time what He wants back for eternity — and what He wants back *with interest*. How can you "double" this talent in flesh and blood which you call your child and who is in all truth just a "keepsake for Heaven"? There is only one way: send your child to the school of love — make him a Christian; then fill him with Christ. That is the only education proper for a child of God.

Parents are not only procreators; they are also educators. But *education* means to "bring out." Parents are to bring out the image and likeness of God; they are to bring out the character of Christ. The first was given their children at conception; the second at Baptism. Since God wants your children back "with interest," you can satisfy the Divine Usurer only by making your children grow up "in the likeness of Christ." You can do that by following the direction given by God the Holy Spirit through St. Paul: "Follow God's example. . . . Let your conduct be guided by love."[413]

∽

Married couples should mirror Christ and His Church

Among Christians, no other guide or principle is admissible. Love is your life — the breath of your body, the blood of your heart. For God is love, and Christ is God, and you are Christ. But Paul specifies for married couples, telling them that the ideal to be

[413] Cf. Eph. 5:1-2.

attained by them is nothing short of God. "Let wives be subject to their husbands, who are representatives of the Lord, because the husband is head of the wife, just as Christ is Head of the Church and also Savior of that Body. Thus, just as the Church is subject to Christ, so also let wives be subject to their husbands in all things."[414]

What a directive! Wives are to look at their husbands and see *Christ*. They are to realize that with him they form a miniature Mystical Body. They are to remember that they are to be to him what the Church is to Christ: "a bride without spot."[415] How utterly sacrosanct that woman should be who would call herself "wife" to one who is a Christian!

To the husband, Paul's challenge is that he merit the attitude the wife is to display; that he fulfill the office of "head"; that he *be* Christ!

Pius XI saw the possibility of men and women both misinterpreting this directive of St. Paul, so in his *Casti connubii*, he insisted that "this subjection does not deny or take away the liberty which belongs to the woman both in view of her dignity as a human person, and in view of her most noble office as wife and mother and companion." Neither Christ nor His Church ever weary of proclaiming and insisting upon the inviolable dignity of every human individual and the utter inalienability of his or her freedom.

What Paul was teaching, and what Christ's vicars are always teaching, is the necessity of *order*. Pius XI shows what is meant by the wife's subjection when he says, "It does not bid her to obey her husband's every request if not in harmony with right reason or

---

[414] Eph. 5:22-24.
[415] Cf. 2 Cor. 11:2.

with the dignity due to a wife . . . nor, in fine, does it imply that the wife should be put on the level with those persons who in law are called minors, to whom it is not customary to allow free exercise of their rights on account of their lack of mature judgment, or of their ignorance of human affairs."

You might ask, "What, then, is left?" His Holiness foresaw that and added what is, for the woman, one of the most beautiful passages she will find in any literature, secular or ecclesiastical. Pius XI names the wife and mother "the heart of the body." Now remember, married couples form a miniature Mystical Body. Hence, when Pius says the woman is the "heart of that body," he is saying that she is Christ's "heart." What more could anyone desire?

Thérèse Martin,[416] known to the world as "the Little Flower," claimed she had solved all difficulties once she had found her place in the Mystical Body. She said that place was "love." The Christian wife and mother has not to ponder or puzzle. Christ's own Vicar has told her that "if the man is the head, the woman is the heart, and as he occupies the chief place in ruling, so she may, and ought to, claim for herself the chief place in love."

∽

Husbands and wives should make each other holy

Ignoring these directives for married life, many human beings have enacted tragedy. The woman who follows Paul's precept, far from suffering any indignity, will garner every possible gain — not only supernatural, but natural as well. For, by submitting, she will actually rule, because every man worthy of the name is won completely when he finds such an attitude in the woman he calls wife. By such a display of dependence, a woman can make a man. For it

---

[416] St. Thérèse of Lisieux (1873-1897), Carmelite nun.

calls up all the chivalry latent in his being and summons every last atom of strength in his moral make-up. She can so shape his character that he will be all he should be: he will be Christ!

Wives, be not taken in by the world. Let no false notions about liberty deceive you, nor any clever catch phrases about the "equality of the sexes" blind you to the beauty of the vision that can be yours and the life of happiness to which that vision can lead you. Look on your man and see the God-Man!

Let this doctrine of the Mystical Body rule your life, and let the fact that you are His member give sacred meaning to your every moment. Do not think that it will take away from your human love to look on your husband and see him for what he is: Christ's vicar; rather it will ennoble, increase, and sanctify it. And should a perfect Christian woman happen to have married a Christian man who is as yet far from perfect, the human disappointment can be dissipated and the human void filled if she will realize that in him, imperfect though he be, she can love and be loved by the all-perfect Son of God, Jesus Christ.

But once He has laid down the law for the woman, God the Holy Spirit, through St. Paul, goes on to address the husband. And no man, listening to Him, can be without a gripping, ever-growing sense of unworthiness and genuine awe. No human male could dare face the challenge implicit in the words of Paul unless he were vividly conscious of the truth spoken by this same Paul when he said, "I can do all things in Him who strengthens me."[417] The strength of God is necessary, for the assignment given the husband is nothing short of divine.

"Husbands, love your wives, just as Christ loved the Church, and delivered Himself for her, so that He might sanctify her by

[417] Phil. 4:13.

cleansing her in the bath of water with the accompanying word, in order to present to Himself the Church in all her glory, devoid of blemish or wrinkle or anything of the kind, but that she may be holy and flawless. Even so ought husbands to love their wives as their own bodies. He who loves his wife, loves himself. Now, no one ever hates his own flesh; on the contrary, he nourishes and cherishes it, as Christ does the Church, because we are members of His Body."[418]

What unselfishness is demanded from ever-selfish man! He is to love his wife as Christ loves His Church and for the same purpose: to make her ever more glorious and more beautiful, to make her more holy. Now, many a man loves his wife to make her more glorious and more beautiful; but how many have loved their wives just to make them more holy? No man will so much as think of it unless he remembers that Matrimony is God's great sacrament, and in it, every Christian man should be a "sacrament" to his wife — a channel of grace, a veritable reservoir whence she can draw sanctity freely and copiously.

How can man do or be that? By loving as Christ loved, and Paul tells you explicitly how that was: "He delivered Himself up for her." A husband must be ready for a *kenosis*; he must be ready for Calvary and the Cross if necessary for the sake of the woman he loves and calls wife — and all so that she may be holy — or else he is not a Christian husband.

What heights you are on now! Christ's Vicar Pius XI amplified Paul's teaching by telling you: "The love [you should have for your wife] is not that based on the passing lust of the moment, nor does it consist in pleasing words only, but in deep attachment of the heart which is expressed in action, since love is proved by deeds.

[418] Eph. 5:25-30.

This outward expression of love in the home not only demands mutual help but must go further; must have as its primary purpose that man and wife help each other, day by day, in forming and perfecting themselves in the interior life, so that through their partnership in life they may advance more and more in virtue, and above all that they may grow in true love toward God and their neighbor, on which indeed 'dependeth the whole Law and the Prophets.' For all men of every condition, in whatever honorable walk of life they may be, can and ought to imitate that most perfect example of holiness placed before man by God, namely, Christ our Lord, and by God's grace arrive at the summit of perfection."

How many young men and women in modern society contemplate Matrimony as a means of perfection — especially the perfection shown by Christ Himself? Yet, what other motive should induce, or be dominant in the thinking of a member of Christ? Marriage is not a physical union; it is a union of souls brought about by a mutual surrender of wills. It is a spiritual thing that finds expression in the physical, and even a sort of consummation there; but basically it is of the spirit. That is what the Pope and the apostle — and God Himself through them — are driving home.

That ideal is obviously above nature. But so are the men and the women to whom the letter and the encyclical are addressed. Every baptized human is above nature. Every Christian is more than human. And that a husband and wife should mutually help one another to become holier day by day means that they are in a holy *state*. There is a sacramental permanency about Matrimony.

When his world was falling apart much more evidently and really than is yours, St. Augustine taught this truth to his people, saying, "Just as by Baptism and Holy Orders a man is set aside and assisted either for the duties of the Christian life or the priestly office, and is never deprived of their sacramental aid, almost in the same way [although not by a sacramental character] the faithful, once joined by marriage ties, can never be deprived of the help and the binding force of the sacrament."[419]

St. Robert Cardinal Bellarmine, S.J., drew a more startling parallel. He did not point to Baptism or Holy Orders, but to the Eucharist in order to alert married couples to the sacramental permanency of their state. He said, "The sacrament of Matrimony can be regarded in two ways: first, in the making, and then in its permanent state. For it is a sacrament like that of the Eucharist, which is a sacrament not only when it is being conferred, but also while it remains; for so long as the married parties are alive, so long is their union a sacrament of Christ and the Church."[420]

Under the human "appearances" of your marriage, you have the sublime "substance" of God. Paul's ideal can be realized by you! But only if you live as a branch on the Vine. Matrimony not only gave you sanctifying grace, as do all the Sacraments, but yet gives you "that peculiar internal grace," as Pius XI calls it, "which perfects natural love, confirms an indissoluble union, and sanctifies both man and wife." Moreover, you are entitled — and God will always respect your title — to constant actual graces to fulfill your state. So day by day you *can* make one another holier and holier. And your marriage can be the living image of that most fruitful union of Christ with the Church.

◌৪०

Couples can make their marriages holy and fruitful
Pius XII has shown you how to implement this directive from God the Holy Spirit and how to reduce Paul's words to works. The

---

[419] St. Augustine, *De Nuptiis*.
[420] *Casti connubii*.

first requirement is a *strong faith*. In a sermon preached July 24, 1949, in St. Peter's, His Holiness pointed to a materialism that can creep into the most Christian of homes and ultimately ruin a good Catholic family. "For this evil," he said, "there is only one remedy: the strong faith of the parents which, through example, religious instruction, and moral education, will produce in children a solid faith. . . . Strength of Faith!" he cries. "Therefore, no superficiality, nor mere formality without substance, and not even a piety of mere sentiment!" His Holiness knows modern times. He knows men and women. So he plunges deep into reality as he says: "Pious and traditional customs of Christian families, beginning with the Crucifix and sacred pictures, must, of course, be held in the highest honor; but they have their true meaning only if they are based on a deep and interior faith, at the center of which are the great religious truths. How great, for example, is the value of the thought of God's omnipresence for the active and believing man, and what an incomparable aid it is in the education of children."

This strong faith and a lively sense of the presence of God will lead you to an *awareness of the Trinity*.

In giving instructions to some newly married couples, on June 19, 1940, Pius XII said, "Man, the masterpiece of the Creator, was made in the image of God. Now, in the family this image acquires, so to speak, a particular resemblance to its divine model, because, just as the essential unity of the Divine Nature exists in three distinct Persons, consubstantial and co-eternal, so the unity of the family is effected in the trinity of father, mother, and offspring. Conjugal fidelity and the indissolubility of Christian marriage constitute a principle of unity which may seem contrary to man's inferior nature, but is in accord with his spiritual nature. The command given to the first couple: 'Increase and multiply,' making fruitfulness a law, assures the family the gift of perpetuating itself through the centuries, and places in it a sort of reflection of eternity."

That same day, His Holiness summed up all you have been learning in this chapter by saying, "The sacrament makes them collaborators with the Father in His creative work; with the Son in His redeeming work; and with the Holy Spirit in His work of illumination and education. See the triple surrender God has made to you, and how each Person in the Trinity has placed His future in your hands! The Pope then asked a question you are now in a position to answer: "Is not this truly a predilection of God, the love of His Heart . . . ?"

You show your appreciation of that love by making your home like the one Pius XI told of when speaking to priests. "In an ideal Catholic home," he said, "the parents strive to instill into their children from their earliest years a holy fear of God and true Christian piety; they foster a tender devotion to Jesus, the Blessed Sacrament, and the Immaculate Virgin; they teach veneration and respect for holy places and persons. In such a home the children see in their parents a model of an upright, industrious, and pious life; they see their parents holily loving each other in our Lord, see them approach the holy Sacraments frequently and not only obey the laws of the Church concerning abstinence and fasting but also observe the voluntary spirit of Christian mortification; they see them pray at home, gathering around them all the family, that common prayer may rise all the more acceptably to Heaven."[421]

Pius XII followed that lead when talking to pastors in March 1949 and said something every husband needs to hear. "Taught to worship and love the Holy Sacrifice of the Mass," says His Holiness,

---

[421] *Ad Catholici sacerdotii* (On the Catholic priesthood), December 20, 1935.

"your menfolk will easily become men of prayer and will make their homes shrines of prayer. How greatly that is needed! Who can deny that the spirit of prayer languishes, while the spirit of the world is gaining ground even in families that claim still to be Catholic and faithful to Christ? Men who give themselves seriously to a deep study of the meaning and the purpose of the Sacrifice of the Mass cannot fail to kindle in themselves the spirit of self-mastery, of mortification, of the subordination of earthly things to heavenly, of absolute obedience to the will and law of God. This, no less than a renewal of zeal for prayer, is a need of the present day, since many, nowadays — among whom it is painful to see not a few Catholics — live as though their only object was to make themselves a paradise on earth, without a thought of the last things, of the hereafter, of eternity."

So you are back to the Mass and the Eucharist. It is inevitable, for no matter from what angle you approach this doctrine of the Mystical Body, you end at its Head and its Heart.

Implicit in all that the pontiffs have been teaching is the realization that you may have married one who is as yet not a perfect member of Christ. That does not change the truth about the sacrament nor your view of your state; for it is still Christ, only Christ, always Christ. He had a Gethsemani and a Calvary. You may have to save your soul and the souls of others by living a whole lifetime in that garden or on that hill. But if you live there ever conscious that you and your family are a miniature Mystical Body to whom God has entrusted His future, then the invisible Head, Jesus Christ, will make up to you even in time for all that your visible "head" — or if the roles are reversed, all your visible "heart" — lacks.

Chapter Fourteen

∞

You are one who can
bring Christ to the world

But you, if you should happen to be single and neither a cleric nor a religious, are not without your specific vocation — your God-given vocation!

It is indeed unfortunate that the idea of a divine vocation has been limited to those who have been called to the priesthood or to the religious life. It is more unfortunate that the idea and the term are not more universally applied to those who have been called by God to be His collaborators in the act of procreation. But it is most unfortunate that such labels as *bachelor girl, career woman,* and *single blessedness* have been coined and enjoy such currency even among those who should be intimately acquainted with what Paul said to his Ephesians, Thessalonians, Corinthians, Colossians, Philippians, Hebrews, and to Timothy — namely, that each Christian, each baptized soul, shares "in a heavenly calling";[422] that each and all are to "live lives worthy of the God who calls";[423] that each man, woman, and growing child can imitate Paul himself

[422] Heb. 3:1.
[423] 1 Thess. 2:12.

and press on "to the prize in store for those who have received from above God's call in Jesus Christ."[424]

Yes, *you*, whoever you are, have a divine vocation — a doubly, and even triply, divine vocation, for it is God the Father who has called you into fellowship with His Son"[425] and has "selected you from eternity to be saved through the sanctification which the Spirit effects. . . . To this has He called you."[426]

Like Paul, the prisoner in the Lord, we "exhort you to conduct yourselves in a manner worthy of the calling to which you have been called."[427] Like him, we urge you on to "fight the noble fight that the faith inspires, lay hold of eternal life to which you have been called."[428]

And Paul is not alone in telling you this truth. Peter, the Prince of the Apostles, taught the identical doctrine when he said that God "called you out of darkness into His marvelous light"[429] and then told you the purpose of the call by foretelling your end. "God, the source of all grace," he says, "who has called you to His eternal glory in Christ, will Himself, after you have suffered a little while, perfect, steady, strengthen, and firmly establish you."[430]

There can be no doubt that you have a divine vocation, for was it not God who called you out of nothingness? Was it not God who called you out of sin into His Christ and that Christ's sanctity? Was it not God who called you "to mature manhood, to the

---

[424] Phil. 3:14.

[425] 1 Cor. 1:9.

[426] 2 Thess. 2:13-14.

[427] Eph. 4:1.

[428] 1 Tim. 6:12.

[429] 1 Pet. 2:9.

[430] 1 Pet. 5:10.

measure of the stature of the fullness of Christ"?[431] God is still call-ing you, whoever you are, be it pope, prelate, prince, or ordinary person. He is calling you to "grow up in every respect in love and bring about union with Christ," calling you to go on "building up the body of Christ until we all attain to unity in faith and deep knowledge of the Son of God."[432] God is always calling you and every other member to "put on the Lord Jesus Christ, and to take no thought for your lower nature to satisfy its lusts."[433]

That vocation is definite enough. Its general outline and its spe-cific principles are in the Gospel. The character of Christ is clear. But just what your individual task as "Christ" is may never be known to you until you stand face-to-face with Christ to receive your eternal judgment, which should be your eternal reward. But that lack of clarity is anything but obscurity. One hundred, sixty-four times does God call you through St. Paul to "put on Christ";[434] twenty-four times in the Gospel of St. John, the identical call, but in other words, is issued. So in the New Testament alone, God has called you no less than one hundred, eighty-eight times "to put on the Lord Jesus Christ." That is your divine vocation.

∞

You are called to total interior change
Now, do not be deceived by terms. When St. John or St. Paul speaks of "putting on" Christ, they are using a metaphor taken from the stage, but the reality to which they are calling you is any-thing but stage play! Through them, God is calling you to a new

[431] Eph. 4:13 (Revised Standard Version).
[432] Eph. 4:12.
[433] Rom. 13:14.
[434] Paul uses "in Christ Jesus" — or its equivalent — 164 times.

life; and since every life principle is interior, God is calling you to a total renovation of your *inner being*. "Yes, we were buried in death with Him [Christ] by means of Baptism," says St. Paul, ". . . so we also may conduct ourselves by a new principle of life. . . . Consider yourselves dead to sin, but alive to God in Christ Jesus."[435]

Why is it that while Christ's life can be summed up in the line: "He went about doing good,"[436] the lives of so many Christians have to be summed up by saying that they simply "went about"? Most of these men and women have the best will in the world. But they have no realization of all Paul meant when he said, "Put ye on the Lord Jesus Christ." They were never told that Baptism was really a divine vocation to a complete *metanoia* — a change of mind and will. They were never told that they are to think with the mind of Christ and throb with all the desires that filled His Heart. They have never been told that they are to replace all their natural, instinctive, impulsive reactions to people, things, and events with the responses of Jesus Christ. Most of them have heard the divine call as it issued from the pens of Paul, Peter, and John, but they have mistaken it to be nothing more than a summons to imitate Christ; they have never realized it was a command to become totally "new creatures,"[437] to live only with the life that Jesus, the Head, pours into His members.

∞

You must bring Christ to the world

One must know what he is aiming at if he is ever to hit the target. So you must know precisely what your purpose is and have

[435] Rom. 6:4, 11.
[436] Acts 10:38.
[437] Cf. 2 Cor. 5:17.

your means as definite as the fingers on your hand if you are to achieve that purpose. That knowledge can be gained from the Gospels and their complementing Acts of the Apostles and letters. There is where you can come to know the character of Christ, learn His principles, and see His reactions to people, things, and events. There is where you will learn how to "put on Christ."

Once you have put Him on, you will "take no thought of your lower nature" for its lusts will be without real life. Once you have attained clarity on the nature of your divine vocation to "put on Christ" and have acquired some skill in "radiating Christ" you will thank God warmly for having called you to fulfill such a vocation in the midmost years of your turbulent century; for a more stimulating time to be "alive to God in Christ Jesus"[438] would be difficult to discover or even imagine.

You have lived, and are yet living, at a time when, as Cardinal Suhard, Archbishop of Paris, said in a pastoral letter in 1949, "a new world has been in the making." What can be said about that world? As yet, nothing with any degree of certitude. But, as this same cardinal pointed out, "Catholics cannot look upon the ever-increasing number of modern inventions as accidental happenings or scientific curiosities." You can't. Not after all you have been pondering about God's Providence and His continued creation. The cardinal is most right when he says, "These discoveries are very significant. They have to be integrated into an apostolic vision of the world's redemption. For, indeed, they do not merely ornament the world, but are actually building a new universe. And it is that universe, and no other, that we, in our time, are called upon to save. I say *save*, for its salvation has not yet been effected. But neither is its salvation impossible. We Catholics realize

[438] Rom. 6:11.

that the direction in which the world is moving is neither wholly good nor totally perverse. As realists, we know that, of itself, the world tends neither toward a golden age nor toward nothingness. It contains within itself, just as the men who shape it, a mysterious duality: it is capable of grace or sin. That world that is in the making may turn out to be the City of God or the City of Satan."

That statement should not kindle fear. For as the cardinal said, "It is not a new dilemma. Ever since the Crucifixion, history has recurrently presented these fundamental alternatives. But this is the first time that they have been presented to men on a global scale; for the world, for the first time, has become a unity. Who, therefore, shall lead the world out of this inherent dilemma? Who shall save the world from catastrophe and lead it to the unity of truth and love? Christ, for He is the sole Mediator. But Christ comes to us only in and by the Church, which is the continuation of His life through time. . . . The specific task of the Church is to effect a penetration of the world in extension and depth, so that nothing of it will remain unregenerated by grace."[439]

The cardinal is talking directly to you and about you; for you are the Church! You are the "continuation of the Christ-life in time." So your specific task is to penetrate the world in such a thorough manner that nothing in it will remain untouched by grace! "Realizing that is no easy task," the cardinal continued. "This work of total consecration presupposes that the Church, while growing, keeps true understanding of God, so as not to naturalize herself while endeavoring to supernaturalize profane things. At all costs, the Church must remain what she is: transcendent and

---

[439] Emmanuel Cardinal Suhard, *The Church Today*, ed. Louis J. Putz, C.S.C., and Vincent J. Giese (Chicago: Fides Publishers Assn., 1953), 219.

mysterious. This is a difficult task, but an exalted one. She has the negative duty of purging the world of atheism, and the positive duty of fulfilling man's relentless desire for holiness, so evident in the torture humanity is experiencing because of the absence of God."[440]

Your specific vocation is to relieve that torture by bringing Christ into your world. You are always a Christian, one who bears Christ within so that you may radiate Christ outwardly.

You are living in a "new universe." Under God's almost universally unperceived guidance, men have made discovery after discovery and presented their fellowman with invention after new invention until the face of the world has been almost completely changed. You drive luxury cars and ride in airplanes today, but it was only yesterday that you or your parents or your grandparents were riding in horse-drawn buggies. You touch a silent switch and your home is flooded with electric lighting. Perhaps this same house and these same rooms knew gas light and even oil lamps. At the beginning of the century it took fifty-four days to make a speedy round-the-world tour. Today your jets do not need three.

∽

God is more manifestly
present in today's world

You live in a "new world." But do not think for a moment that it is a man-made world, lest you become Manichaean. God is not only behind the scenes; He is the center of the stage. Leo XIII used to call every new invention a "spark of divinity." Pius XII says, "The natural sciences are making astonishing progress, and each one of their discoveries prompts men to exclaim, 'Here is the hand of the Creator!'" Most thoughtful men will give vent to such

[440] Ibid., 220.

349

exclamation and, with the Pope, see in every new discovery "one more trace of the Divine Intelligence, one more token of the power of God." To those who think aright and see clearly, God has been in your world and your century more manifestly than when He led His Chosen People by a cloud by day and a pillar of fire by night.

God is back in His world as He has not been for four, perhaps five, full centuries. And the remarkable part of His resurgence is that it is evil that has brought Him to the fore as good never did.

As your century opened, science banished God from His universe, and men were taught to aspire to the only heaven they would ever know: the one they would build on earth. Those were the dogmas and the dreams your century inherited. And how the men of those early years hugged that heritage and even capitalized on it. As the decades formed, universities boldly taught that humans had no souls; that they were only higher anthropoids; that instinct, animal appetite, sense, and especially sex were their guides. Free will was only a myth.

But look what has happened: actually it is Godlessness that has brought back God, for atheistic Communism has forced mankind to re-examine its conscience. Immorality so sickened and even frightened whole nations that they begged for a return to morality and the sanctions of religion. The neopaganism of your college campuses finally boomeranged, so that now chapel attendance is not only mounting, but is considered a mark of real intelligence and worthy of high merit.

How subtly and in what strange ways God works! He has been in those movements which have appeared as entirely man-made; for Nazism, Fascism, and even Communism have sprung from an impulse that is good because it is God-implanted. Deep in mankind is a desire for and an impulse toward unity. God put it there for man's good and His own glory. If followed rightly, it will fuse the teeming millions of the world into a oneness that will be absolutely unshakeable, because it will have been founded on Him who is immovable: Jesus Christ.

Christ-consciousness is deepening throughout mankind. Gradually the realization is growing that today you need no new Savior, but need to go back to Him who twenty centuries ago merited the name of Savior by winning the possibility for salvation for each and every member of the human race.

With the growth of that realization, a conviction is forming that the men of your century have been on the right road, but have been going in the wrong direction; that they are right in working for — and when necessary, in warring for — solidarity; but they have been working and warring under wrong colors. In your day, men are beginning to see that salvation lies not under black or brown or red; that what your world needs is not separate colors, but the fusion of all colors into Christlikeness. The more-advanced thinkers are turning to the past so as to assure progress in the future; they are growing ever more and more conscious of the fact that Christ was bled white on Calvary, and that in His bleeding was Redemption; that today Christ is in that Vicar who speaks from a heart that is overflowing with love for mankind and bleeding in a certain sense for each individual man; that unshakeable solidarity is possible only in and through the Mystical Body of Christ.

You and your times are moving into the Age of the Mystical Body; and in that movement you have a part to play, a definite contribution to make, which can be done only by an ever-keener consciousness of the fact that you are His member with a divine vocation to put on Christ and help build up His Body. You are called by God to do it in what is one of the very real major crises of history and which some wise men have rightly named the "crisis of puberty," which means that mankind and the Mystical Body of Christ are still very young. The fact that you have something to do for God at a time when His Son's Mystical Body is just issuing into its "young manhood" should thrill you.

That the Mystical Body of Christ is moving into its vigorous young manhood would seem evident from daily facts. What other explanation can be given for the energy, intellectual aggressiveness, and manifest self-assurance, so typical of early manhood, that is seen today in the Roman Catholic Church, which is the Mystical Body of Christ? At a time when those who are not Christ's members stand not only bewildered but paralyzed by a discouragement that borders on despair, the Mystical Body shows a fearlessness and a determination to accomplish great things that are proper to and characteristic of only young men.

Pius XII seems to have had this very analogy in mind when in June 1949 he said, "The Church, the Mystical Body of Christ, is, as the men who compose it, a living organism. . . . But the living body grows, develops, and tends toward maturity." The analogy is sound and has a piercing point for you, because it tells you that your call from God is to see that His Christ manifests His strong, young manhood in ever-wider circles, and that His maturing goes on.

That constitutes the high and exciting challenge of your vocation and your times, for young men can become sick and decline just as they can go on maturing and growing more robust. You are positive that the Mystical Body of Christ will not die. But you have no dogmatic assurance whatsoever as to the state of its health as it moves on into greater maturity. That is why, perhaps, God is calling more insistently in your day than He has called since His Christ died. You are one who can answer that call!

You are one who can bring Christ to the world

∞

Your vocation is to make
Christ present to others

Your vocation is clear. The general outline is unmistakable. Even many particulars are most evident. Yet while you live on earth, you may never know in its ultimate individuality just what your precise vocation as Christ's member is. That vocation is your real name — which is known to God alone. Just when the most important hour of your life is striking you may never know. That bit of divinely planned obscurity is what gives your life and your vocation its most real zest, for it is deep with mystery. When are we most needed by God — and men?

Father Robert Greene, the Maryknoller who was so viciously brainwashed in China, but who managed to hold on to his sanity despite the Reds, tells you in his book *Calvary in China* that as day succeeded day while he was under house arrest, he wondered if his life was not a waste. What was he doing for God or neighbor as he lived under guard? Then slowly the thought came — and grew — that possibly God was keeping him there, alone, a prisoner, a subject for torture, just so that in that God-hating land Christ might live. By clever maneuvering he managed to celebrate Mass, consecrate an extra Host, and reserve this Blessed Sacrament. Christ was then doubly alive: mystically and sacramentally, in a land that had brutally exiled Him.

Who can say that the hour in which Father Greene said that Mass and reserved that Sacrament was not one of the most important in the history of China and the Church in China? Thanks to that courageous young priest, infinite praise, infinite thanks, infinite adoration and reparation, along with infinite petition went up to God from the infinite Christ in a land where God was being hated. Since man is made to glorify God, what greater work could

353

any man do than what Father Greene did in that dark hour of seeming uselessness?

Think of Charles de Foucauld[441] out in the desert. What was he doing for God, himself, or his neighbor as day followed day and the slow years mounted? Nothing that would stir the United Nations. Nothing that would interest the International News Service or the Associated Press. Yet, thanks to his Mass, Charles de Foucauld brought Christ to that desert.

And so with *you!* Your employment may seem utterly colorless; your life, weariness and a waste. But you can always bring Christ into that part of the world where you are. It might well be that God wants you in that office, that factory, that workshop because you, by being a vital member of His Mystical Body, are the only one who can bring His Christ to that particular spot. Never doubt for a moment the dogmatic fact that you have a vocation and it is from God. Believe with all your being that so long as you make an honest effort to "put on Christ" and "take no thought of your lower nature to satisfy its lusts," you are fulfilling that divine vocation, pleasing God, and helping save your world, which is in such need of salvation.

Fill yourself not only with conviction, but with the courage those convictions give. Then go on bravely saving your world, confident that it can be saved! Realize that the very excesses to which your generation has gone — the hideous struggles of races, classes, nations fomented by the wild "isms" of your day: the first world war that brought into being trenches, tanks, flame-throwing, mustard gas, and air raids; the latest, which introduced mankind to the unbelievable atom bomb; your tragedies on the money

---

[441] Charles de Foucauld (1858-1916), French explorer who became a hermit in the Sahara.

market; your worse tragedies in the realm of Matrimony — all testify to one thing: the deep abyss in the human soul that cries incessantly to the other Abyss, the only One who can fill it, the God who called you into Christ Jesus. If God is calling to the world, never doubt that your world is calling to God. The very evils from which you and your world are suffering are evidence that there is a bleeding going on in the human heart. It can be stanched by you and your fellowmen, but only if you live under Him as Head who had His Sacred Heart emptied of blood.

∞

Peace requires that you "put on Christ"

Be realistic. You and your world want peace. But neither you nor your world can have it so long as matter reigns supreme. And surely you will not question the supremacy of matter in your groaning world. Belloc unquestionably was right when he said that ultimately every war is a religious war. But his friend Chesterton was not wrong when he pointed out that the wars of your day have also been economic wars — utterly inexcusable wars that were begun and viciously pursued for sheer materialistic ends. You yourself must see that such wars will go on with the best of your youth taking up arms, knowing not exactly why, and going out to massacre and be massacred by the best of the youth of some other country, equally ignorant of why they are under arms. This madness will not only perdure; it will worsen unless mankind undergoes a *metanoia* — a complete change of mind and heart, which will set the minds and hearts of men on their proper object.

This earth, your entire universe, is not big enough to fill the heart of one human. Alexander wept when he had conquered the world of his day, for his heart was still empty. The same would have been true of Napoleon, Hitler, Stalin, and any other would-be world conqueror if they had enjoyed the success which would have made their megalomaniacal dreams come true. This universe has bounds; the human heart has none, except God — and He is boundless.

Peace is possible for you and for your whole world, but only on God's terms. Peace will be had when all men follow the legitimate and absolutely limitless ambition of their hearts and become like unto God by putting on Christ.

Imagine your world if every individual in it knew that he had a divine calling, a command to complete Christ. Imagine the race of men laboring only to build up the City of God, and living only to bring the Mystical Christ to maturity. Vain imagining? Perhaps. But for twenty centuries now, Christians have been echoing Christ and crying, "Thy kingdom come!" You may reply that His kingdom is not of this world.[442] It is not of this world as it is now. But never forget that at Patmos, John saw a "new Heaven and a new earth." Never forget he also "heard a loud voice from the throne say, 'How wonderful! God's dwelling place is among men; He shall make His home among them. They shall be His people, and God Himself will abide in their midst." And "He who was seated on the throne said, 'See, I make all things new.' Then He added, 'Write, because these words are trustworthy and true.' "[443]

There is testimony from Truth itself. It should fire you with the determination to do your part in the bringing into being of this "new Jerusalem." Be Christ everywhere, to everyone, at all times, and you will not only enjoy that peace which comes from having answered God's call, but you will be flooded with surprise and excitement to learn how contagious this thing Christianity is, once

[442] Cf. John 18:36.
[443] Apoc. 21:1, 3, 5 (RSV = Rev. 21:1, 3, 5).

it is really lived. As Chesterton said, "Christianity has not been tried and found wanting. It has been found difficult and left mostly untried."

See what happened when Christianity was tried. When Saul of Tarsus brought to Ephesus the Good News that mankind had been redeemed, and now needed only to be saved by incorporation in that Redeemer, Ephesus was one of the most important of the great Asiatic cities. It held the Temple of Diana, one of the Seven Wonders of the World. But perhaps nowhere else in the world, save possibly at Corinth, was idolatry so passionately cultivated or shocking immoralities so openly and universally performed. It was to such a city that Paul taught the truths you have been learning; for to them, perhaps more than to anyone else, did he teach the doctrine of the Mystical Body.

What happened? In less than three years, he had founded and formed one of the greatest Christian Churches of his day. The people were not only won from their shocking immoralities but completely divorced from their idolatries. The heights to which Paul raised them is evident from the depths he opens out to them in his majestic letter to the Ephesians.

Read the introduction to this letter: "Blessed be the God and Father of our Lord Jesus Christ, who in Christ has blessed us with every manner of spiritual blessing in the heavenly realm. These blessings correspond to his choice of us in Christ before the foundation of the world, that we should be holy and without blemish in His sight. Out of love He predestined us for Himself to become through Jesus Christ His adopted children. . . . In Him we have our redemption through His Blood, the remission of our transgressions, in keeping with the riches of His grace. With this grace He has inundated us, by imparting to us all manner of wisdom and practical knowledge, making known to us, in keeping with His good pleasure, the mystery of His will. And this good pleasure He decreed to put into effect in Christ when the designated period of time had elapsed, namely, to gather all creation both in Heaven and on earth under one Head, Christ."[444]

That is not only deep doctrine; it is a call to highest sanctity. And Paul was one of the most practical of preachers! He tells you in those lines how contagious Christianity can be and what a revolution it can bring about.

Corinth may be even a more encouraging example. St. John Chrysostom pronounced Corinth "the most licentious city of all that are or ever have been." The guardian deity of this seaport was none other than Aphrodite, the goddess of lust and sinful love. Unrivaled as it was in wealth, Corinth was unsurpassed in profligacy. "To live like a Corinthian" was the proverbial way of saying one was leading a lawless and dissolute life. During the day, the streets of Corinth were packed with soldiers, sailors, foreign and domestic traders, idlers, slaves, gamblers, and the like. At night, the city was one concerted scene of drunken revelry and rioting in every kind of vice.

Paul lived there long. He knew what was going on. Hence the vigor and vividness in his letters to the Corinthians. But it was to such a city that Paul preached the doctrine of the Mystical Body of Christ, and preached it so successfully that the size and fervor of the Christian community enraged the Jews there and stirred up a persecution against the apostle.

What has been done can be done again. History can repeat itself with ever-greater emphasis. Your world is certainly no worse than Ephesus or Corinth. You have more than Paul had when he began to preach and teach; for the Mystical Christ has grown to

---

[444] Eph. 1:3-5, 7-10.

young manhood since the tentmaker from Tarsus first spoke to Gentiles about incorporation in Christ.

Hence, courage, confidence, and great expectations are your three stimulants to an energetic, enterprising, and never-flagging prosecution of your vocation. "He who was seated on the throne said, 'To him who thirsts I will give the water of life, free of charge, from the fountain.' "[445] Let your thirst be as maddening as a desert thirst, and God will give you your fill of Christ, for He is faithful to His promises. Then you can go forth and conquer for Christ by radiating Him everywhere.

"To him who is victorious," says God the Holy Spirit — and we take Him to mean those who reach Heaven — "I will give the hidden manna, and I will give him a white stone, and on this stone is a new name written, which no one knows except him who receives it."[446] That will be your real name, the one by which God calls you. That name will reveal what your vocation was. More than likely, that name will simply be *Christ*, for you are a Christian, and you already know that "there is no other name under Heaven appointed among men as the necessary means of our salvation."[447]

You may never know your real name this side of Heaven. You may never know your specific task for God and man this side of the grave. You may never know the unique purpose God had in mind when he called you into being and then into His Christ, until you see both God and His Christ face-to-face. But you do know you are to put on Christ and that you are to build up the Body. And you learn from Paul how to do that: "Whether you eat or drink, or

[445] Cf. Apoc. 21:6 (RSV = Rev. 21:6).
[446] Apoc. 2:17 (RSV = Rev. 2:17).
[447] Acts 4:12.

do anything else, do everything for God's glory."[448] "Whatever you do or say, let it always be in the name of the Lord Jesus, while you give thanks to God the Father through Him."[449] "Let the ruling principle of your heart be the peace of Christ, to which you were called as the members of one body; and be thankful."[450]

Even historian Arnold J. Toynbee is aware of what is going on in your century. His awareness led him to a diagnosis which reads like a tentative prognosis or even a prophecy. "In our war-ridden generation," he writes at the end of his six-volume book, A Study of History, "in which the lately brilliant prospects of a neopagan dominant minority have been rapidly growing dim, the sap of life is visibly flowing once again through all the branches of our Western Christendom; and this spectacle suggests that perhaps . . . we may live to see a civilization that has tried and failed to stand alone, being saved, in spite of itself, from a fatal fall by being caught up in the arms of an ancestral Church which it has vainly striven to push away and keep at arm's length. In that event a tottering civilization may be . . . given to be born again as a Res Publica Christiana [a Christian State] which was its own earlier and better ideal of what it should strive to be."[451]

You are called to see that your civilization falls into the arms of Mother Church. You answer that call by "becoming what you are" — Christ!

"For you, to live means Christ, and to die means gain."[452]

---

[448] 1 Cor. 10:31.

[449] Col. 3:17.

[450] Col. 3:15.

[451] From D. C. Somervell's abridgment (New York: Oxford University Press, 1946), 403.

[452] Cf. Phil. 1:21.

You are one who can bring Christ to the world

There is your divine vocation and your eternal destiny in a line. To answer the call, to achieve the destiny, you must realize that you can do neither alone. You need the "Help of Christians," the *Omnipotentia Supplex* — "the all-powerful Suppliant" — the woman who is mother of all men because she is the Mother of God. You can "become what you are" only through the help of your Mother.

Chapter Fifteen

You are one born of a Mother most powerful

You are on the last step of your climb. Your pedestal touches the gates of God. You are now in position to answer that searching question "Who are you?" with clarity and completeness. You know now that you cannot begin to tell anyone anything vital about yourself without mentioning God, His Christ, and that Christ's Mother, for your roots are in eternity; your substance is from the creating hand of Divinity; your dignity, destiny, and all real living lie in your incorporation in Him to whom Mary gave birth. For, thanks to Him, you can look straight into the eyes of God the Omnipotent and say, "*Abba*, Father!"[453] You are a child of God working out your destiny. That destiny is nothing less than a divine vocation to be to your contemporaries what Mary's firstborn Son was to His: a manifestation of God. You live to praise His glory, to be a revelation of His paternity to your fellowmen.

Because you have such a vocation from God, you are, needless to say, a very important person. You mean much to God and — much more than they realize or appreciate — to your fellowmen.

[453] Rom. 8:15.

You live among realists who demand facts, for your contemporaries are more than wary; they are cynical about the value of mere words. Having been subjected to so much propaganda and pressure from all sides, they shy from and are skeptical about all catch phrases, even as they are inclined to be somewhat pessimistic about verbal promises.

So now you are surrounded by sharp and somewhat embittered realists who demand facts, not nice-sounding phrases. In all truth, they do not want Christianity; they want Christ. They have seen something of the first. It did not show them the Latter as He should be shown. So your vocation will have to grip you the way Christ's gripped Him; and you will have to follow and fulfill it with the same stoutness of heart and fearless fixity of purpose. No other attitude of mind or manner of acting will impress your fellowmen and women in this century.

∞

Deeds, not mere words, will convert the world

Edgar Guest's piercing comment: "I'd rather see a sermon than hear one," will serve as your directive. Your contemporaries will not learn the real truth about Christ and Christianity from mere books. The Bible was the first book ever printed and remains today a bestseller. But in spite of its widespread diffusion, mankind has not yet been converted. To be effective, truths must be lived here and now! There is only one script from which the truth about Christ and Christianity will be universally accepted — that is the souls of saints. The witness the world wants and will listen to is the member of Christ who always, at all times, and with all peoples acts as Christ's member. The witness your contemporaries will believe is the Catholic who meets all men without regard to surface appearances and greets each as a manifestation of God, as a being of real worth, as a person who is of great importance to God and man. In other words, your world will accept Christianity only when Catholics look and see in every man the Christ, then act toward each and every one as they would like to have been able to act toward Mary's Son.

The realists among whom you live size up the insincere in a flash and recognize the weak compromiser at first glance. They are hard, but they are fair. Once they see the genuine, their applause is quick and generous. That fairness is a foundation on which you can build. Your contemporaries may seem irreligious, but that is only because true religion has not been presented to them by witnesses who testify by deeds. The apologetics that will win your world are those apologetics that breathe in flesh and blood, walk on two feet, and use two hands to minister tenderly to every wounded wayfarer — and your world is filled with them.

Christianity is Christ — not His teaching so much as His Person. His teaching can be found in books. But books do not breathe; they have no hands that can be tender; they lack the heart that can be warmly sympathetic; they have not the eye nor the voice that can be as human as God's Son was human. But the Person of Christ is in Heaven. So if your fellows on earth are to see Him, you will have to be Jesus Christ.

Very specifically that means you will have to present the one argument no one can rebut, show the one mark that is the authentic mark of Christ and Christian, testify to Truth with the testimony everyone must accept: you must love as He who "emptied Himself" loved; you must show your fellowman the kind of love that will go to the Cross so that they may live. But you will never be able to do that unless you live ever dependent on your omnipotent Mother, that maid who by a *fiat* became Mother of God — and simultaneously Mother of all Christ's mystical members.

∞

Mary is truly your mother

Now you are in dogma that is deep and faced with truth that staggers. So approach gradually. It says that you, who were born of the flesh, who were born of human parents in this century, were also born twenty centuries ago, and that you came forth from the immaculate womb of the peerless Virgin, Mary.

The twentieth century had hardly dawned when a man who would be canonized was sitting in the Chair of Peter: Pius X. But, lauded as he will be for all ages for the many brave and even bold moves he made in his short and often stormy pontificate, he can never be shown gratitude enough for the encyclical he wrote before he had been a full year in office. It is called *Ad diem illum laetissimum*[454] and tells much about you and your Mother.

From the following brief section, you can see of what import it is to you and to Mary: "Is not Mary the Mother of God?" asks St. Pius. "Then she is our mother also. And we must hold in truth that Christ, the Word made flesh, is also the Savior of mankind. He had a physical body like that of any other man; and again, as Savior of the human family, He had a spiritual and mystical body, the society, namely, of those who believe in Christ. 'We, being many, are one Body in Christ.' Now, the Blessed Virgin did not conceive the eternal Son of God merely in order that He might be made man, taking His human nature from her, but also that by means of the nature assumed from her, He might be the Redeemer of men. For that reason, the angel said to the shepherds, 'Today is born to you a Savior, who is Christ the Lord.' Wherefore, in the same holy bosom of His most chaste Mother, Christ took to Himself flesh and united to Himself the spiritual body formed by those who were to believe

[454] On the Immaculate Conception, February 2, 1904.

366

in Him. Hence, Mary, carrying the Savior within her, may be said to have also carried all those whose life was contained in the life of the Savior. Therefore, all we who are united in Christ, as the apostle says, are members of His body, of His flesh, and of His bones, and have issued from the womb of Mary like a body united to its head.

"Hence, although in a spiritual and mystical fashion, we are all children of Mary, and she is mother of us all. Mother, spiritually indeed, but truly mother of the members of Christ, who we are. If, then, the most Blessed Virgin is the mother at once of God and men, who can doubt that she will work with all diligence to procure that Christ, Head of the Body of the Church, may transfuse His gifts to us, His members, and, above all, that of knowing and living through Him?"

Your God-given vocation is to live as Christ. But that is impossible unless you know Him. And no one knows Him save those to whom God reveals Him. The Gospel tells you that these are always the *parvuli* — "the little ones," the men and women whose spirituality, or contact with God, is childlike.

As always when dogma deepens, paradoxes pile up. You have just learned that you are to bring Christ to maturity. No one need tell you that that can be accomplished only if you yourself are a mature Christian. But now you are being made to realize that such maturity can be reached only by your becoming like a little child. Such revelations can be upsetting at first. But that is only because the "child of Adam" in you has not yet fully yielded to the "child of God," which you were made by Baptism.

∽

Piety will make you Christlike
If you wish to rid yourself of that instinctive recoil from this call to childlikeness, deeming it something beneath the dignity of

a mature adult, look at Jesus Christ. Study His attitudes toward God the Father. Never in all time did a more mature Person walk our earth than Jesus Christ. Yet, who could be more childlike toward God than this same Christ Jesus? Jesus never did a single thing that was not bidden Him by the Father. "I tell you the plain truth," said this incarnate Son of God. "The Son can do nothing on His own initiative; He can only do what He sees the Father do. Yes, what He is doing — that and nothing else, the Son does likewise."[455]

Count, if you can, the number of references Jesus made to the Father. The very first words recorded as from His lips are those Jesus addressed to Mary the day she found Him in the Temple after three days and three nights of anguish. " 'Child,' said Mary, 'why did You behave toward us in this way? Oh, our hearts were heavy — Your father's and mine — as we searched for You!' He said to them, 'Why did you search for me? I had to answer my Father's call, and did you not know it?' "[456]

If ever there was a "keynote," that is it. With Jesus, it was always the Father. There is one word that sums up Christ's character perfectly, but unfortunately, in English, certain connotations have obscured its real meaning. In Latin that word is still resonant with holiness and reverberates with a hundred connotations that actually open to your view the very Holy of Holies. That word is *pietas*. It tells of a virtue man has from his very nature, one that prompts him to have an affectionate regard for his parents. But it also speaks of a special gift God the Holy Spirit seeded in your soul along with sanctifying grace the moment Baptism cleared that soul of sin and made it proper soil for such a seeding. It is a gift that turns you to

[455] John 5:19.
[456] Luke 2:48-49.

God as your Father, floods your soul with filial affection for this omnipotent Father, and orients your entire life and being to Him and His paternal care.

Theologically looked at, it has nothing whatever to do with clasped hands, bowed head, lowered eyes, arched neck, and that odd and forbidding aura of unnaturalness some people carry about with them as they try to be holy. It is more distant from plaster statuary and those so-called pious prints and holy cards than is the brilliance of a noonday sun from the blackness of a burned-out star.

Pietas is virile and vigorous. It demands stoutest heart and strongest will. It calls for a keen mind and arrow-straight direction of warm affection, for it bespeaks faultless evaluation of love received, even as it tells of the return of love to God in God's own measure: "pressed down, shaken together, running over."[457]

In its perfection, *pietas* is found, perhaps, only in the sinless soul of the Son of God and the Immaculate Heart of His Virgin Mother. Yet it is a gift the God of Fire set burning in your being when He branded you as a child of God and began to breathe in you because you were a member of Christ.

Thomas Aquinas tells its nature briefly. "The Holy Spirit," he writes, "moves us to this effect among others, of having a filial affection toward God according to Romans 8:15: 'You have received the spirit of adoption of sons, whereby we cry, "*Abba*, Father," ' and since it belongs properly to piety to pay duty and worship to one's father, it follows that piety, whereby, at the Holy Spirit's instigation, we pay worship and duty to God, is a gift of the Holy Spirit."[458]

[457] Luke 6:38.
[458] *Summa Theologica*, II-II, Q. 121, art. 1.

∽

Christ is the model of childlike love for the Father

In two short articles on this tremendous gift, St. Thomas opens broad vistas. He proves that, as a gift, *pietas* — a true piety — is greater than religion as a virtue. By this latter, you pay worship to God as Creator and fulfill the first Commandment of the Decalogue God gave Moses on Sinai. But by piety, you worship God as Father, and fulfill the first commandment Christ gave to all men. For *love* permeates piety as redness does a rose. Since both justice and love embrace your relations with your fellowman as well as with your God, it is not surprising to learn that the gift of piety enables you to pay worship and duty, not only to God, but also, as St. Thomas put it, "to all men on account of their relationship to God." So this one gift will assist you in the fulfillment of the second commandment Christ gave about loving your neighbor as yourself.[459]

Thanks to this gift, there is a possibility of one day being able to apply to you in all literalness the adage "like Father, like son," for this gift comes from Omnipotence and is a share in that power which is God. But it must never be forgotten that its function is to enable you to express your childlikeness to God, your Father.

Christ once set a child in the midst of His disciples. Follow His example now. Study some unspoiled child who loves his father, and learn how to use your gift of piety toward God. You will find that the child trusts absolutely. He considers his father omniscient and omnipotent; a man who knows all the answers and can do all things quite easily. In his father's presence, this child is fearless, for he believes with all his being that this man can, and will, shield him from every harm, come to his rescue in every predicament, and either preserve him from error, or effortlessly right every mistake.

[459] Cf. Matt. 22:37-39.

See that child now as a mirror reflecting truth, and not as a lens giving you sharp focus of immaturity's illusions. Since "all paternity comes from Heaven,"[460] this child is showing you that there is a Parent both omniscient and omnipotent, a Parent who is eternally alert and keenly alive to your every predicament, a Parent whose love is not only ever watchful, but utterly tireless.

Such a child was Jesus Christ, not only at Bethlehem, Egypt, and Nazareth, but right on through His public life up to that last moment when the child in Him cried, "Father, into Thy hands I commend my spirit."[461]

It is Jesus Christ who will teach what maturity is required of you so that you may live as a child of God. You have seen Him in the Temple telling His Mother that He "must be about his Father's business" as the Douay-Rheims translation has it. Watch Him at Cana, at that beginning of miracles. Why does He, at first, refuse His Mother? He tells you. His "hour," that is, the hour appointed by the Father "had not yet come."[462]

Follow Him through His three years of teaching. Hear Him again and again insisting that the teaching is not His, but the Father's. "The things, therefore, that I speak, even as the Father said to me, so do I speak."[463] "My doctrine is not mine, but His that sent me."[464] He goes so far as to say He lives by the Father: "As the living Father hath sent me, and as I live by the Father . . ."[465] Could a loving child say more?

[460] Eph. 3:15.
[461] Luke 23:46.
[462] John 2:4.
[463] John 12:50.
[464] John 7:16.
[465] John 6:58.

Christ Himself summed up His life for you, in the words: "I do always the things that please Him."[466] That kind of living is expressed perfectly by the one word *pietas*.

In your day, rife as it is with independence, both correct and incorrect, the call to childlikeness is too often repudiated before it is in any way understood. So let it be said again: There never was a more mature, more adult, more fully grown and perfectly balanced human being than Jesus Christ; yet never was such perfect childlikeness shown to God the Father than that shown by the same Christ Jesus. Hence, if to be childlike is to be weak, Jesus Christ, the strongest human character in all mankind's history, stands condemned as weak. But if childlikeness toward God the Father is the acme of perfection for a human, you have your model in the Man who said, "Unless you become as little children, you shall not enter into the kingdom of Heaven."[467]

The virility and perfect piety of Jesus is emphatically revealed at the Feast of the Dedication, the last He celebrated in Jerusalem the winter before He died. Pressing Him to end the suspense, the Jews angrily demanded that He declare openly whether He was the Messiah. "I told you," replied Jesus, "but you refuse to believe. The things I am doing in the name of my Father testify on my behalf. The pity is, you refuse to believe, because you do not belong to my sheep. My sheep listen to my voice. I know them and they follow me; and I give them eternal life; they will not be lost in eternity, for no one can snatch them out of my hand. The Father, who has entrusted them to me, is all-powerful; and no one can snatch anything out of my Father's hand. The Father and I are one."[468]

[466] John 8:29.
[467] Matt. 18:3.
[468] John 10:24-30.

This is piety at its bravest. For Jesus faces the possibility of brutal death because of this superb filial tribute to His Father. "Once again the Jews brought stones, ready to stone Him to death. Jesus remonstrated with them. 'Many a kindly deed have I performed under your eyes, with power from my Father; for which particular deed do you wish to stone me?' 'Not for a kindly deed,' the Jews retorted, 'do we mean to stone You, but for blasphemy and because You, a man, make Yourself God' "[469]

The Jews understood, then, what Jesus meant when He said, "The Father and I are one." Now read the reply of the God-Man and learn what an adult thing childlikeness is. "Is it not written in your law, 'I said: You are gods'? If it called 'gods' those to whom the word of God was addressed — and the Scripture cannot be annulled — will you then say, 'You are a blasphemer,' to Him whom the Father has consecrated to His service and made His ambassador to the world, just because I said, 'I am the Son of God'?"[470]

Nothing childish about that. It is proof positive that courage, and even heroic courage, is required if one will be as a child toward God. But Jesus did not stop with that one refutation. He went on boldly: "If I do not act as my Father does, then do not believe me; but if I do, then believe me on the strength of my actions even if you do not believe my words. Thus the truth will dawn on you, and you will understand that the Father is in me, and that I am in the Father."[471]

Christ Himself tells you that, with people, actions speak louder than words. His magnificent stand against hostility also tells you that you can show God the Father to your contemporaries while

[469] John 10:31-33.
[470] John 10:34-36.
[471] John 10:37-38.

showing them God the Son, for He and the Father are one. Childlikeness toward God is what your world needs to see. You can make that revelation to it.

Do you recall the scene in which the disciples return from their mission journey? They were exulting in the fact that demons obeyed them when they used Jesus' name. "Inspired by the occasion," says St. Luke, our Lord "exulted in the Holy Spirit," then gave vent to a prayer of praise that is typical of true piety. "I praise you, Father, Lord of Heaven and earth, for hiding these things from wise and prudent men and revealing them to little ones. Yes, Father, for such has been your good pleasure! All things have been put into my hands by my Father, and no one knows who the Son is except the Father or who the Father is except the Son, and anyone to whom the Son decides to reveal Him."[472]

You can begin to understand now why St. Jerome proffered the peculiar explanation that when Jesus stood a child in the midst of the disciples, and taught them that spiritual maturity is reached only when one becomes "like this little child,"[473] He pointed to Himself. He Himself was "this little child." Certainly you must admit that the Gospels give irrefutable testimony that Christ's soul was ever oriented to God as His Father, and that is the essence and the acme of *pietas*, or true piety, the gift you must use incessantly, the virtue you should cultivate unwearyingly.

∞

Childlikeness requires three qualities

Before turning to your all-powerful Mother and learning what *pietas* you are to show toward her, take one more glance at the

---

[472] Luke 10:17-22.
[473] Matt. 18:4.

qualities that are necessary for genuine piety, or childlikeness, toward God.

First, you must realize vividly that God is your Father and that you are His child. Hence, dependence! It is not enough to address God as *Father*. A parrot could do that! You must have the mind and the heart of a child toward Him — a mind and heart that will have you turning to Him for everything; looking to Him to supply your real needs; calling to Him in every danger and difficulty; clinging to Him when in distress; showing Him your hurts, and expecting Him to heal them.

Such an attitude of mind and heart will give you a trust in God that nothing can shake, and a peace of soul that can never be disturbed. For you will depend on God for everything, not because you know Him to be wise enough to lead you aright, rich enough to supply your every want, and powerful enough to protect you from every real harm; no, your dependence will rest on something more potent than the omnipotence of God, on something more stable than the immutability of God; your dependence and trust will be based on His never-failing *paternal* love. You will know yourself to be a child who is in all truth a "favorite child," and you will live as Christ lived: free and unafraid.

Next, your Father, God, will be the sun of your world. Living in that Light, you will never know the darkness that comes from the unfounded fears of the neurotic. Like every young child, you will be anything but an introvert. Your gaze, like his, will always be outward. The adolescent, and even the adult, is too often preoccupied with self, grows calculating, ambitious, cautious, and reserved. The child is just the opposite; for the springs of his life are outside himself. His thoughts are on his wonderful parents, and his trust is centered there. You are a child of God. You will live in His light and let your world have no other sun.

Finally, your conduct toward God is to be characterized with the same generosity that marks the conduct of a little child toward his loving father. The child not only gives what he has, but yields all that he is to his parents. In a mature member of Christ, no other attitude toward God the Father is admissible.

Father Edward Leen, C.Sp.S., once remarked on the strangeness of the fact that men are much more ready and willing to adopt almost any other attitude toward God than this only proper one of childhood. They are ready to look upon Him as a just and severe Master, to whom they must one day render a rigorously exact account of their lives. Many more readily regard Him as the rich and openhanded Owner of the vineyard who rewards the lightest labor with lavish generosity.[474] Still more look upon Him as a Sovereign to whom they must pay tribute. Each and all of these attitudes they consider proper to grown men — but not the attitude of a child.

They will even read the parable of the Prodigal Son wrongly. They see the boy after he has wasted his substance by "living riotously," reflect that many servants in his father's house are better off than he. They hear him say, "I will rise and go to my father and say to him, 'I have sinned . . . make me as one of your hired servants.' "[475] And they think that is the precise lesson in this moving story. They fail to see that the point of the parable and the protagonist in the story is the prodigal's Father — who is your God! He will listen to no such nonsense as the boy would pour out. He runs to meet his son, throws his arms around his neck, kisses him, and excitedly orders the ring for his finger, the best garments for his back, shoes for his feet, and a feast. His child is home! That is what

[474] Cf. Matt. 20:1-15.
[475] Luke 15:18-19.

you are to learn from that best of short stories: God is your Father, who loves you to the pitch and point of folly!

Cardinal Newman, in showing how the child is the fit emblem of the mature Christian, intimated, perhaps unwittingly, just what disciplining of self you will have to do to arrive at the perfection of this virtue and gift of *pietas*, which alone can give you the child-likeness proper to the adult Christian.

"The child," says the cardinal in one of his sermons, "seems to have come lately from God's presence, and not to understand the language of this visible scene, or how it is a temptation, or how it is a veil interposing itself between the soul and God. The simplicity of a child's ways and notions, his ready belief of everything he is told, his artless love, his frank confidence, his confession of helplessness, his ignorance of evil, his inability to conceal his thoughts, his contentment, his prompt forgetfulness of trouble, his admiring without coveting: and, above all, his reverential spirit, looking at all things about him as wonderful, as tokens and types of One Invisible, are all evidence of his being lately (as it were) a visitant in a higher state of things. I would only have a person reflect on the earnestness and awe with which a child listens to any description or a tale; or again his freedom from that spirit of proud independence, which discovers itself in the soul as time goes on."[476]

❧

To become childlike, you need Mary

You know how strong that spirit of "proud independence" is in you and in your day. By now you must realize how completely

[476] John Henry Newman, *Parochial and Plain Sermons*, Vol. 2, Sermon 6: "The Mind of Little Children."

opposed it is to the virtue and gift that are to dominate your life. Hence, you must see that if you are to become and remain a child in the eyes of God, and if you are ever to look to God with the eyes of a child, you will need a veritable flood of grace. That is where your all-powerful Mother comes in — and where you are to manifest *pietas*, or the attitude of a loving child, toward her, too. For the hand that opens the floodgates of grace is the hand of Mary Immaculate.

If you are to live as Christ, grow up "in Christ," mature like Christ, and attain the stature of God's only Son, then you have constant need of Mary. In all theological truth, it can be said that your *pietas* — your childlikeness toward God — rests on Mary's *maternitas* — her very real motherhood of God. So if you wish to be a child of God, live ever conscious of the fact that you are a child of Mary.

St. Pius X said essentially the same in his encyclical *Ad Diem Illum Laetissimum* when he wrote, "There is no more certain and steady way of uniting all to Christ and of reaching that perfect adoption of sons [true *pietas*] so that we should be holy and immaculate in the sight of God, than by Mary. . . . For since it is the will of Divine Providence that we should have the God-Man through Mary, there is no other way for us to receive Christ [and Christhood] except from her hands."

∾

Mary became your mother on Calvary

To the living and life-giving belief that God is your Father add the belief that must be just as vital: that Mary is your mother. She conceived you, as St. Pius X taught, when she conceived Christ. But she did not bring you forth to life in Christ and as Christ until she saw Him die. You were born of Mary on Calvary.

You are one born of a Mother most powerful

Leo XIII told you this in his *Quamquam pluries*,[477] writing, "The Most Holy Virgin Mother of Jesus Christ, is also Mother of Christians: for she has given birth to them on Mount Calvary amidst the extreme sufferings of her Son, our Redeemer. Jesus, then, is, as it were, the first born of Christians, who by adoption and redemption are become His brothers." Like all children of a pain-filled and difficult birth, you are a favorite child. Mother Mary can never forget the hour of your birth, nor all that it cost her.

Can you, if you will pose as mature and be possessed of real *pietas*, ever be unmindful of the same hour? You cost your brother, Christ, a heart broken by a lance thrust. You cost your Mother, Mary, a heart broken by the stabs of Seven Sorrows. You were born in blood. It was Mary's blood, both that which flowed upon the Cross and that which came from the sorrowing heart beneath it. This makes you doubly dear to Mary and should win from you a double share of *pietas*: one you give to God, your Father, the other you give to her whose Child gave her to you as Mother!

This truth points the way to your sanctity. God gave you Mary so that she might mother you unto eternity. As long as you live on earth, you are nothing but a child to God, constantly dependent on Him for supernatural life. Mary is the channel through which that life flows. Early writers used to call her the "neck" of the Mystical Body, and St. Pius X recalled this fact in that encyclical quoted so often already. "Mary," he wrote, "as St. Bernard fittingly remarks, is the 'channel' or even the neck through which the body is joined to the Head, and likewise through which the Head exerts its power and strength on the body. 'For,' as St. Bernardine of Siena said, 'she is the neck of our Head, by which all spiritual gifts are communicated to His Mystical Body.' "

[477] On devotion to St. Joseph, August 15, 1889.

This same St. Bernardine[478] was quoted by Leo XIII in his Rosary encyclical:[479] "Every grace which is communicated to the world has a threefold course. For, in accord with excellent order, it is dispensed from God to Christ, from Christ to the Virgin, from the Virgin to us." Two years earlier, this same Pontiff, in an encyclical called *Magnae Dei Matris*,[480] had been explicit about your order of approach, saying, ". . . one can affirm that absolutely nothing of that great treasury of grace which the Lord brought to us (for 'grace and truth came by Jesus Christ') — nothing of it is given to us except through Mary, for such is the will of God: so that, just as no one can go to the Most High Father except through the Son, in much the same way, no one can come to Christ except through His Mother."

The popes are telling you to found your piety on Mary's maternity, to approach your God through His only Son, but approach that Son through His and your Mother. They are also telling you with full authority that you are using no figurative language when you address Mary Immaculate as "Mother." A mother is one who gives life, and Mary gave you yours. A mother is one who sustains life once it has been given, and Mary sustains you in the life of all living, the life of grace, the life that is yours as Christ's mystical member.

Could it be otherwise? Could the branches be given life from any other earth than that which nourishes the vine? Could the Head of the Body have one mother and the members of that same Body, another? If Christ could call Mary nothing less than Mother,

---

[478] St. Bernardine of Siena (1380-1444), Franciscan missionary and reformer.

[479] *Iucunda semper expectatione*, September 8, 1894.

[480] On the Rosary, September 8, 1892.

what can Christians do but follow His example? If there is only one Christ — the whole Christ — then Mary is the Mother not only of Jesus, but also of everyone incorporated in Him.

Now you can understand why Mary must be tender toward you. She sees the same lights in your eyes as she saw at Bethlehem that first Christmas night; for in all the world there is only one Child as far as Mother Mary can see — her Jesus — and that is you! So whatsoever she does to the least of mortals, she does to Him, the greatest! Hence you can be absolutely confident of always being tenderly loved by and ever welcome to Mary.

Of course you differ from her sinless Son. Still, be confident! For no child is ever too dirty for a mother to wash; too bruised by any fall for her not to kiss away the hurt; too headstrong and self-ish for her not to love. You are Mary's child just as much as you are God's child, by every title save that of creation.

St. Albert the Great, the teacher of St. Thomas Aquinas, brings you back to the opening pages of this book, and to that page which Father McNabb tore out of the child's catechism, as he says, "It has been the will of God that Mary should have share in the re-creation of our nature, and that, too, according to the four kinds of causality. She has been, after God, with God, and un-der God, the *efficient* cause of our regeneration, because she has given flesh to our Regenerator, and because, by her virtues, she has *merited*, congruously, this incomparable honor. She has been the *material* cause, because, acting on her consent, the Holy Spirit took of her most pure flesh and blood to form the body immolated for the salvation of the world. She has been the *final* cause, be-cause this great work, directed principally to the glory of God, contributes, in a secondary manner, to the glory of the Virgin. She is the *formal* cause, for, by the light of her life, of so divine a form, she is for all an example which shows the way to emerge from darkness, and the direction we are to take to arrive at the Beatific Vision."[481]

In another passage, this great saint and theologian said, "Mary is the 'form' of God, the form of Christ — the mold divine by which Christ was fashioned, and the elect are fashioned into the image of Christ." That is why you must cling to your heavenly Mother. She can fashion you into the image of Christ. She can do it with ease; for she is all-powerful, a suppliant neither God the Father, God the Son, nor God the Holy Spirit can refuse; for she is the daughter of the First, the mother of the Second, and the spouse of the Third.

∞

It is right to honor Mary

That fact enables you not only to refute the slurring charge of "Mariolatry," which some bring against you for your cult of Mary Immaculate, but to explain why you can call her "omnipotent." You may even convince your hearers that God Himself, not only the God-Man or the Man in God, but God Himself, has a "cult" of Mary.

You will have to know your Mother very intimately in order to sustain such a statement as that; for *cult* is "paying honor to a superior because of the excellencies in that superior," and everyone knows that no one is superior to God. Yet, you will welcome such an objection and make of it an opportunity joyously to tell your objector just who your Mother is. You can do so by arguing that the essence of "cult" is paying honor to another because of the excellencies in that other, and then hurry on to tell how God gave

[481] St. Albert the Great (c. 1200-1280; medieval theologian, philosopher, and scientist), *Quaest.*, Q. 146.

Mary the honor of being conceived without Original Sin — the only human person so conceived in all creation! He gave her the honor of being free from all concupiscence; the honor of being full of grace; the honor of being free from any slightest shadow of ignorance in those things that appertained to her role; the honor of being, in all truth, and in many ways, "our tainted nature's solitary boast." And all this honor because of one thing: the fact that she was to be the Mother of His only Son. Mary's maternity was the wellspring of all her surpassing prerogatives. Because of this excellence, God gave her all those other honors. That is "cult."

Once he sees that God has so honored Mary and why He did so, no honest man will fail to do the same. Grasping the fact that she is the God-bearer, every real man will gladly yield that cult to Mary, which is called by Catholics *hyperdulia*. It is a special kind of cult, for she is a very special person. Yet it is infinitely different and distinct from the cult Catholics pay to God. St. Thomas says that Mary, your Mother, "borders on the infinite." But no child of God is ignorant of the fact that that border is infinitely long, infinitely wide, infinitely high, and infinitely deep. In other words, while Mary, your Mother, is truly Mother of God, she is in no sense a mother goddess. The distance between her and the Infinite on whom she borders is infinite! Nevertheless, because she did bear such a unique relation to each of the Persons of the Trinity, since her divine maternity terminated in the Hypostatic Union,[482] since, in all truth, she is *Theotokos* — "Mother of God" — she is above all angels and saints; she is in a realm of her own: above every created being, above every existing being save God Himself. Hence, the cult she calls forth is less than *latria* — the worship — we give

---

[482] The substantial union between the human and divine natures in the Person of Christ.

to God alone — but higher than *dulia* — or honor — we so honestly pay to all God's heroes and heroines — the angels and the saints. It is *hyperdulia,* a cult different not only in degree from what we pay the saints and angels, but different in kind, yet infinitely different, too, from what we pay to God.

Yet the end purpose of this cult of *hyperdulia* is not Mary, just as the end purpose of the cult called *dulia* is not the angels or the saints. It is always God. Your worship of Mary because of her divine maternity terminates not at that maternity but, as always, at divinity. You worship your Mother; you do not adore her. And far from detracting from the worship due to God alone, it more surely promotes it; for she is the way to the Son who named Himself the only Way to the Father. You are being just, honest, and Godlike, when you love and worship your Mother like a child.

When Mary's place in God's plan is known, it is readily seen why she is called "omnipotent." God had prevision not only of Creation, the Fall, and Redemption, but also of Redemption's mode — and that was *through Mary!* With that in mind, you can reread the Old Testament and find your Mother on countless pages; for just as you can recognize Jesus in the many men and things that were figures and types of Him, so you will recognize Mary in many women and things that were but types and figures of her.

Your Mother is mentioned in the earliest chapters of Genesis, not only in the promise about the "crushing of the serpent's head,"[483] but in Eve herself, the mother of all the living; for this first woman was but a figure of that second Eve who would mother all men to supernatural life and living. You will recognize your Mother in Sara, who conceived so miraculously; in Rebecca, the

---

[483] Cf. Gen. 3:15.

beautiful, the figure of her who would give you the Font of Living
Water; in Rachel, who saw her son sold into Egypt, a foreshadow-
ing of Him who would go down into Egypt so that one day He
might save all His brothers; in Ruth, who won the heart and hand
of her lord by declaring herself his handmaid; in Abigail, whose
humility appeased the wrath of a king; in Bethsebee, sitting on the
throne beside her wise son, Solomon. You will recognize your all-
powerful Mother in Judith, as that heroine stands holding in her
hand the head of the enemy of God's People; in the comely Esther,
whose loveliness so pleased the king that he rescinded the order
that her people should be destroyed.

Rereading the Old Testament this way, you find your Mother
prefigured in such things as the Garden of Eden, Noah's Ark, the
rainbow after the flood, Jacob's ladder, the burning bush, Gideon's
fleece, the Tower of David, and the Ark of the Covenant — for
each of these betokened in their own way life, peace, union with
God, motherhood in an inviolate virgin, the strength of omnipotence, and the immanence of the Almighty. If you bear the word
Theotokos in mind, each of these sacred figures takes on a beauty
that is transcendent and a meaning that is most personal. God had
that word in His mind *ab aeterno* — "from the beginning, from the
unbeginning of endlessness and eternity"! That is why St. Bernard
described your Mother as "a work of Eternal Counsel and an Affair
of the Ages."

∽

Mary had a significant role in Christ's Sacrifice

When you listen to Isaiah telling of "a virgin who would conceive and bring forth a son,"[484] and to Jeremiah foretelling that "a

---

[484] Isa. 7:14.

woman would compass a man,"[485] or to that darker, yet, in a way, more beautiful prophecy of Ezekiel wherein he describes the east gate of the sanctuary which "shall be shut, it shall not be opened: because the Lord, the God of Israel, hath entered in by it, and it shall be shut,"[486] you realize that your Mother's place in the plan of God is all-pervasive.

In the New Testament, from the Annunciation and Nativity to the Ascension and Descent of the Holy Spirit, your Mother Mary is far front in the picture. The Gospel story of Christ's infancy and hidden life are completely dominated by Mary. In His public life, she is quite silent, but others speak out for her, crying to Christ, "Blessed the womb that has borne You!"[487] Of Christ's culminating hour you read, "There stood beside the Cross of Jesus His Mother."[488]

How could that last line be otherwise? Mary had given birth to a Child who would be a Priest. She had mothered a Son who would be a sacrificial Victim. And as at His birth in Bethlehem, she was the only one who really knew what was taking place, so on Calvary, as He died, she was the only one who knew what was really going on. She, His Mother, would be present at His first Mass. Not as mere spectator, however, but as you should be at every Mass: as co-offerer and co-offered! Like all her children, Mary was both priest and victim. She had to be "beside the Cross of Jesus."

From that reality, you must learn what is the reality of all your life and all your living. St. Albert the Great called your Mother

---

[485] Jer. 31:22.
[486] Ezek. 44:2.
[487] Luke 11:27.
[488] John 19:25.

"the mold of God." She can shape you, then, only in the mold of Christ. If she is to mother you to maturity, she must bring you up for only one purpose: the same for which she raised Jesus — to be priest and victim! Life on earth has only one object; human existence has only one end: you were brought into being to glorify God as Christ and His Mother did.

In other words, you live just to say Mass. That is what Christ did. That is what Mary did — like Mother, like child. Hence, that is what you must do.

Perhaps you have already read passages in which Mary was called a priest. Usually they are rhetorical passages and refer only to a figurative priestliness. For instance, the Pietà furnishes opportunity to describe your Mother as a priest holding in her hands the broken Host of the world's first Mass, her lap being the world's first corporal to hold the bloodless body of God. It is legitimate language, but it is far from being deep or accurate theology. Mary is really a priest. She had to be, for she is Co-Redemptrix of mankind; and mankind was redeemed only by the Mass, and the Mass is offered only by priests.

If you are priest in the real sense of that word — and you are! — Mary is the same in a pre-eminent manner, since she was ever so much more closely associated with Christ in the offering of His Mass than any other member will be or can be. She is not priest in the sacramental sense — namely, that of bearing in her soul that character of Christ which only men who have received the sacrament of Holy Orders bear — but she is priest in the sense that she offered her Son and herself to God for the reparation of His glory, which sin outraged, and for the redemption of the sinners who were guilty of the outrage.

In fact, her Immaculate Heart was the most completely sacerdotal heart that ever beat, save that of her Son. The virgin disciple

John, to whom the Virgin Mother was given by Christ from the Cross,[489] was priest in the fullest sense of the word, for he was ordained in the Cenacle. But his great heart, priestly though it was, was not, nor could it ever be, as sacerdotal as that of your Immaculate Mother.

∞

Mary will help you to become Christlike

The point is stressed for a double purpose. First, your heart will never beat aright until it beats as a sacerdotal heart, one whose systole is oblation and whose diastole is immolation. That is how the Sacred Heart of Jesus beat from the moment Mary said *fiat;* that is how it beats in Heaven today. That is how Mary's Immaculate Heart always beat, and that is how it is beating this moment as she stands beside her Son doing exactly what He is doing: "ever living to make intercession for us."[490] Second, the point is stressed to show you the power of your Mother.

You are playing a part in the drama of salvation. You will never portray what you were born to portray without the help of this all-powerful Mother. You are on earth this moment to say Mass. But in the New Law, there is only one Mass, and only one priest who can say it: Jesus Christ. So you are on earth to be Jesus Christ. How can you be Jesus Christ unless you have the Mother of Christ as your Mother, and allow her to mother you even as she mothered Him? The necessity for this must be realized. Just as all human life on this globe is traceable to Adam and Eve, so all divine life in a human being is traceable to Jesus as Redeemer, and Mary, His Mother, as the new Eve.

[489] Cf. John 19:26-27.
[490] Heb. 7:25.

St. Ephrem[491] once put this in the form of a prayer, crying, "Since the first Adam, even to the end of the world, all glory, all honor, all sanctity has been carried, is carried, and ever will be carried to us through thee, O Mary!"

So if you would live, and complete your life's work with any finesse, you will cling to your all-powerful Mother even as does a newborn baby. You will beg her to mother you unto mature Christhood. And ultimately that means only one thing: the Mass.

St. Bernard of Clairvaux gives you your life directive in one of his most powerful sermons on the nativity of Mary. He says that it is the will of God that you receive everything from Mary, who, as Mother of mankind, knows all the graces in which you stand in need. As your Mother, she wishes you to receive them and asks them for you from her Son. As the Mother of that Son of God, she is all-powerful and, therefore, can quite easily obtain them for you. Those were the sentiments that led many to attribute to St. Bernard that meaningful, powerful, and moving prayer the *Memorare*.[492]

But another bit of Mariology is one that will focus all your thoughts on Mary, and refocus all your devotedness to her. It comes from Cardinal Lercaro, Archbishop of Bologna, who developed it in a paper he gave at the Mariological Congress held in Rome in 1950. At one point in his conference he said, "Now, the Virgin remains ever the Mother of Christ, and her will continues

---

[491] St. Ephrem (c. 306-373), Syrian biblical exegete and ecclesiastical writer.

[492] "Remember, O most gracious Virgin Mary, that never was it known that anyone who fled to your protection, implored your help, or sought your intercession was left unaided. Inspired with this confidence, I fly to you, O Virgin of virgins, my Mother; to you I come, before you I stand, sinful and sorrowful. O Mother of the Word Incarnate, despise not my petitions, but in your mercy hear and answer me. Amen."

to be intimately united to the will of her Son. Therefore, just as on Calvary, in a union of will, she offered with Jesus the life of her Son, so also at the altar, still in union of will, she offers Jesus in mystical immolation. For she is present at the altar as at Calvary, and in the same role." That means your Mother is present at every Mass!

That fact will prompt you to pray before Mass as every priest who is to consecrate is urged to pray, saying, "Stand beside me, Mother Mary, and beside every priest offering here and all over the world, just as you stood beside your Son on Calvary."

∽

You are called to be Christ

The theology of this fact is sound: Mary was on Calvary in a leading role; the Mass is Calvary; Mary is there in the same leading role. The application of that sound theology is simple: the Mass is your life, and your life is a Mass. Rejoice, then, for your Mother is with you, and she is all-powerful!

Now you should be able to answer exactly the question "Who are you?" by saying, "I am a child whose Father is God Almighty; whose Mother is the all-powerful Mary, the Mother of God; whose Brother is Jesus Christ, the only Son of God; whose breath of life is the Holy Spirit, the Third Person of the triune God; and whose life, both here and hereafter, is love of God and every creature made by God."

In brief, you are a member of Christ with a work to do. You have an omnipotent Mother who will help you do it. You are a person important to God and man because your life must be a Mass that is offered "through Christ, with Christ, and in Christ," so that all honor may be given to the Father in union with the Holy Spirit, and real life, the life of grace, may be given to men.

You are one born of a Mother most powerful

What a person you are! But never forget you live to "become who you are." Yet, remember also that life's work can be done only in a life's time. So be patient. But above all: *Be yourself* — that is, *Christ!*

Biographical Note

∞

Father M. Raymond
(1903-1990)

Father M. Raymond's long years devoted to prayer gave him a profound knowledge of the tremendous dignity of each person, made in God's image and likeness. But his insight into human greatness never blinded him to the reality of the struggle that man must wage in order to live up to that dignity. He was forthright about his own spiritual battles, once remarking, "Perhaps I'll become a cloistered contemplative in earnest only when cloistered in Heaven and contemplating the Beauty 'ever ancient, ever new.'" In line with this, he firmly believed that the saints should be shown to be fully human, with the same difficulties that we all experience.

Born in Roxbury, Massachusetts, this remarkable monk was baptized Joseph David Flanagan. Long before he discovered his vocation as a Trappist, he entered the Jesuit order in 1920. There he benefited greatly from the influence of Father Francis P. Donnelly, S.J., author of *How to Love as Jesus Loves* (Manchester, New Hampshire: Sophia Institute Press, 1999). Young Flanagan studied literature in New York, philosophy in New England, and theology in the American Midwest and in Rome. He observed that he got more of lasting value from the variety of schools he attended than from the schools themselves. He was also an accomplished debater: from 1927 to 1930, he held the Chair of Rhetoric at Holy Cross College in Worcester, Massachusetts and acted as moderator of the college's Debating Societies. All this still left him time for his central duties as a Jesuit missionary and retreat master.

In 1936 he entered the Cistercian Order of the Strict Observance at Gethsemani Abbey in Kentucky. He later noted that only in the silence and solitude of the Cistercian Order was he finally able to live what he had learned from St. Ignatius Loyola, the founder of the Jesuits.

Father Raymond wrote more than twenty booklets and several books, including *The Man Who Got Even with God: The Life of an American Trappist* and *God Goes to Murderer's Row*. He read many of the writings of the classical authors, but also found much enduring wisdom in the works of modern writers such as Leon Bloy, G. K. Chesterton, and especially Archbishop Fulton J. Sheen and Caryll Houselander, who shared his great devotion to the Mystical Christ.

Indeed, Christ's Mystical Body is a recurring theme in many of Father Raymond's works. He found this doctrine to be both the heart of theology and the only satisfying explanation of life, for it alone revealed the fullness of man's dignity, destiny, and duty. Engagingly and with wonderful clarity, and drawing especially on the wisdom of the popes, in his writings Father Raymond leads readers step by step into the mystery of the Mystical Body. He instructs, convinces, and inspires them to rise — even in this life — to the immense weight of glory to which God calls us all as members of that Body.

An Invitation

Reader, the book that you hold in your hands was published by Sophia Institute Press.

Sophia Institute seeks to restore man's knowledge of eternal truth, including man's knowledge of his own nature, his relation to other persons, and his relation to God.

Our press fulfills this mission by offering translations, reprints, and new publications. We offer scholarly as well as popular publications; there are works of fiction along with books that draw from all the arts and sciences of our civilization. These books afford readers a rich source of the enduring wisdom of mankind.

Sophia Institute Press is the publishing arm of the Thomas More College of Liberal Arts and Holy Spirit College. Both colleges are dedicated to providing university-level education in the Western tradition under the guiding light of Catholic teaching.

If you know a young person who might be interested in the ideas found in this book, share it. If you know a young person seeking a college that takes seriously the adventure of learning and the quest for truth, bring our institutions to his attention.

www.SophiaInstitute.com
www.ThomasMoreCollege.edu
www.HolySpiritCollege.org

SOPHIA INSTITUTE PRESS

THE PUBLISHING DIVISION OF

 THOMAS MORE COLLEGE *of* LIBERAL ARTS    HOLY SPIRIT COLLEGE